Out of Darkness

OUT OF DARKNESS

Rumana Monzur's Journey
through Betrayal, Tyranny and Abuse

DENISE CHONG

RANDOM HOUSE CANADA

PUBLISHED BY RANDOM HOUSE CANADA

Published in 2024 by Random House Canada, a division of Penguin Random House
Canada Limited, Toronto. Distributed in Canada and the United States of America
by Penguin Random House Canada Limited, Toronto.

www.penguinrandomhouse.ca

Random House Canada and colophon are registered trademarks.

LIBRARY AND ARCHIVES CANADA CATALOGUING IN PUBLICATION

Title: Out of darkness : Rumana Monzur's journey through betrayal, tyranny and
   abuse / Denise Chong.
Names: Chong, Denise, author.
Identifiers: Canadiana (print) 20220263272 | Canadiana (ebook) 20220263310 |
   ISBN 9780735274150 (softcover) | ISBN 9780735274174 (EPUB)
Subjects: LCSH: Monzur, Rumana. | LCSH: Abused wives—Bangladesh—
   Biography. | LCSH: Family violence—Bangladesh. | LCSH: Women—Violence
   against—Bangladesh. | LCSH: Women—Bangladesh—Social conditions. |
   LCSH: Women—Bangladesh—Biography. | LCSH: Women social reformers—
   Bangladesh—Biography. | LCSH: Social reformers—Bangladesh—Biography. |
   CSH: Bangladeshi Canadians—Biography. | LCGFT: Biographies.
Classification: LCC HV6626.23.B3 C46 2024 | DDC 362.82/92092—dc23

Text design: Kate Sinclair
Cover design: Kate Sinclair
Image credits: 'Nakshi Kantha (Tablecloth?), Unknown artist, Gift of Richard L.
   Simmons in memory of Roberta Grodberg Simmons, 2004.169.23, Minneapolis
   Institute of Art
Typeset by: Natalie Shefler

Printed in Canada

10 9 8 7 6 5 4 3 2 1

Penguin
Random House
RANDOM HOUSE CANADA

For Anusheh

prologue

A BLUR OF SOUND NIBBLED AT HER CONSCIOUSNESS: MACHINE beeps, alarms and hisses. Voices fading in and out. Then, unmistakably: drawers sliding open and closed. Paper packages being ripped open. Water splashing. Paper towels rustling.

She could hear.

That must mean she was still alive.

A specialist from ophthalmology, Dr. Niaz Rahman, accompanied by a junior doctor, made his way to the intensive care unit. He'd been the day before to see the patient, but the bleeding and swelling of her eyes had made any examination impossible.

"Rumana, can you open your eyes?"

". . . No?"

"Can you see any light?"

"No."

"I need to see inside your eyes."

The specialist dampened a gauze pad with saline and reached down to clean the patient's eyelids of encrusted blood.

She screamed and jerked back into her pillow.

He was puzzled. He thought he'd barely made contact. Forgo the cleaning, he decided. Just get a look inside. With his ophthalmoscope in one hand, he reached again with the other.

This time her scream was chilling. Tears gushed from her eyes as if from a burst pipe.

Neither the specialist nor the junior doctor spoke.

She wanted to know. "What's happened to my eyes?"

"More tests are needed."

Out of earshot of the patient, the specialist spoke to the junior doctor. Any pooling of blood inside the globe of the eye does not normally cause pain. "The damage has to be extensive." What with the many road accidents in Dhaka's chaotic traffic, he'd seen horrific injuries. Once, a metal rod that split the globe of the eye. He knew vision could return after trauma. But this was the worst.

Never had he seen a gouging.

Silence enveloped Rumana after her transfer to a private room. Finally, a heavy clunk of what sounded like a door handle. Then a rush of air into the room, and the footfall of a purposeful walk.

A metal tinkling, then footsteps in the opposite direction, and the same tinkling and swoosh of air.

Drapes being drawn. Open or closed?

"Are you the nurse? Can you tell me, is it morning?"

A cheerful male voice confirmed yes.

Rumana felt a stab of panic. Why couldn't she see the daylight?

With every new visitor to her bedside, Rumana heard anew the sharp intake of breath and the stifled tears, and felt the tremor of their hands on hers. She did not have to ask how she looked. She'd heard the MRI technicians talking to each other. "What could have happened? Was she attacked by a wild animal?"

One week on, a morning nurse burst in. Her words fairly tripped over each other. "Rumana, your picture is all over the news! There are pictures of you with your daughter. You were so beautiful!"

Rumana plunged into sorrow. Would anyone even recognize her now? What if she didn't recover her sight? She'd never see her daughter's face again; Anusheh was only five years old. What if *his* face, contorted with evil, was the last thing she ever saw of the world?

Rumana forced herself to turn away from the memory of the attack. She put her mind to doing what, as a student and a teacher, she knew how to do best: pose a question, answer it with research. Try, she told herself, to locate the beginning of the trail that led to the attack. But where did the trail start? With her agreement to marry, or when she first indulged his attentions? Or were there clues deeper in the past?

one

SATELLITE IMAGERY ON SUNDAY, NOVEMBER 8, 1970, PICKED
up a tropical depression centred over the warm waters of the Bay of
Bengal. A day later, it strengthened to the intensity of a storm, while
continuing a slow drift north toward the coast of East Pakistan.
On Tuesday, meteorologists classified the swirling cloud mass as a
cyclone; every year an average of five cyclones funnel into the Bay
of Bengal. Late on the afternoon of Wednesday, November 11, the
winds rapidly intensified. Heavy, lashing rains began. For the three
million who lived on the islands and tidal flats, there was no higher
ground. That evening, East Pakistan's storm warning centre broadcast its highest alert: Moha bipod shanket. "Great danger coming"
was hardly sufficient: at midnight, coinciding with an above average
lunar high tide, winds reaching 240 kilometres an hour slammed
into the coast. Storm surges as high as nine metres bludgeoned
villages and swallowed islands.

On Friday, handicapped by downed communication lines, the news in the capital, Dhaka, more than 240 kilometres inland, reported mild damage. By evening, the estimate was as many as fifty lives lost. In the morning, it rose to tens of thousands dead. On Sunday, talk was of a death toll in the hundreds of thousands. The international community rallied, but the military government of Pakistan in Islamabad, in the west and separated from East Pakistan by 1600 kilometres of Indian territory, did not mobilize the army to the stricken areas until the tenth day after the cyclone struck. By then, the landscape was an apocalyptic scene of suffering and death.

One month later, Pakistan went ahead with a scheduled general election. Anticipation was high for the first election since 1947, when Partition had dissolved the British Raj and hived off areas of Muslim majority from India to create the independent state of Pakistan. Partition landed two strangers in the same house: Urdu-speaking Punjabis lived in the province of West Pakistan; Bangla-speaking Bengalis in the province of East Pakistan.

Voters in the East went to the polls angry. To Bengalis, the ruling Punjabis' callous indifference to the plight of cyclone victims mirrored the subjugation of the East since Partition. The final tally gave the Awami League of East Pakistan a majority of seats in the planned National Assembly. However, neither it nor its rival party in West Pakistan won seats in the other's province. Loath to be governed by Bengalis, the leader of the rival Pakistan People's Party vowed to "break the legs" of any of his elected members who took their seats.

For weeks, the president of Pakistan dithered on convening the assembly. In protest, people in East Pakistan took to the streets, only to be met by police gunfire. With tensions already running high, the Awami League leader, the fatherly Sheikh Mujibur Rahman (Mujib), gave a fiery speech on March 7 at the Dhaka racecourse to a crowd two million strong, more than the city's population. He exhorted Bengalis to set their sights on self-determination. The only question: how much Bengali blood would have to be spilled to birth the nation of Bangladesh.

On the night of March 25, the military government of Pakistan responded. In a ruthless attack codenamed Operation Searchlight, the Pakistan Army arrested Mujib, and summarily executed members of the Awami League and hundreds of Dhaka's intellectuals, targeting, in particular, teachers and students at Dhaka University. Hours later, a clandestine rural radio station calling itself Radio Free Bengal broadcast Mujib reading a prerecorded proclamation declaring East Pakistan as independent Bangladesh. It was the point of no return: the war for Bengali independence was on.

Second Lieutenant Monzur Hossain, a twenty-four-year-old Bengali engineer in the Pakistan Army, sat at his desk at the Jessore Cantonment. He agonized about whether to heed Mujib's cry; droves of young Bengali men were travelling for the other side of East Pakistan's border with India to encamp there and train as freedom fighters with the Mukti Bahini.

Under oath to serve the constitution, Monzur kept his face expressionless. Should he stay with his fledgling career, or should he shed his uniform, desert and join the war against the Pakistan Army? "Stay with my unit, and nothing will happen to you," his commander had assured him. True to his word, he protected Monzur when an order came down to take all Bengali officers into custody for interrogation. Of the forty officers, only Monzur, the cantonment's supervising engineer, was exempted.

On his graduation from university, Monzur had worked for the local council of the district town of Jessore. Two years into the job, he answered an ad by the Pakistan Army for engineers. Fresh out of six months' training at the military academy in West Pakistan, where he'd excelled, he was awaiting a posting when the cyclone struck. The Pakistan Army command in Dhaka assigned him to manage the transfer of overseas emergency aid. Blankets, food, water and medical supplies arriving at Dhaka Airport were loaded onto trucks then river barges for distribution to civilian authorities and relief workers along the coast and on islands off-shore. After twenty-five days of taxing and grim work, Monzur was rotated out, leaving with commendations for his leadership and cool head. His superiors rewarded him with a posting to Jessore—a garrison of strategic importance because the district town anchored a main through road to the border of India, 50 kilometres away. The posting was a nod also to his obligation as an eldest son; the district town was home to his widowed mother and five younger siblings.

Monzur considered the grievances of his fellow Bengalis to be undeniable. After Partition, the ruling Pakistanis had tried to impose Urdu as the national language and outlaw Bangla; the outcry when police shot dead four student protesters from Dhaka University gave rise to the language movement of 1952. Over the decades, West Pakistan had grabbed the lion's share of foreign aid and the nation's budget, fattened on export earnings from the East's jute plantations. The East remained mired in grinding poverty. Against such grievous insults—the tortured screams of his fellow Bengali officers under interrogation still ringing in his ears—Monzur considered the cost to his mother should he join the resistance. As long as the conflict raged, he'd leave her and his younger siblings without their sole provider. What if Pakistani soldiers decided to take revenge for his defection? They knew where his family lived. What if he were killed in the war, where would that leave them?

Monzur saw only one choice, to stay put.

His decision seemed the right one. In late May, the Pakistan Army, having moved on after Dhaka to the countryside, declared that the last major town in the hands of rebel Bengalis had fallen to its control. The war in a lull, Monzur resumed his routine after work of pedalling his bicycle down an ox-cart-rutted road to join his mother and siblings for dinner. On days off, he travelled to Dhaka to stay with the eldest of his eight siblings, Jolly, and her husband, Maqsood.

As it happened, Jolly had plans for her visiting brother.

Spring had brought violent street protests, so Jolly had taken in a younger sister, Molly (the parents nicknamed their daughters Jolly, Polly, Molly, Dolly and Colly), and her roommate at Dhaka University, Rahima Khatun, whose family lived far from Dhaka. "During the war, I will be your mother," Jolly told Rahima. Seeing how well the nineteen-year-old girl, with her serene manner and temperament, fit into the household, Jolly enlisted Molly to scheme. They showed Rahima family albums and lingered on images of Monzur looking smart in his army uniform, which gave them opportunity to laud the security and benefits, including a pension, of a career in the military.

In August, Monzur was spending a week's leave with Jolly. She asked his opinion of Molly's friend Rahima. Only then did he realize she had been something of a fixture at his sister's. "We like her," Jolly declared. Monzur did not see it as his place to determine the timing of his marriage or whom he would marry. "If you and Mother judge this girl to be the right choice, I have no objection."

Jolly took a proposal to Rahima's maternal uncle. The uncle, who had raised her, was accustomed to fending off families looking to make a match with Rahima. She was exceptionally pretty, if thinner than custom would prefer. He'd insisted her focus was her studies, an attitude contrary to that of most rural parents. Those who did put their daughters in school withdrew them at puberty and told them more education would only make them unhappy. Uncle told Jolly he was open to the proposal, but marriage could come only after Rahima had completed a master's degree. Jolly had anticipated this demand. "Fine, but she has been more or less living in my household in the presence of an unrelated unmarried man. For the sake of the reputations of both our families, the two ought to become engaged." Uncle relented.

In September, Monzur's life took an unexpected turn. The army ordered him to report by month's end to the Peshawar Cantonment in West Pakistan, to join the engineering battalion there. His wedding would have to wait.

In November, Monzur noticed that troops were being sent from the Peshawar Cantonment to border areas of West Pakistan with India. India, which was already sheltering millions of Bengali refugees, declared war against Pakistan, for the third time since

Partition, on December 3. By then, Monzur had received a letter from his mother, written a month earlier, that she'd taken the children and fled Jessore for Jolly's place in Dhaka.

The Indian air force and troops soon overwhelmed the Pakistan Armed Forces. On December 15, with a joint effort of Indian troops and a force made up of the Mukti Bahini and Bengali defectors from the Pakistan Army on the verge of capturing Dhaka, Pakistan conceded defeat. The war was over, only nine months after it had begun.

At the Peshawar Cantonment, the commander asked each Bengali officer, did they want to stay in what was now Pakistan or return to the newly independent Bangladesh? Monzur opted to go home. For two months, he and his fellow Bengalis were garrisoned in a corner of the fort before being flown to Lahore. From there, instead of being sent home, they and thousands of Bengali military personnel and bureaucrats were dispersed to prisoner-of-war camps around the country.

In Monzur's camp, 150 men were packed 30 to a room. Sanitation was poor; the toilet, two holes in the ground. Prisoners slept head to toe on sagging charpoys—it would take Monzur six months of scrimping on the meagre prisoners' allowance to buy a thin cotton mattress. Television and newspapers were denied, and no mail to or from Bangladesh was permitted. A few prisoners had transistor radios. At seven every evening, others crowded around to hear a thirty-minute broadcast from Dhaka of prerecorded greetings by relatives of POWs. Months passed before Monzur took comfort in a few seconds of hearing Rahima say his name and send blessings.

With no idea when his captivity would end, Monzur vowed to make good use of his time by defining a problem to solve: how to progress in one's maturity while living in close quarters with persons not of one's choosing. In February 1974, Pakistan finally recognized Bangladesh. The prisoners of Monzur's camp were flown home. He was able to take home two lessons from his deliberations during his two years in custody: mix with all persons but judge carefully their strengths and weaknesses of character, and do not act in haste. However honourable these two lessons, Monzur could not know then that searing consequences would come of his later failure at one and his fidelity to the other.

Monzur arrived home to a war-ravaged country. Everyone in Bangladesh was touched by death and loss and living uneasily with the tens of thousands of war babies born of rape by Pakistani soldiers. The economy, battered by global inflation, was afloat only because of foreign aid. The government was plagued with corruption and incompetence. After Mujib's release from a prison in Pakistan, he had returned to serve as the country's first prime minister; while a charismatic leader, he proved inept at governing.

The Bangladesh Armed Forces gave returning prisoners of war a false choice: join the army or be considered a deserter. Monzur chose the army. He had another—long overdue—decision: setting a date to marry Rahima. Hewing to economy, he brokered a match between a friend and fellow POW, Captain Haque Nazim, a signal officer from Dhaka, and Molly—the two same age and both fun-loving—and they agreed to a double wedding. He set a date in September, limited the guest list to 250 and arranged for a friend to lend the courtyard of his house for a dinner.

Monzur began his marriage when the purchasing power of his monthly pay lasted only ten to twelve days. Since April, Bangladesh had been in the grip of a devastating famine brought on by heavy rainfall and a series of massive floods, and worsened by the government's mismanagement of rice stocks. For months, Bangladeshis had to scrimp and scratch for most everything. Monzur was forced to borrow heavily from his brother-in-law Maqsood and rural relatives. Another sister, Polly, and her diplomat husband let him move his bride, his mother and now four siblings still of school age into the finished part of a house they were building in Dhaka. Monzur joined the family only on his days off; the army had assigned him for the next year to the air force base in the port city of Chittagong, to oversee the construction and maintenance of infrastructure.

It was three and a half years before Monzur was back on secure footing. His debts squared, and his younger siblings in high school, he was ready now to take on the responsibility of starting his own family.

In 1978, during the monsoon season when the nights stay stubbornly hot and leave the earth steamy by dawn, one hour after midnight on the ninth of June, Rahima gave birth to a girl. She named her Rumana. Its meaning—"heaven's fruits"—acknowledged her arrival as a salve for the loss Rahima felt at not having truly known her own parents. Her father had succumbed to liver disease when she was three, and her mother was taken by cholera one year later. The first-born of the eldest son was a child to be cherished, but

Rumana arrived to even greater excitement: she was the first girl in more than a dozen years to be born in the next generation of the extended family. Rumana would be known by family as Hema, a "milk" nickname (bestowed at birth) meaning gold.

Everyone who set eyes on baby Hema was besotted. "There has never been a child who smiles more." "This child is the most angelic ever." "A more contented, adorable child cannot be found." Her smile became her trademark: it began with a crinkle at the edges of her eyes, settled into her deep dimples in her cheeks, then burst forth. Smitten with his niece, Maqsood entered a photograph of her in the competition for the most beautiful baby of the month sponsored by his employer, Glaxo, a British pharmaceutical company for which he was the representative in Bangladesh. Originally a general trading company, Glaxo turned excess fresh milk from family farms into dried milk and marketed it under the slogan "Glaxo builds bonnie babies." The company calendar would hang for years in Jolly and Maqsood's home, open to the month of June and his niece's winning photograph. In it, a chubby, smiling baby Hema sits plopped on her diapered bottom, a shock of black curly hair framing her big brown eyes.

In happy synchronicity, Molly and Haque were expecting a baby the same year. Three months after Rahima gave birth, Molly had a baby boy. She and Rahima, once roommates and best friends, then sisters-in-law and now first-time mothers together, would raise their first-borns almost as twins.

"I live like a queen!" Rahima exclaimed. By the time Rumana was born, the Monzur household employed a live-in cook and a maid. Domestic help was not an indulgence; even poor rural families took in an orphan child as help in exchange for food and a place to lay their head. In the city, help was a necessity. Any one of the daily chores of shopping, cooking, and cleaning could take a full day, especially in the winter when there was no rain to wash away the dust.

Three years after Rumana was born, the Monzurs had a son, Mashrur. Despite her mother's time being consumed by her brother, Rumana did not lack for maternal attention. Jolly gladly took her overnight. At home, by day, Rumana retreated to the room of Grandmother Momena. She sat at her feet while the old lady brushed her waist-length hair, redolent with coconut oil. Hours were passed listening to stories of her grandmother's beginnings, the grandfather Rumana had never met, her life as a young widow. Momena had met Golam Hossain when she was a student at the Lady Brabourne College for Muslim women in Calcutta, as the Indian city was then called, and he was serving with the British Reserve Forces in the Second World War. They married and returned home to East Bengal to raise a family. The youngest of their nine children was only two months old when Golam died prematurely.

Childrearing was a Bangladeshi mother's domain; a father's responsibility took hold only when the children's lives took them outside the home. Now that he was a father, Monzur assessed his ambitions for his children.

Two things his father told him echoed in his mind. He spoke of growing up in a remote village where he dreamed of attending school, unlike his two brothers who wanted no more out of a day than the time to sit and gossip. He went on to become a lawyer. "I got myself an education so that my children could have an education," he said. The second was a final piece of fatherly advice, though neither Monzur nor Golam knew it at the time it was given. Golam was visiting Monzur at his high school hostel, where as usual, he was lazing rather than studying. "Educate yourself, that's capital," Golam said. Not long after, Monzur's sister Polly showed up with news that their father was dead from a ruptured chronic ulcer. In the way that a flood can change the course of a river, Monzur's keening grief would change his attitude toward learning.

In his careful, calculating way, Monzur considered his ability to afford his ambitions. He wanted to be able to afford the fees of the better schools, whether public or private. Middle and upper class families who eventually wanted to send their children abroad to study favoured private schools, which went by the UK curriculum and taught in English. These schools had sprung up since independence as investors saw opportunity in the country's poor education system and in the aspirations of parents. But what Monzur wanted most was that his children develop a broad and enlightened outlook—which he felt would be best accomplished through travel. He set a goal: to take his children, while still in grade school, and wife on an extended trip overseas.

For a second time in his career, Monzur questioned the viability of remaining in the military. Although he had reached the rank of major, his salary afforded him less and less, and the army had eliminated most benefits. But monetary issues were not his biggest disappointment with military life. It wasn't the well-ordered culture he'd known when first recruited by the Pakistan Army. Respect and discipline were sorely lacking. Still, Monzur took pride in the quality of his work and maintained his passion for engineering. He saw a compromise: he could start his own business, as Retired Major Monzur. When he had first returned from captivity, he had to win over former freedom fighters who were suspicious of men like him who'd not fought in the War of Independence. But in the years since, his professionalism and reliability earned him respect in every branch of the military, respect that could now help him secure army engineering and construction contracts.

Monzur was decided. In 1982, after twelve years in the military, he took voluntary retirement and launched his company. He set up an office in Dhaka. To minimize risk—his family's future rested on his business—he started small by sourcing and delivering bricks, transformers and rivets, deciding to scale up only as he built a record of success.

When the time came to choose a school for Rumana, Monzur decided that his business, expanding as it was, had not yet grown to the point where he could afford the better private schools. He opted to send Rumana to the Mohammadpur Preparatory School, a public school that enrolled boys and girls, and that he judged to have a higher standard than lower-ranked private schools. Mohammadpur Preparatory, a half-hour's drive across the city from home, was near Monzur's office and, fortuitously, steps from Jolly and Maqsood's apartment. Monzur, now owner of a reconditioned Toyota Corolla, dropped his daughter at school on his way to work, and Jolly met her at the end of the day and kept her until Monzur was done. During those after-school hours, Rumana gained a mentor: Rashed, Jolly's middle child, a university student. He sat down daily with her to review that day's school work—emulating the example of his mother, who required that the orphan children she brought from the village for a year of schooling account for their progress by demonstrating a grasp of the day's newspaper headlines. After their studying, Rashed then rewarded his young cousin with a double-ride around the block and a visit across the road to the sport field to fly a kite or, what she liked best, to coach her in cricket.

Monzur's business prospects kept looking up. The government, aiming to quell a separatist movement among tribes in the Chittagong Hill Tracts, had ramped up its military presence in the region, beginning a building spree expected to last years. When in the army, Monzur had been second-in-charge of the construction of a forty-five-kilometre road to link police outposts to the Burmese border along a route known to be used by insurgents, which ideally positioned him to supply the new government effort. Assured of a flow of steady contracts to build water and gas pipelines, roads, offices, houses and barracks for army personnel, Monzur was able to enrol his son, Mashrur, in a private school.

His children now going to school in opposite directions, Monzur chose to move the family closest to Rumana's school so she could be walked there and back. He rented an apartment in the building next door to Jolly and Maqsood's. To accompany Mashrur to and from school, either Monzur would drive or Rahima would take him by rickshaw. For two years, Monzur's and Jolly's homes were revolving doors of adults and children and visiting family from Dhaka and relatives from abroad. Rumana would remember that time as the idyll of her childhood. Always, she had cousins to play with, enough to field a cricket team to play at the sport field across the road.

Abruptly, Rumana's life quieted when her aunt and uncle moved to a house of their own in a new neighbourhood. As the only girl among the four families in the building, and her brother busy with younger friends—especially once a wealthy family across the road bought their son an Atari game console—Rumana was left without a playmate. Her mother encouraged a new favourite way to spend free time: drawing and colouring. At a parent-teacher meeting, Rumana's fourth-grade teacher praised her student's landscapes, so Rahima bought coloured markers and drawing paper for use at home. Rumana's interest in art grew as an outlet for her creativity, especially in the use of colour.

When Rumana was in fourth grade, boys who weren't family disappeared from her daily life. Her parents transferred her to an all-girls school. Molly, a teacher, had advised it, telling Monzur that students at Agrani School, established in 1957 in the Azimpur neighbourhood, always performed well in the nationwide tenth-grade tests, the first hurdle in the path to university.

In sixth grade, Rumana's education took a turn away from the classroom. Financed by his successful business, Monzur had accomplished one of his life's goals: raising a building for a primary school in his late father's village. Now he was ready to realize another goal: to take his family abroad. After seven years of saving, he could afford a trip of four months and cover the loss of income while he was away. "You can learn by reading," Monzur intoned to his children, "but you must also learn by seeing." He told them he'd already informed their teachers that they would be away from October to January and had pledged that both children would work hard to catch up when they returned.

Monzur drew up a meticulous itinerary, leg by leg, day by day. Travelling by rail, car and ferry, the family covered the breadth of Western Europe, from Rome in the south to the Danish city of Aarhus in the north, then across the English Channel to London. At every stop, he had identified landmarks for the family to see. The Vatican, the Colosseum, the Eiffel Tower. The headquarters of the United Nations in Europe. Buckingham Palace, Trafalgar Square. He explained historical figures commemorated with statues, from Julius Caesar to Admiral Horatio Nelson. He spoke of turning points in history as the family climbed the slope of the Lion's Mound, marking where Napoleon met his downfall in the Battle of Waterloo. He shared lessons for low-lying Bangladesh gleaned from the dams, floodgates and storm surge barriers holding back the North Sea from the Netherlands. In England, he took the family to Folkestone to see the English side of the Chunnel under construction.

In the Netherlands, the Monzurs stayed several weeks in Utrecht with his brother, Moynul, fulfilling Monzur's responsibility as the eldest son in the family to check in on his siblings. Moynul and his Danish wife, Anne Marie, led the Monzurs on a bicycle tour of the "cyclists-first" city and took them to Denmark to visit Anne Marie's family. English being the only language in common, Rumana had a chance to put her conversational skills to practice. The Monzurs' trip wound down with a last stop in the US, in New

Jersey, to visit Dolly, the youngest sister, and the youngest brother, Mostaque, whom Monzur had sent to live with Dolly and her husband for his last year of high school.

So that his own children understood the value of the experience abroad, Monzur told them on the plane ride to Bangladesh that with what the trip cost, he could have purchased a lot on the outskirts of Dhaka and built them a modest house. To go from renters to homeowners would have vaulted the family into the city's upper class. At the time, the remark went over Rumana's head. Years later, she realized her father's choice underscored how their family, for generations, valued education more than any material good.

Rumana was determined to improve her comprehension of English. Lonely again at home, she made her way through the shelf at the local library that contained a young adult series of condensed Western classics in English. Among her favourites, Alexandre Dumas's *Count of Monte Cristo*, *Man in the Iron Mask* and *Three Musketeers*, and *The Blue Lagoon* by Henry De Vere Stacpoole. And she worked on her art. When her uncle Moynul was next visiting Bangladesh and asked what he could bring her, she asked for coloured pencils. The sixty Dutch-made pencils were suited to Rumana, given her streak of perfectionism. It was Grandmother Momena who noticed how a slip of her young granddaughter's crayon to the wrong side of a line could bring her to tears. The pencils from Moynul, prized by professionals for their buttery soft lead and intense hues, became the staple of Rumana's art supplies.

Rumana finally gained the company of another girl when a new family moved into the building. They had returned to

Dhaka after the father's stint working in the Middle East. The mother knocked on the door to ask Rahima if their two daughters could be friends. Though Basma, a fifth-grader, was two grades lower, Rumana was happy for company. The mothers allowed them to go outside to ride their bicycles, but no more than a block from home, with strict instructions that they stay together and avoid the intersection where large trucks carrying loads of bricks rumbled through. Mostly the girls played at one or the other's apartment or climbed the building's stairs to the rooftop terrace. A ubiquitous feature of Dhaka's residential buildings, the terraces offered residents a secure place to be outside, above the dust and noise and chaos of the street below. Mostly, Rumana and Basma whiled away time sitting at the railing, four storeys above the street. If feeling energetic, they took their badminton racquets to the rooftop, chalked out a makeshift court and anchored a net between the water tank and the mounting pole of the television antenna. Or they played Twister, or, weary of tying their bodies into knots, Monopoly.

If ever her brother said he was going to the sport field to play cricket, Rumana joined him. One day, on their return home from a game with some neighbourhood boys, Rumana's mother made what struck her as an odd comment. "You don't want to be the only girl out there." Rumana couldn't think why her mother would say that. After all, she fancied herself a rather good batsman, able to time her stroke to use the speed of the bowler's ball to lift it to the boundary and score a six. Sometime later, in the midst of another game of cricket across the road, Rumana felt the eyes of male passersby who were standing on the other side of the two-metre wire fence. She didn't recognize them as being from any of the neighbourhood families. They're not looking at me in a good way, she thought. Puberty had come early for Rumana but only now, for the first time, was she feeling self-conscious about her billowing blouse.

Rumana didn't make a conscious decision to avoid the sports field, but she never went back.

In the playground at Agrani, girls wondered aloud whether their parents loved their brothers more than them. Rumana couldn't discern the feelings of her father. Anything personal he had to say to her or her brother was conveyed by their mother. He bypassed that only when Rahima brought what she deemed a misbehaviour to his attention for him to hold them to account. It had happened to Mashrur once: when called before his father to explain why he'd broken another child's toy, he'd quaked so violently that he never wanted to find himself in such a position again. As for the feelings of Rahima, Rumana felt she and her mother were close but her brother absorbed all her energies. Then again, he was demanding, loud and boisterous, where she was docile, soft-spoken and uncomplaining.

At school, it was unthinkable to Rumana's classmates that she would do or say anything to sadden anyone. She exuded positivity. The students confided in her freely. They went to her for comfort. Rumana was the voice of reason, the shoulder to cry on, the one to lift them up. She assuaged their fears and uncertainties. "This is not something you have control over." She was reassuring. "It will work out." If someone felt aggrieved, she persuaded them to find their way back to happiness. "Don't dwell on feeling wronged. Let it be." In her presence, girls found themselves on their best behaviour. They didn't use slang or utter a mean or ill-tempered word. One particularly rebellious classmate, Zana Shammi, liked to pinch Rumana's dimpled cheeks in affectionate greeting. "Hema, how come you're so-oh nice?"

When Rumana was in eighth grade and Mashrur in fifth, Monzur moved the family closer to the centre of Dhaka to Dhanmondi, a planned residential area developed in the 1950s. With its well-lit and wide roads, it was considered one of the city's safest neighbourhoods. Home was now a ground floor apartment in one of two 2-storey buildings that stood behind a shared wall. As added security, the occupant of the apartment above was their landlord, and in the building behind lived two brothers, one of whom had been a former engineering classmate of Monzur.

One afternoon, Rahima, as she did every day, took a rickshaw to pick up Mashrur from school. Twenty minutes later, two blocks from home, a motorcyclist pulled alongside and forced their wallah to stop. Three men emerged from the roadside. One brandished a pistol. "Don't shout," he told Rahima. "You have a son." She did as he demanded and handed over her purse and jewellery.

When Monzur learned of the robbery, he marched to the Dhanmondi police station. He didn't expect the culprits to be caught. As a consequence of the country's deteriorating social security system, petty crime was on the rise. Snatchings were commonplace. Passengers on a rickshaw could easily lose a purse or a bag to a passing rider on a Vespa. Rather, Monzur thought because Dhanmondi was an upscale neighbourhood, the local police would want to monitor such street crime.

The moment Monzur entered the station, he was treated with suspicion. The officer impugned his motives for coming in. Why was his wife on that block? Why did she have that much cash? Why was she wearing her jewellery? Monzur could see where the officer was headed; he was trying to frame him for collusion with the perpetrators. Monzur left hastily, before the officer could force a bribe out of him to disentangle himself from a contrived conspiracy. At home, Monzur told Rahima that going to the police had been a waste of time. He advised her to leave her jewellery at home in future and to take a chequebook and a minimum of cash.

Monzur pondered his first-ever experience with police. It was true what people said: educated people do not go to the police. He expected to never have need of them. Monzur knew that any person contemplating harm to his family would soon learn that the head of the family was Major Monzur, whose engineering business was built on military connections. That ought to make them at least think twice.

Now that Rumana's home was located more conveniently, she could invite friends from Agrani after school. Her two best friends came with her when her father picked her up. The arrangement helped their families, as the parents kept odd working hours. Shehneela Tilat's belonged to a local theatre troupe; her mother was an actress and her father did lighting and sound. Farzana Morshed's mother, who was divorced, worked as a clerk at Imperial Tobacco. Her workday started early and it ended late. Both girls' mothers gave their approval for their daughters to go home with Rumana; her home had supervision, since her mother didn't work.

Rumana had befriended the pair when she first arrived at Agrani and students were clamouring to sit beside the pretty new girl who'd joined midway through fourth grade. Seeing one of them, Shehneela, reduced to tears at being elbowed aside, Rumana told everyone that tomorrow it would be her turn. Farzana, meanwhile, had many friends. It was not always so; in first grade, girls whispered about her coming from a broken home, and before her father disappeared from her life, teachers had not hidden their confusion about which parent was picking her up on any given day.

In accordance with the household's inviolable rule of study before play, the three girls first tackled their homework. Unlike her friends' homes, Rumana's had window air conditioning units in the bedrooms, which allowed the girls to work more comfortably and, therefore, more productively at their homework. They then moved on to watching a DVD or making greeting cards on Monzur's Compaq 386. Or they turned to what was forbidden by the dress codes at Agrani: trying different hairstyles, hair clips and coloured elastics, and experimenting with lipsticks and face powder from Rahima's dressing table.

The three friends sometimes mused about becoming brides, when, for a day, they'd each be transformed into a beautiful goddess. They gave no thought to the identity of the groom; that was a matter for their parents.

For a young woman, marriage was not always the stuff of teenage fantasies. One recent story that was impossible to avoid as a subject of gossip was a husband's murder of his wife, a crime case that pitted two prominent families in Dhaka against each other. Sharmin Rima, a graduate of one of Dhaka's top colleges, was the daughter of a martyred journalist and correspondent with the BBC who'd broken stories of Pakistani atrocities during the war. Munir Hussain, a graduate of an American university, was the son of a renowned gynecologist and the owner of a major textile factory. In 1989, after only four months of marriage, Munir stabbed Sharmin and dumped her body in a roadside ditch between Dhaka and Chittagong. Dramatic headlines accompanied every revelation of the police investigation, including a reported trove of nude photos and obscene videos that implicated the husband in a long-running affair with the middle-aged wife of a disabled man. The husband's trial resulted in a death sentence. When the government carried out the sentence in 1992, disbelieving crowds, wanting proof, chased the truck carrying his body.

Rumana, on the cusp of her teenage years when news of the murder broke, had little interest in the lurid details. She thought only of how the young woman's life could have turned out differently. Had the two families not forced their son and daughter into an arranged marriage, the beautiful Sharmin could still be alive.

As Rumana's life took her beyond home and school, Monzur and Rahima, like other parents, worried that the outside world could be hostile—even dangerous—to their daughter. The greater visibility of females—more girls enrolled in and stayed longer in school, and girls and women worked in the garment factories—fed into a notion of a female in public as a temptress and deserving of whatever vulgarity came her way. In Rahima's youth, delinquent boys might try to get girls' attention by calling out to them or throwing a shower of pebbles in their direction. In

Rumana's time, boys and men, from rickshaw wallahs to bus drivers, even traffic police, felt at liberty to whistle, hoot, stare, shout obscene words, make lewd gestures or expose themselves. At its most threatening, "Eve-teasing" escalated to sexual assault. Police could not be expected to help. A girl or woman going near, much less into, a police station put her at risk of rape by police themselves. Either way, the victim's future would be ruined. She would be dogged by blame, rumour and gossip. Her family's ability to marry her into a good family would be gone.

Living in the safety of Dhanmondi and moving in the educated circles the family did, Monzur's only worry was that Rumana might become so afraid of encountering harassment or teasing that she'd not want to leave the house. If so, her education would be jeopardized. "I'm not willing to chance it," he told his wife. Accordingly, Monzur set strict rules for his daughter travelling in public: whenever he was available, he would drive her to and from any destination, door to door, a rule that would hold at least until she started university. He set different rules for his son. He permitted Mashrur, once he turned thirteen, to take a rickshaw alone to and from school, then farther afield once he turned sixteen.

Parents of girls at Agrani could expect that their daughters did not have to contend with a mixed setting until they graduated and went to college for grades eleven and twelve. However, many parents allowed their daughters in ninth grade to participate in tutorials offered at the homes of moonlighting teachers, to get a head start on the fierce competition for acceptance to Dhaka University. Every year, some two hundred thousand students vied for fewer than five thousand first-year seats. Admission was based on a student's scores on nationwide exams in tenth and twelfth grade, and the score on the university entrance exam.

As Rumana always placed in the top three or four of her class, she was left by her parents to select tutorials, which teachers offered to groups of eight or ten students, girls and boys. Rahima weighed in only to ensure Molly's son, Rana, signed up for the same sessions, allowing Rumana to travel with Molly's driver and in her cousin's company. By Monzur's rules, Rumana could ride with another family's driver but never alone—drivers came and went so often it wasn't worth the effort to investigate them or their family's background—so Molly's driver would pick up Rumana only once Rana was already in the car and drop her at home first.

Rahima's first mention of the opposite sex to her daughter ought to have been years away, when she and Monzur decided the time had come to think about arranging a marriage for Rumana. But one day, Rahima put a pointed question to the teenager. She named a boy and asked Rumana if she knew him.

Rumana did not; she assumed the boy had to be from one of the tutorials.

Rahima explained. A letter addressed to Major Monzur had arrived at the house. The boy who'd written it had enclosed a photograph of himself and asked for an introduction to his daughter. He wasn't the only boy asking after her. Another had telephoned the house and asked to speak to Major Monzur. When Monzur got on the phone, the boy asked permission to speak to his daughter.

At that explanation, Rahima, whose serene temperament had

much to do with her avoidance of confrontation, brought an end to an uncomfortable subject, for both mother and daughter.

Rumana knew her parents trusted her to steer clear of any impropriety. She went to the tutorials with a strictly academic purpose. At school, while other girls were eager to gossip about boys in each other's tutorials, Rumana did not let the subject cross her lips. However, the tutorials had opened her eyes to what the "cool" girls were up to. A parent would drop their daughter at the tutor's home and return to collect her two hours later, none the wiser that she'd skipped the session and gone off to meet a boy.

Of course, no girl or boy would ever tell.

Dating was a Western concept. Parents disapproved of an unmarried boy and an unmarried girl alone together and in close proximity because it could spiral into physical contact, which was haram (forbidden by Islamic law). Yet, such subterfuge of teen boys and girls meeting was often no more than curiosity about what it would be like to speak to someone of the opposite sex who wasn't family. A person could have friends only of the same gender.

Rumana had no interest in meeting "outside" boys (unknown to the family) on her own. Even if she did, she reasoned, she wouldn't be able to discern which boy would make for a "special relationship." She saw herself as too trusting, unable to sort good people from bad. Anyway, she did not like to waste time.

One day after school an Agrani classmate was visiting. She asked for Rumana's help; she wanted to meet a boy without her mother finding out. She had tried before, phoning her mother from the house of another friend to ask if she could stay later. Her mother, immediately suspicious, had said no.

"I'll have a better chance with you," the friend said.

Rumana could not imagine herself engaging in such deception. If her parents found out, she'd lose their trust, to say nothing of how she'd hurt them. But at the chance to show solidarity with the rebel crowd, Rumana agreed to her friend's plan.

The telephone was in her parents' bedroom, the room where families who could afford a landline installed them so the adults could monitor who was calling the house. Rahima and a visiting neighbour had settled in the lounge, out of earshot.

The friend dialed her mother. She asked if she could stay one hour longer. "Auntie said I could."

A pleading look came over Rumana's friend's face as she handed her the receiver. Hardly had she begun to repeat the story they'd rehearsed when the mother abruptly refused. Rumana couldn't be convincing, not when she ventured so close to what her father called the "sin of all sins"—telling a lie.

two

RUMANA KNEW ONLY A FEW THINGS ABOUT THE FAMILY friend her father spoke of. They'd been close since their university days, and he now lived with his family in Chittagong. And her father had now invited Syeed Ahmed and his wife, Hasina Begun—Kabir and Ruby to family and friends—and their two sons, to join them on a long weekend getaway. Courtesy of Molly and her husband, Haque, the extended Monzur family were planning to spend several days together in Mymensingh. To Dhaka residents wanting to escape the city and its summertime sweltering heat, the scenic city of Mymensingh, located three hours north of Dhaka on the banks of the Old Brahmaputra River, promised cooler temperatures. Like Monzur, Haque had been released from the POW camp after the war and joined the new Bangladesh Armed Forces. Now a colonel, he was serving with the Bangladesh Rifles, a border security force, as commander of the district of Mymensingh. Molly and their two sons joined him on the weekends.

Had Monzur flipped through one of the family's photo albums with Rumana, she would have seen a photograph recording her first introduction to the Kabir family: at six months she sits propped between their daughter, Sabira, and their second-born child, Sumon, respectively aged eight and four. The families had last gathered six years ago at Sabira's wedding, when Rumana was in the wedding party. She could remember being spellbound at how beautiful Sabira was as a bride and how she'd fussed over Rumana as if she were a little sister. She had no memory of Sabira's young brothers from that time, but Mashrur did, because Sumon had been tasked with keeping him and the Kabirs' youngest son, Shawon, out of trouble.

Since Monzur and Kabir's days as roommates at the Pakistan University of Engineering and Technology (after independence renamed BUET—Bangladesh University of Engineering and Technology), Kabir had been known to the entire Monzur family. Everywhere Monzur went he collected friends. None, however, had remained closer than the three he lived with during his university years. From their first days together, the foursome told each other they had a bond for life: Monzur was the open-hearted one; Kabir, the wisecracker with leading-man looks; Mustafizer Rahman, the poet and idealist; Farrukh Mohsen, the gentlemanly genius.

The other three had a special admiration for Kabir as someone who seemed to persevere in life through sheer force of will. Orphaned young, he had run away at age fifteen from an unkind older brother and presented himself at a madrasa—a religious school that opened its doors to the poor and homeless—where he became a devoted student of orthodox Islamic theology and religious law. At age twenty, astute enough to recognize that without a broader education he wouldn't be able to support himself, he enrolled in a public school. On graduation from university, he married Ruby, to whom he was engaged while a student, and took a job with the government water development board. Monzur was hired by the council in Jessore. The other two went abroad for their doctorates and stayed overseas. The pair left behind drew only closer.

On Monzur's first chance following his release from captivity, he reunited with Kabir in Chittagong. Only then did he meet his friends' first two children. And now the Kabirs were soon to be left at home with only Shawon, their third and youngest. Sumon was eighteen and about to head off to India for university.

Monzur organized two microbuses from Dhaka and had the Kabirs meet them there for the trip north. He divided the crowd departing Dhaka—his family and those of Molly, Jolly and Polly—between the two buses.

On Rumana's bus, Monzur put Rahima, Ruby, each with their children, and Jolly. He added Jolly's son, Rashed, so that there was an adult male with them. Rashed sat next to the driver. The three mothers shared the seat behind, and in the rear seat Rumana and Sumon sat against the windows, their little brothers squeezed between them. Rumana thought the ride felt like a party. Her lively recounting of a Hindi movie she'd just seen kept everyone entertained. Jolly added explanations and filled in details— "Hema, how will anybody understand if you don't say. . . "

Everyone, adults and children alike, chimed in, taking on the roles of the characters.

On arrival, Rumana could see how Molly and Haque were able to throw large parties on their family's weekends together at Mymensingh. Haque's posting came with a four-bedroom house on sprawling grounds that sloped down to the wide river. The property included manicured gardens, an ornamental pond and a tennis court. The couple were all for it when Monzur asked if he could invite the Kabirs.

Haque encouraged everyone to enjoy the fresh air, the gardens and the tennis court. He had planned two excursions: a tour of the area, which was dotted with mouldering palaces dating back to when Hindu zamindars administered swaths of the Bengal region of the Indian subcontinent; and a trip two hours west to Madhupur National Forest for a stroll through its moist groves of towering sal trees, where they hoped to spot brown wood owls sleeping in their branches. To cap off the weekend, Haque had scheduled a cruise on the Old Brahmaputra River.

For Monzur, the days away were a much-needed break.

Where he had once prided himself on keeping a balance between work and family, the balance had tipped sharply toward work. He was now not only in the engineering business, but as of several months ago, had ventured into the ready-made garment business. He had thought it prudent to diversify as the prospects of military contracts in the Chittagong Hill Tracts had waned with recent peace talks between the government and insurgent tribal groups. Monzur had been keeping an eye on the garment industry since Bangladesh's first joint venture in 1980 with the

South Korean conglomerate Daewoo to sew jackets for export to Sweden. Satisfied with the industry's decade-long track record, Monzur had joined with two investors. One was a silent partner, the other provided the building for a factory, and Monzur's role was to set up and oversee the business. He outfitted the building with cutting tables and sewing machines and hired 250 workers.

Monzur soon learned that the garment industry's complicated supply chain allowed him none of the control to which he was accustomed in his engineering business. The local agent he hired could land contracts with only low-budget retailers interested in cheap jeans, jackets and polar fleeces. Only zippers and cardboard packing cartons could be sourced locally. Everything else—fabrics, fleece, buttons, thread—had to be imported from Hong Kong or China. Supplies would finally arrive in the port of Chittagong only to be tied up in customs, incurring storage costs and running out the clock on clients' deadlines, and on the letters of credit that covered the cost of supplies. Meanwhile, he had to meet payroll.

His long days at the factory forced Monzur to give up looking for contracts for his engineering business and left him in a constant state of tension at work. The effort required to keep his ill mood from following him home only made it worse. So when Molly and Haque's invitation came, he felt he owed it to his family to accept. And he looked forward to seeing his close friend Kabir. Rarely did the two see each other, and usually only if one had business where the other lived, although Kabir never let more than two weeks go by without speaking to Monzur on the telephone.

As happened at every family gathering, the adults started together. Soon enough the men and women congregated separately.

Rumana noticed that the Kabirs' eldest son, who stayed with the children rather than the adults, was taking it upon himself to see that she was happy. Seeming not to mind the four years between them, Sumon showed her extraordinary consideration. He asked whether she liked the food. Her aunt's aloo chaat was delicious. Was she thirsty? Would she like a lemonade? Rumana had a sense of awe at doing something novel: she and the Kabirs' son were actually having a conversation. When Sumon was invited to join a tennis game, he offered to forfeit his turn for her. In a game of Monopoly, in which Rashed and Mashrur teamed up against her and Sumon, he asked Rumana what she thought their strategy should be, then lauded her response: "Oh, I hadn't thought of that." Rumana again was awed. Uncle's son not only asked her questions, he listened to her answers. She thought about how her parents never asked her opinion, as if children were not supposed to have any.

Sumon's attentiveness caught the amused notice of Rashed. "Hema, Sumon's trying to impress you."

On the last day of vacation, Haque engaged a tabla player and a singer who also played the harmonium for the river cruise. Haque directed the women and children to take the shade of the canopy in the middle of the boat and to sit on the large cushions he'd put there. Gliding across the serene waters took everyone far from city life. Fishermen poled their black wooden boats while scanning the riverbanks for villagers who would signal they wanted to be ferried across. Nearby, cows and goats stood placidly in the shade of gnarled banyan trees. At the magic hour around sunset, iridescent stripes of pink and purple etched the sky and danced in the water.

If only the musicians did not play and sing so often, thought Rumana. It made conversation difficult, and she would have liked Sumon to speak more to her.

The Kabir family had slipped from Rumana's mind when, months later, she overheard their names in a conversation between her father and mother. It seemed some kind of crisis had developed. It sounded serious; Kabir was in Dhaka and her father had arranged to go meet him.

On her father's return, Rumana listened keenly as he spoke to her mother. Apparently, Sumon had come home mid-semester from India and was refusing to go back.

The next day, Kabir joined them for dinner. At one point he turned to Rahima. "Have you heard? Sumon's back."

"Why do you think he returned home?" Rahima asked.

"He says he can't eat the food there. He says he has to walk long distances from the hostel to where his classes are."

Rumana heard in Kabir's dismissive tone that he thought these were excuses. He said that he and his wife were at odds, that she defended their son and believed him to be simply homesick.

It didn't make sense to Rumana that Sumon, newly enrolled in a prestigious university, would cut short his studies. More incomprehensible, that he'd defy his father's wishes. There has to be more to the story, she thought.

Not long after that, from what she overheard, the crisis had blown over. Sumon was resuming his studies in Dhaka. On his own initiative, he'd written the university entrance exam for BUET, with plans to study engineering.

The date of the nationwide tenth-grade exams fast approaching, Rumana had devised a strict study schedule when her mother asked if she could spare some time off. Ruby had proposed another getaway, a long weekend with her and the boys in Chittagong. Kabir was working upcountry, and Monzur could not afford to take time off work. It would just be mothers and children.

Rahima offered an inducement to help persuade her daughter. They could afford to travel first-class on the train because they would stay with Ruby. Rumana considered her upcoming exams but allowed that some rest before she got down to studying would be welcome.

The Kabirs' driver collected the guests at the Chittagong station. The high status of the Kabirs was evident to Rumana when the car entered a gated community. The driver stopped in front of a two-storey house. It was modest, but the Kabirs owned it.

For much of the weekend, the two mothers were joined by one of Ruby's younger sisters—her husband was too busy at his job as Chittagong's chief public prosecutor to even drop by—and her son. The same age as Shawon, he had been company for Sumon's much younger brother during his otherwise lonely childhood. When Shawon was age four, Sumon had left for boarding school, and their sister and her new husband had moved to Texas, leaving Shawon to grow up like an only child.

Ruby's hospitality rivalled Molly and Haque's. She reserved a microbus for a tour of the city. The driver also took them past its busy port and followed the road by the sea to see the beaches that lay beyond the boulders that protected the road from the tides. Next came a day trip to see the massive lake created by the Kaptai dam, the country's only hydroelectric plant. The sixty-five-kilometre drive there threaded through the lush jungle of the hill district of Rangamati, home to eleven Indigenous hill tribes.

On this visit, Rumana found herself homing in on the ways of the Kabirs' eldest son. At mealtimes, Sumon rose to serve his mother before serving himself. He used a fork and spoon to eat, in the Western fashion, and not with his fingers. With the same relaxed manner, he injected English words into the conversation. He spoke of "world politics," of "capitalism" and "socialism." He cited "contemporary issues" and gave as an example "feminism."

Rumana wondered why members of her own family didn't exhibit some of the same polish. They'd long been anglicized. Grandmother Momena and her husband had started their lives under the British Raj. Her father was perfectly fluent in English, her mother marginally less so. Both read daily papers in Bangla and in English. Both watched CNN and BBC broadcasts relayed on Bangladesh Television, the state-owned network. Yet, in the Monzurs' home, only Bangla was spoken. Cutlery stayed in the drawer, brought out only for guests who did not eat in the Bangladeshi way.

Rumana concluded that Sumon was the product of his cadet school, the premier boys' private school in the country. As the train from Dhaka had rolled into Chittagong, she had glimpsed the Faujdarhat Cadet College and its vast grounds, which included a track, a football field and a parade ground. The school, which was established by the Pakistanis in 1958 with a view to grooming future civilian and military leaders, required students to board in order to fully absorb the military-like discipline. In the vision of its first principal, an air force colonel from New Zealand, its graduates would be as renowned for gentlemanly etiquette and athletic prowess as for academic brilliance. In addition to sports, the boys had to prove their endurance by swimming rivers and learning to survive in the wilderness.

One evening in the lounge after dinner, the mothers and children were chatting together until, eventually, the three women became engrossed in their own conversation. Sumon's audience now only Rumana and the three younger boys, he started to tell stories of wars fought over control of the Holy Land. The boys grew bored, but Rumana was paying close attention. Sumon spoke of Saladin, the Muslim Sultan of Egypt and Syria, who led forays against the Christian Crusaders and, using his skills in warfare and politics, set about unifying the Muslim world. That was the first Rumana had heard of Saladin. When she returned home, she searched out a book in the library about the ancient leader. She delighted in how her passion for learning had been fuelled by Sumon sharing his knowledge.

Recalling Ruby's claim that her son had been homesick in India, Rahima made a point of inviting Sumon to join the family on special occasions. She thought he'd also appreciate relief from the monotony of canteen food at his hostel at BUET.

This new proximity to the Monzur family gave Rumana her first peek at university life. Ruby appeared at her parents' home one day with an invitation to join her in delivering a new mattress to Sumon for his dorm room.

Rahima also offered to take Sumon in on holidays or during any sudden closure of the campus because of a hartal (a twenty-four- or thirty-six-hour general strike called for by the opposition) or political turmoil in the city. It was an offer he had several occasions to accept. If Grandmother Momena's room was free—she had taken to spending months at a time with Moynul in the Netherlands—Rahima assigned him her room. Otherwise, she had Rumana give up her room. She bunked with her grandmother, and the maid, who normally laid her bedroll on Rumana's floor, moved to the cook's space in the storage room off the kitchen. Mashrur was relegated to a space open to the veranda—thus to mosquitoes—a space too small to share.

When attending gatherings at the Monzur home, Sumon gravitated to the women. Witty and charming, he held court. He endeared himself to Momena, showing her the deference that befit her status and age. The two fell into conversation about India, comparing their experiences five decades apart. Listening in, Rumana was bemused by his accounts of senior students ragging incoming freshmen—making the new students dress in white or black, oil their hair and address the seniors as sir. On special occasions when Rahima took over from the cook, Sumon made runs to a neighbourhood shop for missing ingredients. Wanting to make sure the younger ones were enjoying themselves, she'd ask him to go to the video store to get them a movie, or go buy them Fanta drinks or take them to the ice cream parlour. Sumon made an outing of every errand, joking and entertaining his charges as he shepherded them along.

Only sometimes did Rumana go with them. If she had free time from studying, she was eager to get back to her art projects.

One day, Rumana was sitting with her friend Farzana Morshed and her mother. She blurted out, "I've been outside with Sumon."

Farzana's mother had remarried and moved into an apartment in the building beside the Monzurs. Since the buildings were enclosed by the same security wall, Farzana and Rumana went freely between each other's homes. Each girl was as much at home in the other's apartment as in her own.

Perhaps because Farzana's upbringing was unconventional, Rumana felt safe to raise or voice aloud what she kept to herself at home. Out of necessity as a divorced woman, Farzana's mother had taught her and her sister, once they turned ten, to travel on their own, on foot and by rickshaw and public bus. They were not yet teenagers when they shopped from footpath vegetable vendors and at markets for meat and fish, and paid bills at the bank.

Farzana wondered if her friend's mention of Sumon was deliberate, to elicit a reaction from her mother. But the remark seemed to pass Farzana's mother by. Farzana thought it might. After all, her mother knew the Kabirs and Monzurs were close family friends.

Sometime after her friend's pointed remark, Farzana was asked by her mother if she'd like to have Rumana for company at a daylong picnic with relatives, in a celebration for a cousin's birthday. When she said yes, her mother asked Rahima's permission. In an exception to the Monzur family's rule that their children could not attend any non-family party where there was mixed company, Rahima gave her approval.

The day after the picnic, the cousin, who was three years older than Farzana, called her. He liked her friend. Could she ask Rumana if they could meet or speak on the telephone?

Farzana was torn. If she followed through and was discovered, Rumana's mother would be angry at hers, because Rumana was to have been supervised. Farzana could ask her mother's opinion about the cousin's request, but she could already hear her response, that even if Rumana's mother did come around, the cousin wasn't good enough for Hema. And Farzana would have to agree. The boy came from a good family and his good looks would stand out in any crowd, but he didn't go to university and wasted his time staying out late and driving around to show off his new car.

Rumana's comment stuck in Farzana's mind. Perhaps her friend really was curious about boys. Farzana had noticed of late how eagerly Rumana told her and her mother about the gifts Sumon's mother brought when she visited—one time gold jewellery, another time a pair of shoes in soft yellow leather from the UK. At first she thought Rumana was simply enthralled with the gifts, but now she wondered if she was interpreting them as a sign that Sumon's mother approved of her as a potential match for her son.

She elected to at least let Rumana know of her cousin's request. To Farzana's surprise, Rumana said she'd think about it.

As Rumana mulled how she might respond, a mutual friend of the two girls teased Rumana about her interest in the cousin. It brought Rumana to tears. "How could you say that?"

She told Farzana she was not interested in the cousin. "I don't want a special relationship."

Farzana had expected as much. Hema is not one to invite trouble, she thought. As long as she has her studies, her parents will not want any boy bothering her. She's going to do the right thing.

In tenth grade, two years later than most girls gave up wearing Western clothes in public, Rumana finally acquiesced to convention.

Beyond that, her mother left her free to appear as she liked. If anything, Rahima was more liberal in that respect than other mothers, who believed the safest way to avoid the male gaze was to disappear into anonymity. Shehneela Tilat's mother imposed rules for her when in public: "Cover yourself to the ankle. Tie your hair back, don't make it fancy." Zana Shammi's mother subjected her to a once-over before she left the house: "I don't want you to look pretty!"

Rumana went to the tailor with her mother, armed with sketches to customize her shalwar kameez so they would flatter her full figure—by Bangladeshi standards, desirable in a woman. She explained her designs: to give her a lengthening and thinning look, the kameez tunic top should hug her bosom and flare slightly above the knee, and a sewn-in belt should replace the conventional knot at the waist. In choosing fabrics, she looked for plain textures in rich, deep colours that complemented her honeyed complexion. Rumana was specific about the hue—a "mossy" green, a "peachy" orange, a "mustard" yellow. Her mother also left her free to express her individuality. She wore her thick, wavy black hair long and loose. She purchased tinted hard contact lenses for cosmetic reasons, to change her eye colour from dark brown to hazel, a less common shade.

In most every other way, Rumana's parents were more strict. When travelling in public, she had to be driven and picked up by her father, and she could go nowhere alone. In a singular exception, if within five minutes of home in the immediate neighbourhood, once Rumana turned thirteen, by then in eighth grade, she was permitted to walk or go by rickshaw there and back with her brother (their destination usually the video store or library).

Other parents, once their daughters reached eighth grade, gave them freer rein, allowing them to travel without a parent and with another girl or girls. One occasion not to be missed was Pahela Falgun, a daytime street festival held annually near Dhaka University, to welcome the first day of spring. On that day, young and old turn out dressed in a blaze of red, yellow and orange, to enjoy a day of poems, song and dance, and food. In eighth grade, when friends invited Rumana, she had to say no, that by her father's rules, any number of girls together counted as being alone. Rumana's friends started calling her "Baby."

Her parents loosened the restrictions when she turned fifteen and was in eleventh grade: they extended the distance she could go within the neighbourhood, if keeping company with one or more girls.

The Snow White Ice Cream Parlour, the first in the city to have a soft ice cream machine, was a fifteen-minute walk away. Though a favourite outing, no matter how many times Rumana and her friends went, she was too nervous to look at or speak to the male server. Her friends ordered for her. Always it was the same: "She'll have a chocolate soft ice cream cone, with chocolate sprinkles." It was not lost on them that Rumana's great modesty epitomized the way a perfect girl ought to behave in public on encountering a male stranger: quiet and shy.

The more relaxed rules of Rumana's parents only marginally extended her horizons. Her parents' rules denied Rumana the opportunity to join friends when they moved on from whatever destination Rahima had approved. Occasionally, as her friends exchanged ideas about what they might do next—go shopping, take in a film, meet up with other friends—she contemplated calling her mother to ask her approval to go with them, but she worried that the request itself could make her mother suspicious.

Even once school turned coed in eleventh grade, the nickname "Baby" hung on. So she devised a strategy to rid herself of it. When going out with friends, she declared a later commitment in the day. In that way, she shielded herself from having to decline any talk of onward plans, and could keep to the prearranged time her father was to pick her up. Always, her commitment had something to do with the Kabir family visiting. Mostly, "Sumon's coming." True or not, she won in two ways. In arriving home at the hour she'd agreed with her mother, she kept safe what she valued most: her parents' trust. If, in fact, Sumon was to stay and it was her room to be given to him, she had time to make sure any clothing, books and half-completed art projects she'd left lying about were put away.

"Baby" gave way to other teasing.

"Oh, so Hema, you'd rather be with Sumon than hang out with us?"

"What's the hurry, make him wait for you."

In her wake, her friends smiled at each other. "She's falling for him."

None took it seriously. Their comments gave Rumana a sense of maturity that was level with her friends'. No one called her "Baby" anymore.

One month before Rumana was to sit for the entrance exam for Dhaka University, she fell ill with a fever. Concerned that she'd fallen behind in her strict study schedule, she deferred her exam to the next intake. To make use of her time until then, she enrolled in a diploma course in computer studies at the new North South University, Dhaka's first private university.

The computer studies program brought Rumana into contact with male students older than her seventeen years. Some had already been out in the working world. Eager to learn and to benefit from the wider experience of fellow students, Rumana participated enthusiastically in discussions in class and conversations in the halls and at the canteen. Her ebullient personality emerged. Soon, a couple of male students competed to fall into step with her between classes and to ask if she'd like to go with them for lunch at the canteen. If she arrived at the canteen alone, others leapt to their feet to offer her space at their table. Though she was flattered, the attention worried Rumana. She cautioned herself to be more wary in her exchanges with male students, so as to not leave herself vulnerable to distraction from her studies.

Finally, Rumana earned admission to Dhaka University. A higher score on the entrance exam would have qualified her to study economics, but she was more than happy to study the second-ranked discipline, international relations. Monzur thought international relations suited her. When she told him that she envisaged a career in the United Nations or foreign service, he suggested that, after a master's degree, she take the highly competitive civil service recruitment exam. Pleased at her ambition, he encouraged her to keep her sights on her goal.

Where once it was his eldest son who had upset Kabir, by dropping out of university in India, now it was the younger Shawon who disappointed, with a poor performance in his tenth-grade exams. Kabir shared with Monzur that he'd decided his son would benefit from the discipline afforded by one of the better private schools in Dhaka.

Accordingly, Kabir set up his wife and Shawon in the capital city, while remaining behind himself in Chittagong. Ruby's mind was eased by her husband's continuing presence there; they owned land, and she worried that if it were left unguarded someone with political clout might try to seize it for themselves.

Kabir purchased a spacious three-bedroom apartment for the family in Paribagh, an area of Dhaka where high-rise apartment buildings first sprouted. The Kabirs' apartment was on the seventh floor of a new ten-storey building. At street level was a jumble of small shopkeepers and street vendors. Conveniently for Kabir when he came in from Chittagong, there was a mosque on the corner. With the apartment's third bedroom free, Sumon left his hostel and moved in with his mother and brother.

On a visit with her family, Rumana noticed the Kabirs' new apartment to be a dramatic upgrade from their home in Chittagong. Every room was furnished with custom-made heavy mahogany furniture in a semi-Victorian style. In the living room, a glassed-in buffet stored Waterford crystal from Ireland and museum-quality Steuben glassware from New York. In the dining room, corner cupboards displayed South Asian knickknacks and collectibles on mirrored shelves. Framed artwork on the walls reflected travels abroad.

One of Rumana's visits came at the invitation of the Kabirs' daughter, Sabira. She and her husband were visiting from Texas.

Days before they were to return home, she asked Rumana to come to Paribagh. Monzur drove Rumana and told her to call him when it was time for him to pick her up.

Rumana and Sabira sat with the family in the living room. The visit with her sister-in-law over, Rumana was about to call her father when Sabira begged a favour. Could Rumana stay a while longer to mind her child while she and her mother ran out to the tailor's shop? She had to pick up saris. On every visit to Dhaka, Sabira ordered at least a half-dozen saris; the small Bengali diaspora in Austin held several cultural events and parties during the year.

Left to entertain Sabira's five-year-old boy, Rumana asked him about his school and about his friends in Austin. Then Sumon joined them in a game of Monopoly. At some point, Kabir left the living room to watch television in the lounge. The child, tired of playing Monopoly, picked up his Game Boy. Then Shawon left, disappearing into his bedroom.

The room fell silent but for the electronic music of the game. Finding themselves effectively alone, but for the young boy, made for an awkward moment. Later, Sumon confessed to Rumana that he was trying to hide his nervousness until, finally, he broke the silence.

He inquired after her studies at Dhaka University. She spoke of having finished her first year with a first-class standing, her highest mark in the subject of English. He asked about the second year of her program, what courses she was taking. They talked about how repeated and indefinite closures plagued all universities—causing session jams of program delays and lost classroom hours—which meant no student could expect to earn their degree on schedule. Eventually, Sumon's questions leaned to the more personal. He asked about her aspirations. She told him she planned to pursue a master's degree and a career in international relations. He spoke of his respect for women with ambition. He told her how much he admired her.

Ruby and Sabira returned. Since they were continuing on to the mall, they said they'd drop her home on their way.

Rumana kept to herself that she had spent time with Sumon with neither of his parents present. She pondered what to make of that hour and a half they'd been together. It was unmistakable to her that the look in Sumon's eyes had been one of adoration. He had hung on her every word. When, she wondered, had he gone from seeing her not just as the daughter of his father's close friend, but as a person in her own right?

She thought back to a day some weeks ago when she'd answered the ring at the door—the family didn't let the help answer the door because they wouldn't know who was safe to admit in. She had been taken by surprise to see Sumon standing there. He was not expected. Only she, her mother and her grandmother were home. Her mother offered him something to drink. He declined. He couldn't stay. He'd come to ask Rumana if he could borrow her calculator. He said his was broken and he had an exam tomorrow.

Now, Rumana contemplated his unexpected appearance in another light. Whether or not his calculator had in fact been broken, he knew she'd taken computer studies and would have needed one for her courses then.

Rumana felt a frisson of excitement.

A couple of months later, on a morning in mid-May, Kabir and Ruby came calling on the Monzurs. As etiquette demanded, Rumana interrupted her homework to greet them, then excused herself, saying she had to study.

The Kabirs' reason for visiting caught Monzur and Rahima entirely by surprise. Monzur called for his mother to join them around the dining room table. The Kabirs had come to offer a proposal for marriage between their son and the Monzurs' daughter. Kabir and Ruby hastened to say this was entirely their son's idea, that they had not seen it coming. They said that he had told them that his love for Hema so distracted him that he could not concentrate on his final months of study at BUET.

Both Monzur and Rahima thought of their daughter's education. Early marriage of girls happened in the countryside, not in the cities. In the cities, parents delayed marriage of their daughters until after a master's degree, to prepare her for a career. Rumana had barely started the second year of a bachelor's program. She was only twenty-one, twenty-two in a few days.

Monzur promised that he and Rahima would give an answer by month's end.

After the Kabirs left, Grandmother Momena was quick to give her opinion. She thought Sumon would take good care of her granddaughter, and all she wanted was for Rumana to be happy.

Monzur and Rahima were still trying to absorb what had just happened when the telephone rang. Monzur answered. It was Sumon. He asked for Rumana.

Monzur was curt. "Call back later."

That the boy had called for Rumana confirmed to Monzur that a relationship had already developed.

He wondered, given his strictness and his wife's vigilance, how was it that they had not noticed? When could Sumon and Rumana have had opportunity to develop a love relationship?

Rumana was surprised that her mother did not come to her alone to tell her about the proposal. Even more unusual, that her father should speak to her directly on such a personal matter.

Monzur was brief. He told Rumana that the proposal came from Sumon, that he'd told his parents that his feelings for her were so overwhelming they had put his degree in jeopardy. "Hema, your mother and I would like your opinion. You can tell your mother later."

Rumana looked at her mother.

"Whatever you decide," Rahima said.

Rumana was giddy. Sumon's madly in love with me, she told herself. She would take the promised month, but she already knew what her response would be. She would have not just a husband in love with her, but a marriage anointed with passion.

Monzur kept his opinion to himself. He recognized the foreboding weight of his wife's silence. For his part, he didn't want to speak ill of the son of his close friend. But he thought that Sumon, aged twenty-six, lacked maturity. He laid some of the blame on his upbringing. From what he had observed, Ruby gave in too easily to whatever her sons asked of her, and she did too readily for them what they should be doing for themselves. He had not seen either son say so much as please or thank you to their domestic help. Perhaps such an attitude of entitlement or superiority was typical of children raised in a wealthy household.

Rumana used the time before the month's end to marshal arguments in favour of Sumon's proposal.

What she truly valued was sophistication. Always, Sumon was impeccably groomed and fashionably turned out. His glasses were trendy wire frames. He wore sporty collared shirts with designer logos. His leather shoes shone. If he had on sneakers, they were Nike. He wore a Guess watch on his wrist. His denim jeans were of a quality not found in a regular store in Dhaka. He did not have the body odour of almost every other man she'd encountered (he'd adopted the Western practice of using deodorant). He wore cologne, one scent by day, another by night.

Above all, Sumon embodied what Rumana wanted most in a life partner: he was educated, and he respected her ambitions and intellectual pursuits. He had to be smart; she once was having difficulty with a mathematics problem and he solved it without even taking pencil to paper. He'd been outside the country only to India, but he knew about world affairs; he'd been a valuable sounding board when she was at work on a paper on the Bosnian Serb army's genocide against Muslims.

Two pragmatic thoughts nested in Rumana's mind.

Once in her department at Dhaka University, she saw a boy whom she knew to be from a different department eyeing her. Later that day, alighting from a rickshaw in front of her home, she thought she saw him again. Maybe he was a potential suitor and just wanted to know where she lived. Still, it worried her. To accept Sumon's proposal would remove the burden of having to be on guard against the attentions of men.

Accepting the proposal would also save her parents the trouble—ordeal, even—of arranging a marriage. She would spare her mother having to gather names of potential marriageable partners, then to narrow the field and enlist her father to verify each family's background, financial circumstances and social relationships. Then there was the complication of finding someone they were amenable to and whom they thought she would like. More importantly, marrying Sumon would save her the uncertainty of an arranged marriage and whether it would lead to the fulfilling life she imagined.

Rahima informed Monzur that their daughter wanted to accept the proposal.

Monzur had prepared himself. He'd told his wife that as parents, their opportunity to counsel their daughter on the choice of a future husband may have already passed them by. He relinquished his judgment of Sumon, believing that the young man would change. With marriage, one develops responsibility. With responsibility comes maturity.

Monzur called Ruby.

He told her they had an answer.

She said she would come straight over.

When she arrived, Monzur had Rumana join the three parents.

Monzur told Ruby that he and Rahima accepted that marriage was the choice of her son and their daughter. The parents would give way to the feelings of the young couple but insist on one condition: marriage must not interrupt the completion of their degrees.

Ruby wept tears of joy. She wrapped her future daughter-in-law in a smothering hug.

She pledged to Monzur and Rahima that she and Kabir would support their daughter in her schooling. Her household had several maid servants; Rumana would not have to do anything domestic. "Hema," she promised, "will have all the time she needs for her studies."

three

RUMANA WAS IN NO HURRY TO LEAVE HER PARENTS. SHE decided she would not move to Paribagh until after the wedding celebration, in January 2001.

Sumon was peeved—why not come sooner, in August, right after the Nikah? "Hema, if you don't come to my parents' house right away, it says you're not happy with the marriage."

The religious ceremony of the Nikah, required by Islamic law for a Muslim man and a Muslim woman to marry, is followed by the celebratory wedding reception, usually, but not always, on the same day. With the Nikah, physical contact and intimacy is now permitted between the couple, but by tradition, at night's end of the wedding reception, the bride says goodbye to her parents and goes home with the groom for the first time to begin her new life with her in-laws.

For the sake of propriety, both sets of parents had agreed that the Nikah should happen quickly, even if months before the wedding itself. The families settled on August for the Nikah, but delayed the wedding reception until the more traditional January, when cooler temperatures are promised along with little chance of rain.

The pressure on Rumana to move in August increased. It came from Sumon's mother. Ruby told Rumana that she and her husband would be away starting in September—they were going to visit their daughter in Texas—and she'd feel better knowing she were at their home in their absence, rather than trusting her two sons to mind the apartment alone. Rumana appealed to Sumon's father. She readied her argument: her brother was starting a bachelor's program at Rutgers University in New Jersey in the fall and she did not want to deprive her parents of both children at once, plus she needed time to adjust to leaving her grandmother, to whom she was especially close. "It's valid and logical for me to wait."

To her surprise, Kabir replied that he needed no convincing.

On a hot and humid morning in August, Rumana and Sumon sat, each with their mothers, in separate rooms at the Monzurs' home. An imam came to them in turn and asked if they were marrying of their own free will. On confirmation, the two came together and, in the presence of both sets of parents, signed the contract of the Nikahnama, which was to be filed with the Marriage Registrar of the City of Dhaka.

In a customary small gathering to mark the union, Monzur and Rahima catered a dinner for close relatives of both families on their rooftop terrace that evening. For Rumana, an otherwise blissful day had one blemish: she thought she discerned a coldness between Sumon and his father. In the morning, she overheard a relative tell her father that he found it odd that for the entire day of the Nikah, Kabir and his son didn't seem to be speaking to each other.

Word spread of the coming wedding. Rumana's friends and classmates traded what news they'd heard.

"It's a love story."

"He comes from a wealthy family."

"He's a student at BUET so he has to be smart."

"He and Hema have liked each other for years."

None would have imagined that Rumana, the ideally behaved girl, would be the first to marry. Most surprising, that Rumana, whose parents they regarded as the most strict of any of their parents, would pursue a relationship on her own and have a love marriage.

All agreed, though, that this being Rumana, everything would turn out perfectly.

Her childhood friend Farzana Morshed wondered at the urgency for her friend to get married instead of waiting until she'd graduated from university. Her mother wondered the same, adding that not only was it short notice—the usual practice was to send invitations out a year in advance—but that she thought the hall at the Dhaka Cantonment an odd choice of venue. Wouldn't one of the new community centres be more appropriate for a family of the status and wealth of the Kabirs?

What mattered most to Farzana was that Rumana was in love. She was happy for her. The few occasions that Farzana had met Sumon, she'd found him easy to talk to, and when she'd gone once with Rumana to BUET to see him, she'd enjoyed meeting his engineering friends.

Rumana's other childhood friend, Shehneela, felt differently. She had disliked Sumon from the start. Home on a break from her first year of university in India, she had been eager to make up for lost time with Rumana. At the Monzurs', Rumana introduced Sumon to her as "Uncle's son." Though impressed by his fashionable clothes, Shehneela found him off-putting in almost every other way. She didn't like how he snapped his fingers to punctuate what he said and thought it rude when he joked about bodily functions. It got worse. She felt embarrassed for her friend when Sumon said, for all to hear, that he preferred Rumana's hair long. Shehneela's father had impressed upon her: "Don't ever give a boy a chance to talk about you in front of others." But Shehneela turned resolutely against Sumon when he asked if she had a boyfriend. She did, but it defied all decorum to ask. Why, Shehneela wondered, does Hema have anything to do with such a person?

She debated cautioning her friend but remembered how Rumana had once told her that she would never say something that would sadden someone. She told herself, whatever is going on between those two, it's happening in front of Hema's mother, so Auntie must not have any issue with it.

The head of Kabir's ministry, Faisal Chowdhury was taken aback to hear that the Kabir and Monzur families were to be united by marriage. How could Major Monzur marry his daughter into that family? How could he?

When Faisal and his wife had made a match for their daughter, Samia, they'd seen to it that she married into a noble and honest family. Their son-in-law, Rashed, Jolly's son and the nephew of

Major Monzur, came from a family who led principled lives and were known as having the highest moral character.

When the senior engineer Syeed Ahmed "Kabir" appeared at the door of Faisal's office and asked to come in, Faisal's first thought was, How dare he. Over Faisal's career in the civil service, he had headed shipping, finance, export promotion, and customs and excise. He brought to his newest ministry of water resources a reputation for ethical public service. The ministry had one of the worst records for corruption. But to stamp it out would be no easy task. The ministry's year-round work to contend with the huge loads of silt and algae disgorged from the spring melt, the annual flooding, and the summer monsoon rains presented opportunity at every turn for bribes, kickbacks and fraud. Faisal turned a watchful eye on senior engineers, responsible for projects large and small, from bridges and dams to sluices and culverts.

Kabir said he'd come to deliver a wedding invitation. Protocol required the hand-delivery of wedding invitations to family and close associates. The invitation received, Faisal was only too happy to see the senior engineer's back.

The time after the Nikah had all the blush of romance for Rumana. The interest Sumon had shown in her studies and her aspirations expanded to everything she did. He asked her to explain her art projects. She had gone from acrylics and oil on canvas to painting on glass, on sheets as large as sixty by ninety centimetres. She moved beyond landscapes to abstracts and replications of traditional embroidery. Sumon was interested in the process of painting on glass—a colour could be added only when the adjacent colour dried, and drying time was at the mercy of the humidity. She showed off the large ornamental clay elephants used for home decor that she'd painted for a year-end student art sale at the art school where she'd taken a course. Sumon asked about the saris she custom-designed for family; his mother was among those who'd asked for one. Rumana explained that to make the borders of each sari unique, she perused shops in the neighbourhood for ribbons, buttons, silk threads, sequins and beads.

Sumon couldn't compliment Rumana enough. "You're an amazing person."

More than once he showed up at Dhanmondi with gladiolas in hand. He professed his love for her. He loved her nose, her dimples, her lips, her eyes. Her voice. He loved everything about her. Sumon tried more than once—without luck—to persuade her to stay overnight at Paribagh. When he stayed over in Dhanmondi, Rahima assigned him the space off the veranda that Mashrur had vacated when he left for university.

After the Kabirs returned from Texas, Rahima and Rumana went together to Paribagh to evaluate the space in Sumon's bedroom. Preparing the marital bedroom was the responsibility of the bride's parents. Rumana judged the space too small to accommodate a dressing table. Accordingly, she redesigned one wall to include a floor-to-ceiling closet with his and her shelves and drawers, and a full-length mirror. Monzur paid a carpenter to do the renovations.

Now and again, Sumon had his family's driver take him to Dhaka University to meet Rumana after class. She returned his affections. She met him at his university and sometimes spoiled him with a hot lunch in a tiffin carrier. Sometimes his appearances at her university were a surprise, which complicated Rumana's plans for studying and made it difficult for her to meet deadlines. Or his appearances interfered with appointments she'd already made to join family or friends. Sometimes, since she had no idea he was coming, she had already departed the campus, leaving him to wait for her in vain.

A family get-together gave Rumana a chance to ask a doctor in the family about something that had been on her mind.

There were two doctors in the Monzurs' extended family, a husband and wife. Jolly's eldest, Shoma, met her husband, Fakhruddin Seddiqi, in medical school. After graduation she worked in hospital administration, and he went on to specialize in internal medicine and now had a private practice.

Dr. Seddiqi—Seddiqi to family—had a special fondness for Rumana, of all his wife's cousins. When he came straight from the hospital, typically late, to family gatherings, he'd home in on her lilting voice and laughter. He'd head there, knowing that was where conversation was the liveliest.

Rumana asked Seddiqi if there was such a thing as tunnel vision.

After the Nikah, with no restrictions on her and Sumon being together and alone, she had been able to converse freely with him. Her question to Seddiqi arose from what Sumon had said about abandoning his studies in India, something she had long wondered about.

"Is it true that you were homesick?" she'd asked Sumon.

He had shrugged. "Most of my classes were in the evenings. I have trouble seeing in the dark."

"But the power of your lenses isn't very high. Why do you think this is happening?"

"I don't know. I have something called tunnel vision. It's nothing serious."

Seddiqi was accustomed to fielding questions about medical issues from extended family. Tunnel vision, he explained to Rumana, is a loss of peripheral vision and a reduced ability to see at night. It's not uncommon.

After hearing this, Rumana thought little more about Sumon's eye condition. She imagined it could be a bit of a nuisance if he had to go out at night, but if necessary she could accompany him. Otherwise, she could think of several classmates at her university who wore glasses with lenses much thicker than Sumon's. And it didn't seem to curb his getting around by day. When he came from Paribagh to visit her at Dhanmondi, he sometimes drove himself.

One month before the wedding, Sumon was worried about a cough and chest congestion, so Rumana took him to Seddiqi's office. Sumon feared it was something serious. He was always concerned about staying healthy and fastidious about guarding against germs. But after examining Sumon, Seddiqi assured him that he had nothing more than a cold, common in December when temperatures dip. Regardless, it laid Sumon low enough that he missed sitting for two of his final exams at BUET. He told his parents that it wasn't a problem; his teachers had allowed him to write makeup exams.

Kabir had been entirely amenable to Monzur's suggestions for the wedding. In the interests of economy, he had proposed that instead of the traditional two events—the ceremonial wedding hosted by the bride's family and, the day after, a reception hosted by the groom's family—the two families jointly host a single event and call it a reception. And that they hold it where he could get a reduced rate, at the hall at the Dhaka Cantonment.

In January, on two successive days before the reception, Rumana and Sumon held their separate pre-wedding Gaye holuds. Rumana's party took place on the rooftop terrace of Molly's building. Molly and Haque, operating within the budget given them by Monzur, organized the food, rental of tables and chairs and a canopy to guard against rain. In keeping with the tradition of the bride's Gaye holud, where the women dress in matching clothes, Rumana's side dressed in jamdani saris—made of traditional handwoven fine muslin—with woven flower motifs that appeared to float on the surface of the cloth. Sumon's female relatives, attired in chunri saris—made of cloth dyed a brilliant red and specked with yellow and white—arrived in an elaborate procession, each carrying a tray decorated with flowers and fruits and bearing items that Rumana needed for her wedding day: the veil, sari, shoes and jewellery, and cosmetics. In a nod to guests who'd come from afar, Rumana repeated the beautifying and cleansing ritual of having guests apply turmeric paste to her face and arms; in August, family had dabbed only her forehead. The games and music carried on into the night. Molly's son, Rana, and a couple of his friends played instruments and sang. Even Monzur and Rahima took to the dance floor.

After Sumon's Gaye holud, Rahima told her daughter the Kabirs had put on an extravagant event for their son in a community centre.

They'd had a small stage built for him to sit on and bedecked it with fresh flowers. The family also hired a band and a videographer.

The next day, as co-hosts of the reception, Monzur and Kabir made sure to arrive at the hall at the Dhaka Cantonment in the early evening, well before the eight o'clock start. They positioned themselves on opposite sides of the entrance and greeted guests on their respective sides, of the bride or groom.

Shortly after eight, Rumana entered on the arm of her brother and escorted by her mother. Her bridal sari, chosen by the groom's mother, was of red silk delicately run through with gold zari threads and embroidered in a design of flowering branches. A veil studded with precious stones, beads and sequins traced the outline of her upswept hair. Around her neck hung several strands of thick gold jewellery, and around both wrists were layers of bangles.

Rumana looked like a goddess, her beauty ethereal.

She took her place on one of two low chairs on a small stage, decorated as a garden landscape with an artificial fountain and fresh flowers. In keeping with the practice of recognizing elderly relatives as among the most important of family members at a wedding, Grandmother Momena approached the stage and offered blessings to her granddaughter. She brought with her a few distant elderly relatives from the village whom Rumana would not know without the old lady's introduction. Now that the bride had arrived, friends of Rumana's gathered at the entrance of the hall to create a mock barricade as if to delay the entry of the groom and his family. Ceremony had it that the groom, escorted by his mother, comes to his wedding late, as if the bride's family has had to send for him.

Kabir remained the sole member of his family at the hall.

The wait stretched out for the groom and his mother. There was no sign either of Shawon or Sabira and her family. Nor of Ruby's three sisters and her two brothers and their families. Monzur assumed the delay had to do with the women's preparations. Indeed, a full wedding package at a salon was a daylong affair, involving a brightening facial, makeup, manicure and pedicure and hair setting.

The groom's delay began to border on rudeness.

If Kabir had any explanation, he wasn't saying.

To Rumana's relief, Rashed's wife, Samia, had the where-withal to mask the sight of the empty chair beside her by perching on the edge of the stage. Taking her lead, Rumana's brother and his friends and then her own friends came up to speak to her.

At nine o'clock, unease pervaded the hall. By now, the groom should have taken his seat beside the bride, and the two mothers would have greeted each other. The bride and groom would have ceremoniously fed each other sweets, which would then open the wedding buffet. A feast of biryani mutton and roasted chicken lay ready and, for the head table, a whole roasted goat.

Tossed between deepening embarrassment and worry, Rumana wondered whether there had been a mishap. Some guests her family had invited, ignoring the absence of the groom, came forward to offer blessings and wish her good luck. The elderly and guests with small children began to say their goodbyes and leave. For wedding guests to leave without having been fed was a serious embarrassment. Monzur dropped his original plan to send one-third of the crowd at a time to the buffet. He announced that the buffet table was open to all.

It was well past ten when the groom, his mother and the rest of their entourage finally made their entrance. The glaring looks between Kabir and Ruby made obvious that they had exchanged harsh words.

When Sumon took his place on the chair beside Rumana, she turned to him. "Why were you so late? Half the guests have left."

Why isn't he answering me?

He didn't need to. Ruby blurted out that they'd been held up at the salon and then got stuck in traffic.

The deejay cued up a famous love song. To complete the ritual by which the respective new mothers-in-laws welcome the betrothed of their children, Rahima put a gold chain around Sumon's neck; at the Nikah Ruby had put a gold ring on Rumana's finger.

The brief ceremony concluded, Rumana waited expectantly for Sumon to turn to her, to gaze, starry-eyed, and to tell her how beautiful she looked.

Sumon didn't look at her, didn't say a word.

Rumana felt a rush of anxiety, then told herself not to read anything into Sumon's behaviour, that her reaction was probably natural for a bride at her wedding. In any event, Sumon's obligations quickly commanded his attention. A long queue of guests from the groom's side waited to greet him and offer blessings.

Ruby continued to mill near the stage, her loud voice competing with the music of the deejay as she complained to any and all about the unfairness of her husband blaming her for the delay. It couldn't be helped; after the women were done at the salon, they had to pick up the husbands and children waiting for them at home, and then traffic was bad. "It's not my fault. I tried to push everyone to hurry."

Monzur had been keeping a watchful eye on the clock. Civilians had to be off the cantonment by midnight. The rental contract for the hall specified its use could not extend beyond eleven thirty sharp, to allow time for civilians to leave the vast grounds. With time pressing, Monzur concentrated on rushing the last of the guests through the buffet line.

As the clock neared half past eleven, he brought the evening to a close. There had been no time for the newlyweds and the younger crowd to play word games and sing and dance, as happened at every wedding. The deejay packed up. The stage was dismantled. In the echoing hall, family members packaged up the last of the food. Those going to the Kabirs' loaded their cars with wedding presents and Rumana's many suitcases and left for Paribagh.

At the last minute, Mashrur elected to go along so he could say a last goodbye to his sister; his return flight to New Jersey was the next day. The limousine that Ruby had hired to bring her and her son to the wedding, its floral decorations still fresh in the cool night air, took the newlyweds home, along with Sumon's sister and her husband. On the ride, the mood was jovial, the banter non-stop between the two couples. Only in hindsight did Rumana realize that Sumon had not said anything directly to her.

A flash of cameras greeted the newly married couple as they stepped into the marital bedroom. Some twenty family and guests were crowded in the small room. One of them held a camcorder to capture Rumana's reaction to the matrimonial bed, almost hidden under a canopy of cascading strings of fresh flowers.

Two of Ruby's sisters took Rumana by the hand and gently parted the curtain. They guided her onto the middle of the bed to sit amid roses and marigolds laid out in the shape of a heart. They arranged her sari for the requisite wedding night photographs. Finally, everyone filed out, the last person closing the bedroom door behind them to leave the newlyweds by themselves.

Without a word, Sumon went straight to the closet and gathered his pyjamas. He went into the bathroom and closed the door.

The sound of the shower came on.

Rumana sat on the edge of the bed in anticipation. After the Nikah, Sumon had exercised restraint, gone only so far as a brush of his hand on her back and a tentative kiss or two.

Rather than waiting for Sumon to help remove her veil, Rumana decided she would do it herself. Her scalp ached from wearing her hair up. Because her hair was so thick and heavy, it was a style she'd allowed only for this occasion. As she pulled the bobby pins out, she counted them: thirty-five in all.

The shower turned off.

Rumana was eager to hurry the night along. She searched among her suitcases piled in the corner. The nightie she had chosen for the first time she and her husband would lay together was maroon, made of fine cotton, overlaid with netting dotted with sequins, and bordered in silk.

She stopped when she heard the bathroom door open. She turned round. "You're done?"

She looked into an angry face. She had never seen someone so terribly transformed right before her eyes. Who is this person? I don't know this person at all.

Sumon came straight for her.

Rumana began to panic.

His hand came up. He slapped her, hard, across the cheek.

"It's not our fault we were late!"

Rumana stood frozen, trying to understand what had just happened.

Sumon strode to the bed, tore aside the curtain of flowers, grabbed the decorative bed cover and flung it into a corner of the room. He lay down, turning his back to her.

Rumana burst into tears. No one had ever struck her. She'd never seen anyone strike someone else. No one had so much as raised their voice or spoken an unkind word to her.

Her cheek burned. Her breathing turned ragged.

"Go put ice on your face," Sumon barked. "And don't make any sound."

Rumana shuddered in the effort to stop her tears and control her breathing. How could she possibly leave the bedroom—pass by his parents and his mother's relatives? She could hear voices and laughter on the other side of the door.

And how could she get ice? The kitchen in every home was the domain of the help and out of bounds to all but the woman of the household. Certainly no visitor stepped foot in another family's kitchen.

She could wake one of the maids. But where were the maids' quarters?

Sumon turned off the light by the bed. The bedroom fell into darkness, but for a shaft of light from the open bathroom door.

Rumana saw only one option.

Trembling uncontrollably, her teeth chattering, she groped in the darkness for the suitcase with her wedding nightie and cosmetic bag. She needed a special cleanser to properly remove the heavily layered makeup from her face and the sandalwood paste and kumkum artwork on her forehead. She needed oil to soften her extra-strong hairspray.

She found the right suitcase and started to unzip it.

"Just *get out* then! Make another sound and I'll kick you out."

She reached desperately inside the partially open suitcase, until she felt the cotton of a shalwar kameez, pulled it out, and shut herself in the bathroom.

She looked in the mirror. The imprint of a hand bloomed red on her right cheek. She took off her long necklaces and her bangles and laid them on the counter. It upset her to leave them there, to not put them away properly in her jewellery box. She struggled to remove her heavy sari. The small bathroom made it difficult to keep the length of material from dragging on the wet floor. She tried to clean her face with some toiletries that she saw in a basket—Ruby must have left them for her—but without her makeup remover, she could only do a half-hearted job.

Rumana lost track of how long she was in the bathroom. She quieted her sobbing, then turned out the bathroom light. Navigating the blackness of the bedroom by memory and touch, she found the chair where she had put her veil and now draped her sari over it. She found her way to the far side of the bed and, feeling a scattering of petals on the sheet, gently swept clear a space, lay down and crawled under the covers.

The hum of voices, adults and children, woke her. She reached for her watch.

Half past eight.

Normally by now, she'd have been up for hours. She looked over, saw a sleeping Sumon. She climbed out of bed.

"I told you not to make a sound!"

Rumana looked at her cheek in the bathroom mirror. The redness had disappeared and only a subtle swelling remained. She told herself that no one would notice. She made a valiant attempt to clean her face.

When Rumana stepped outside the bedroom and closed the door behind her, a profound calm settled over her.

A chorus of voices greeted her. "Hema, you're up! Come, join us for breakfast."

Ruby looked askance at her daughter-in-law. "Why aren't you wearing makeup? Where's your jewellery?"

Sumon was still sleeping, she replied.

Ruby's sister teased her. "Hema, go wake your husband."

She just smiled.

Rumana made sure to appear as Sumon's parents had known her: sweet and cheerful. She could make a count of all the Kabirs' guests now: Sabira and her family, and from Chittagong Ruby's sister and one of her two brothers and their families, and three of Shawon's friends.

It was almost noon when Sumon emerged. Ruby herded everyone into the living room to watch Rumana open wedding presents. Sumon took a seat at the far end of the room. The gifts ranged from saris, jewellery, purses and watches to decorative crockery, dinner sets and crystal. Ruby called attention to the Kabirs' generous gifts to their new daughter-in-law of five saris in Katan silk and rich brocade, a pair of imported shoes and two purses, with pointed mention of how much she had paid in each instance. At the announcement of lunch, Rumana rose to help Ruby's sister set out the food, dallying long enough until the seats near Sumon were taken. Over lunch, he asked her several times in a voice ever so sweet to pass a dish down the table.

Rumana, cloaked in fear of her new husband, felt like she'd fallen down a rabbit hole.

All week Ruby complained to her sister about her husband blaming her for the late start to the reception. Kabir maintained his quiet demeanour. At week's end, he returned to Chittagong and the house finally emptied of guests. With the household now down to just herself, her sons and her new daughter-in-law, Ruby made a grumbling comment to Rumana about the wedding: "A wedding is supposed to be fun for a younger brother. The entire time, Sumon didn't say a word to Shawon."

In recognition that his son was not earning an income because he was still in school, Kabir sent five thousand taka (about fifty US dollars) to his wife to give to their daughter-in-law. Rumana was grateful. It was enough to help with incidental expenses like school supplies and rickshaw rides to and from Dhaka University, maybe a new shalwar kameez. However, it was in her hands only momentarily. When she went into the bedroom to put it away, Sumon followed and took it from her.

Rumana began her marriage having given no thought to what life would be like in a new household. Even with just three Kabirs around, the household seemed to have only one volume: loud. Where she'd once regarded their family's noisy and rapid-fire talk as boisterous conviviality, she found living with it unsettling. What to them was talking sounded to her like constant argument.

The contrasts with how her family lived unsettled her further. Ruby went alone to the fish and meat bazaars. In Rumana's family, her father took on that responsibility, adamant that it was no place for a woman. The one time Rumana accompanied him, she saw why: the sellers and crowd were mostly men and boys, and the butchering of skinned animal carcasses sent innards and blood spattering. Rumana wondered why, with his father away, Sumon wouldn't do that shopping for his mother or at least accompany her. As for Sumon and Shawon themselves, Rumana saw none of the closeness she had shared with Mashrur. If anything, the brothers stayed out of each other's way.

It saddened Rumana to see how the help shrank away, even cowered, whenever the two sons came near. Her parents had impressed upon her and her brother that the menial work of cooks and maid servants was not their choice, that it was often the only employment available to girls and women who left their villages to find work and support their impoverished families. Rahima made clear that their cook, who had been with them since Rumana's birth, and their maid were to be treated like family. The feeling was mutual. When Rumana and Mashrur were young, they'd snuggled on the couch with the help when they took a break from their work in the afternoon to watch their favourite television series. When Bangladeshi television picked up the American TV show *MacGyver*, although she and her brother eagerly anticipated the next episode, by their mother's instructions they were not to pre-empt what the help was watching.

Marriage was throwing her daily schedule into disarray. She liked to get out the door early to arrive at the university in good time for her classes and allot a good chunk of time in the evenings to study. She had no idea how Sumon spent his days. Rising at noon as he did on the first morning of their marriage turned out to be his usual practice. He routinely stayed up until three or four in the morning, sometimes even later, then slept until noon or beyond.

Rumana realized that she'd missed a clue to her future husband's odd hours. Soon after the Nikah, she'd telephoned the Kabirs' home and asked the maid to please put Sumon on. "He's sleeping," the maid had said.

"It's three in the afternoon! Tell him his wife wishes to speak with him."

The maid's tone was unequivocal. "He cannot be disturbed." At the time, Rumana had marvelled that anyone could sleep that long.

One night early in their marriage, Rumana was deep asleep, still hours before she had to wake for school. Sumon shook her awake. He hadn't gone to bed yet and now he was hungry. He demanded a cup of tea and a poached egg.

At the confused look on her face, he rained down scorn on her. "You're a woman and you can't do these basic things?"

Rumana froze. She didn't dare admit that she had never touched a stove, had not so much as boiled water.

Other times, Sumon awakened her to demand soup, an omelette.

The Kabirs' cook, a woman a few years older than Rumana's mother, did not ask the new daughter-in-law why she needed to learn how to use the gas stove or how to chop onions, or in what order the garlic, turmeric, cardamon and other spices should be put in the pan. City mothers saw no reason for their daughters to ever go into the kitchen, unless they had an interest in cooking. They themselves went in only to discuss the menu with the cook or to settle accounts. The cook quickly developed a soft spot for the harassed daughter-in-law. The older woman, widowed early, had given up her baby boy to her husband's relatives to raise. On days that Rumana had to be out of the house in the pre-dawn to make her first class, leaving her too pressed for time to take breakfast, the cook met her at the door with a steaming cup of tea, insisting she take a sip before leaving.

One day on her return from the university, Rumana went to the bedroom and, as usual, began to empty her satchel to set out her study materials for later that evening. She stopped, seeing Sumon fixing her with a glare.

"Why aren't you making the bed?"

She hesitated.

"You think you can be spoiled here? You had so many maids that you never had to do anything?"

Rumana soon realized that on top of cooking for her husband when he demanded it, on days he slept so late that the maid had moved on from housecleaning to helping the cook, he expected her to clean their bedroom. She took her instructions from his sideways condemnations. Routinely, he swiped his finger across the top of the nightstand, then uttered in disgust: "I don't know how a woman can expect anyone to live in a home so dusty." He stood at the threshold of the bathroom and turned to her, "How long are you going to leave it like this?" He cast a disapproving eye over the job she had done of scouring the toilet and scrubbing the shower and floor, and said to her: "How come your parents did such a bad job of raising you?"

Between rising in the middle of the night and studying late, Rumana was exhausted. When she had a major assignment due, she dared to ask Sumon if she could forgo cleaning the bathroom. He brooked no excuse. Inevitably, Rumana faltered. Being on edge led to more mistakes.

Used to success, Rumana felt devastated at her failures that Sumon exposed. Society had instilled in her the conduct and behaviour that made for a good girl, but who was supposed to prepare her to be a good wife? She upbraided herself. She'd always governed herself by being prepared. Knowing that the day would come when she would join a new household and embark on marriage, why hadn't she learned the skills to keep a house and cater to a husband? Why hadn't she asked her mother what was expected of a new wife?

There was more to being a wife that Rumana did not expect. At mealtimes, Sumon required her to serve him and his mother before she served herself. He expected Rumana at all times to anticipate his need for water or juice. "Why aren't you asking me if I'm thirsty?" She soon learned that when Sumon summoned her, she should immediately drop what she was doing. He was withering: "How dare you not come when I call you? What's your problem?"

Rumana took comfort that she measured up in one respect of being a wife, when they lay together as man and wife. Sumon found pleasure with her and told her so, and she in turn found him to be a good and gentle lover. That he had waited one month before consummating the marriage, saying he wanted to be sure she was ready, she allowed herself to take as a sign of his consideration.

In the third month of the young couple's marriage, in the early spring, Sumon was planning a trip to India, to the Sankara Nethralaya eye hospital in Chennai. Sometime between the Nikah and the wedding he'd mentioned to Rumana that he wanted to make a change from his regular eye doctor. She had asked Seddiqi for a recommendation in Dhaka. However, for any Bangladeshi with money and wanting the best eye care, going to Chennai was the obvious and preferred choice.

Ruby asked Rumana to accompany Sumon to India. As a new daughter-in-law, Rumana took the request as an order. She did not have the excuse of school; a session jam at Dhaka University had classes cancelled indefinitely.

"Take a few extra days," Ruby told the young couple. "See the sights, all expenses on me."

The idea of being totally alone with Sumon, out of the country in a faraway city with no family at hand, under his scrutiny twenty-four hours a day, totally at his mercy, terrified Rumana. At the same time, she told herself that her mother-in-law must have sensed that she wasn't settling in as a wife and thought some time away as a couple would do them some good.

On arrival at the Sankara Nethralaya, Rumana and Sumon joined the queue for the outpatient clinic. The line snaked for blocks around the vast complex. Once they reached the front, Sumon presented his documents and was given an appointment for a preliminary assessment the next day.

At that appointment, Rumana remained outside in the waiting room. When Sumon came out, she asked, "Everything okay?"

"Just a regular checkup." He said the doctor had ordered several tests, but otherwise didn't elaborate.

Over the next day and a half, Rumana helped Sumon find the right building and the right department for the tests. At the final appointment with a consultant to review the findings, Rumana didn't hear anything to be too worried about, but made a note to talk to Seddiqi about what could be done for Sumon in Dhaka.

Though shadowed by her fear of Sumon, Rumana was hugely relieved that he had found her presence on the trip useful, not just accompanying him at the hospital, but doing all the talking, mostly in English but sometimes in Hindi, with hotel clerks, taxi drivers and the like. She guessed he was less comfortable than she was in another culture.

Emboldened by her success, Rumana shared what she thought they could do with their free day ahead. She started by agreeing with Sumon's only suggestion, a visit to the city's marine and amusement park, recently upgraded with new rides from abroad. They watched performing otters, and Rumana rode alone on a water ride. They had their driver carry on farther up the highway to a go-kart park, where Rumana took out a kart, once again alone. They continued on to a crocodile farm. Back in the heart of the city, they visited the famed Marina beach, its quartz sand stretching thirty kilometres. They took the obligatory stroll on the promenade, lined with shops and food stalls and dotted with fountains and statues. Rumana paused at the granite statue depicting Gandhi mid-stride, walking stick in hand, leading the Salt March in an act of civil disobedience against the ruling British. She explained to Sumon her interest, that she was an admirer of Gandhi.

Back in Dhaka, Ruby did not ask Rumana anything about the trip or Sumon's visit to Sankara Nethralaya. Rumana did overhear Ruby say to him, "Your wife didn't bring me a sari from India. Everybody knows when you go to India, you bring home a Kanchipuram sari." As a student, Rumana didn't have that kind of spending money. She hadn't bought herself anything in India. But she learned a lesson; after a trip she should not come home to Paribagh empty-handed.

Overall, Rumana judged the five days away to have been a modest success. She had slipped up only once, when she couldn't put her hands immediately on her passport, prompting a rebuke from Sumon about her disorganization. She had to admit that to be an area of needed self-improvement.

Shoma knew by the way her husband draped his long frame in a chair, clasped his hands and sat in silence, that something was bothering him and he was gathering his thoughts.

Seddiqi sighed. He told Shoma he had something to share about a patient.

Shoma cautioned him; confidentiality was vital to build a patient's trust.

"This is a matter of family, Shoma. It's about Hema. She came to see me today."

He explained. In the early fall, she had dropped by his office to pick up blood pressure medication for her mother. She said Sumon was looking for a new eye doctor, could he recommend one. He gave the name of Dr. Niaz Rahman. Like Seddiqi, Dr. Rahman, an ophthalmologist, was one of the top doctors affiliated with the private Labaid hospital.

The couple had faith in Dr. Rahman; they funnelled Shoma's aging relatives to him for cataract surgery. A vitreoretinal surgeon, he had, like all the country's best doctors, gone abroad to further his studies. He had a second degree from Johns Hopkins University and had spent a year as a fellow at the University of British Columbia.

Today, Seddiqi told his wife, Rumana came to ask him to recommend another eye doctor. Apparently, Sumon wasn't happy with Niaz Rahman. "I told Hema, 'But Dr. Rahman is one of Dhaka's best. Sumon's not going to learn anything new from another doctor.'"

Shoma knew Dr. Rahman could have an off-putting manner, as if he were always in a hurry.

"I had this feeling, Shoma, that there had to be something Hema wasn't telling me. So I sat back as if I had all the time in the world, and I got her talking."

Rumana revealed that she had accompanied Sumon to Chennai. After his final appointment, the consultant had come out to the waiting room and asked Rumana to speak to her privately. The consultant had questions for her. When did the two marry? Did her husband or his parents tell her that his tunnel vision was an inherited disorder? That its symptoms appear in childhood, that there was no effective treatment, that it can progress—though at a very slow pace? Total blindness was rare, but possible. Maybe, the consultant said, his parents had hidden this information from her before she married their son?

"Hema said to me, 'Maybe the consultant didn't look into it enough. Maybe he was wrong. With a good doctor, Sumon can recover.' I told her, Dr. Rahman is frank and honest with his patients. There's no better eye doctor in Dhaka."

Seddiqi sat shaking his head. "You know Hema. She's not one to give up, not until she's tried everything."

His anger tumbled out. "Shoma, that family, they are big hypocrites. How, how, being a father who knows your son is having vision problems that are only going to worsen, how could you hide that from your best friend and let your son marry his daughter? How could you?"

After a long silence, he said, "Sumon and Hema could divorce."

Another long silence followed. "She's trapped."

four

DURING THE DAY SUMON COULD BE IN A GOOD MOOD, contentedly sitting to talk and joke with his mother. In the presence of the rest of the household, Rumana, still wary of her place in the family hierarchy, was subdued.

Once she and Sumon retreated to their bedroom for the night, more often than not he fell into complaining. Routinely, he griped about his family. He interpreted something his mother or brother had said over dinner as more proof they were aligned against him. He fretted that his mother favoured his brother. She'd bought something for Shawon's room and not for his. His father had yet again pestered him about looking for work. When he called his father corrupt, Rumana steadfastly ignored it; she didn't appreciate such disrespectful talk about her father's friend. Otherwise, Rumana was careful, by way of a well-placed word here and there, to show that she was listening.

One evening behind their bedroom door, Sumon started in on Rumana on some transgression. She was poor at remembering her accumulating mistakes, which she put down to her sadness at Sumon's biting criticism and her instinct to not hold on to anything sad. But at hearing Sumon recite a litany of her inadequacies and failings—she'd left a cleaning rag behind in the bathroom, she'd not risen to serve him dessert at a dinner at the home of his mother's relatives, she had left a book in the middle of the bed—she realized he had been keeping a mental catalogue of his disappointments.

Suddenly, Sumon's anger exploded. He began to yell at her. Then shoved and pushed her. Even as she cowered from him, he didn't stop. He jabbed her, slapped her face.

When his anger was spent, the room fell quiet but for Rumana's convulsive sobbing. Since their wedding night, she had feared another ambush of his hand blazing across her face. She had not imagined that he would do worse.

Two days later, it was a different Sumon who came to her. He looked stricken. He was contrite, emotional, his eyes red and wet with tears. "I feel terrible. What I did was wrong of me."

When he professed his love for her, Rumana broke down in tears. They both wept openly.

"I promise to be better. Hema, forgive me."

Seeing a moment of vulnerability in her husband, Rumana tried to understand. "How could you have done that to me?"

He hugged her, kissed her.

He tried to be intimate with her.

Rumana rebuffed him, and he accepted her refusal.

He promised, and she believed him. She couldn't possibly have deserved him striking and shoving her. At the very least, he'd overreacted.

But he faltered. Or maybe she did? She couldn't remember her misstep or omission, or even if she had done something new. The beating that followed unfolded as before. It was late evening. She and Sumon were in their bedroom, their door was closed. It ended in the same way. Except that Rumana cried even harder, that he'd beaten her again filling her with disappointment as much as sorrow.

As before, two or three days later Sumon came to her, his head hanging in deep remorse. He apologized and asked for forgiveness. Declared passionately how much he loved her, how he was crazy in love with her. Fighting through tears, Rumana tried to take back some ground. "I still can't believe that you'd do that to me."

"I'll never do it again. If I do, just leave me."

Rumana resolved to become better at being a wife, to try harder to overcome her failings.

One night, as Rumana was readying for sleep, Sumon's anger flared. Whatever set him off, he was suddenly screaming at her. In his rage, he shoved her, grabbed her hair and threw her against the wall, hurling indiscriminate invectives at her. "You bitch! You bastard!" His curse words shocked Rumana as much as the escalation in his display of temper: curse words were a sin in her family.

When Rumana saw Sumon reach for the decorative khukuri knife that hung on the wall, she lunged for the bedroom door, flung it open, and ran down the hall.

She burst into the bedroom of her mother-in-law. "I can't lie with him tonight!"

Ruby was in bed watching a Hindi TV series. These dramas from India were almost always about a family embroiled in conflict or plotting against one other. She flipped aside a corner of her covers and Rumana climbed into her bed.

Sumon appeared at the door. He angrily demanded the return of his wife.

His mother spoke firmly. "The girl will sleep with me tonight."

He left without protest.

Rumana felt no need to explain. In a building with walls of cement, sound didn't travel. But once she had opened their bedroom door, her husband's screaming would have echoed down the hall.

Ruby wiped the tears from her daughter-in-law's face. "Can't be helped, Hema. You have two people who have to get used to living under the same roof."

That night Rumana slept soundly.

The next day, she found a piece of artwork occupying the space on the wall where the khukuri knife used to hang.

A few mornings later, Ruby, up early, was watching television in the lounge as Rumana sat eating her breakfast at the dining room table. No one else was awake. Over the din of the television, Ruby said, "After marriage, women have to tolerate a lot. Otherwise, marriages wouldn't last."

The next time Rumana fled a beating, she again sought sanctuary with her mother-in-law. Ruby was again consoling, but also frank: "After marriage, men beat their wives. This happens to everyone. After a while, it gets better. You'll see." She prodded Rumana: "You can be a good influence on him." When she fled to Ruby a fourth time, Rumana knew it had to be her last. Running from her husband had allowed her to avoid responsibility; she needed to ride out the vicissitudes of early married life. Sumon must have thought the same; after the second time she'd fled to Ruby, he didn't come after her.

Her mother-in-law took a firm line. "Marriage is a sacrifice, Hema. If you really want to keep your marriage, you have to take these beatings." She let the advice sit with her daughter-in-law, then added, "But don't tell anyone. People will not understand."

One morning as Rumana was about to leave for school, her mother-in-law asked her, "How long are your classes?" Ruby had never asked her anything to do with her studies. The question was so out of the ordinary it left Rumana feeling as if she stood suddenly outside her marriage and in an alliance of two women. She knew her mother-in-law, caught between her son and his wife, was doing her best. From time to time, Ruby slipped Rumana a cheque, only ever a modest amount, but written out to her so that no one else could cash it. "Out of my own pocket," she'd whisper. Whatever Rumana spent it on, she did not record it in the account book in which Sumon required her daily to enter her every expenditure—as insignificant as a rickshaw ride, even the tip she gave the wallah.

"Fifty minutes," Rumana answered, as all classes were at the university. The exchange ended there, but Rumana heard what the older woman was really saying to her. She's telling me, Breathe, Hema, breathe.

Rumana felt cheered that she had a mother-in-law who offered both comfort and counsel, that she didn't fit the stereotype of the tyrant intent on dominating her daughter-in-law. The next time Ruby was the target of her son's disparagements, Rumana spoke up in her defence. "She wants only the best for you." Seeing her husband's irritation, however, she quickly backed off.

That it was a new husband's prerogative to beat his wife led Rumana to wonder about her parents' marriage. Had they arrived at their happy and loving union only once her mother had come through that early period of adjustment and settled into the marriage? Did that explain why she'd never heard her father raise his voice to her mother? Why she'd not seen evidence that he beat her? Did that explain her mother's determined avoidance of conflict, of steadfastly never taking a position that favoured herself? Was the submission she had thought to be a character trait of her mother instead a wife's necessary accommodation?

Rumana speculated about the marriage of her in-laws. When Sumon's father came from Chittagong on holidays or stayed overnight in Dhaka on business, she regularly heard raised voices as she passed by his and his wife's bedroom that sounded like quarrelling. Was that where her in-laws' marriage had reached its stasis, one of habitual bickering?

In June, on Rumana's twenty-third birthday, Sumon presented her with a bouquet of yellow gladiolas. He did so again in August, on the anniversary of the Nikah. But the flowers were still fresh in the vase when a beating followed. She was left to nurse a sore shoulder, a wrenched arm, a stinging cheek. A few days later, a week at most, came the abject apology. Ever hopeful, she threw him a small party in September for his twenty-seventh birthday.

In an effort to break the cycle of beatings and apologies, she tried a new tactic. In the wake of a beating, she opened the tap wider on her tears and turned up the volume of her crying, hoping he'd feel badly enough to make that beating the last. When that didn't work, when Sumon came with his forlorn apology, she gave in if he wanted sex. This side of him, she could trust. She told herself if such concessions on her part led to less violence the next time, better for them both.

In the early mornings, no matter how carefully she tiptoed around the bedroom as Sumon slept, his voice could suddenly shatter the quiet: "You bitch, haven't you learned not to make a sound!"

In her first celebration with her in-laws of Ramadan, which that year was observed from mid-November to mid-December, Rumana traded off what was supposed to be a joyful time with the stress it brought to both ends of her day: the risk of disturbing Sumon's sleep at the start of the day and again when she retired. During the holy month, Sumon refused to participate with his parents and brother and her in the meal that broke the daily fast. By the time the meal was over—well after midnight—Sumon was already sleeping when Rumana entered the bedroom. A few hours later, she again risked disturbing him when she rose for class. With only a few hours to sleep, the ordeal took a toll on Rumana, leaving her rattled as she headed for school.

She devised a plan to preserve the peace of the night throughout Ramandan. The execution took planning: Rumana packed a satchel and shalwar kameez and undergarments and whatever else she needed for the morning in a paper bag—Ruby's daily routine of shopping at upscale stores yielded all manner of bags, so she wouldn't notice any missing—and stashed the bag behind the couch in the living room. After the meal, Rumana lingered until the others retired, then took to the couch for the night. Come morning, she rose before anybody and hid all evidence of where she'd slept.

Her plan worked. At the end of the holy month, Rumana was in a celebratory mood for Eid al-Fitr to mark the breaking of the fast. Ruby's family from Dhaka and Chittagong were invited. Ruby asked Sumon to pick up lamb kebabs for the feast she'd planned from the popular Star Kabab Restaurant. He told Rumana to do it, since the restaurant was on her way home from the university. Though nervous, as this would be the first time she'd shop outside a neighbourhood where she lived, Rumana didn't dare refuse. At the restaurant, she re-evaluated the quantity Sumon told her to buy. She opted to almost double it. An obligation of Eid was charity to the poor and those less fortunate, and she noted that Sumon's calculation didn't take into account the Kabirs' cook, two maids, houseboy and driver.

On arriving home Rumana offered to help the cook by putting the kababs on a serving dish. Just as she placed the crystal serving bowl on the table in the dining room, Sumon walked in.

He stared hard at the kababs. "How much did you buy?"

At Rumana's answer, he swept the dish onto the floor.

The cook motioned Rumana away when she rushed to clean the mess. "Don't come near. There are too many small pieces of glass."

—

From Rumana's first days as a member of her in-laws' household, she had felt for Sumon's younger brother, who received no encouragement or mentoring in his studies. To make up for his older brother's unattended responsibility, she stepped in. A year into her marriage, she thought she had built up enough trust with Shawon to put a question to him she had long wished to ask.

At the time of the Nikah, had something happened between his brother and father?

Shawon did not hold back.

The trouble started, he said, when his brother told their father that he wanted to marry her. Their father had objected. He wanted him to wait until he graduated. They argued. The argument turned physical, and his father suffered an injured foot.

Rumana waited to ask her husband about this until one evening when Sumon retired to their bedroom in an upbeat mood. He answered as if the conflict with his father was no longer of consequence: he told Kabir he wanted to marry her, his father started to bad mouth him, then physically attacked him.

And his father's injury?

"I had to defend myself."

So, his love for her at stake, Sumon had stood up to his father. Rumana wondered if she'd been fair to her husband, not appreciating the stress he was under. She recalled his answer when she aired her disquiet about his keeping birds as pets. He kept his birds, a cockatoo and a pair of lovebirds that he bought from a bird market he frequented near Dhaka University, in cages on the balcony. He was devoted to their care, checking daily how well the maid had cleaned their cages, and taking them out to perch on his shoulder and nuzzle in the nook of his neck. He defended his hobby to Rumana. "The birds relieve my stress. Just to look at them gives me pleasure."

She still had her studies, but Sumon, though done at BUET, had been sitting idle for a long time. He had to have been feeling the pressure of the commitment his father made to hers that both their children would complete their education—the implication being that an education led to a career. His father nagged him constantly, told him he should be out looking for work. Again, perhaps unfair. Like every graduating student of every university, he was at the mercy of BUET's tardiness in publishing final exam results. Without final marks, degrees could not be awarded, and engineering jobs required verified credentials. But what really upped the tension with his father and led to scenes when they visited was when Sumon divulged that he'd had a change of heart, that he wasn't interested in working as an engineer. His father was finally appeased when Sumon told him that his real interest lay in business and that he was studying for the entrance examination for the MBA program at the business institute at Dhaka University.

Sumon's plans gave Rumana hope that the stress would lift from their marriage, that things would settle down. A degree from that institute held promise. Her cousin Rashed, a graduate from there, was climbing up the corporate ladder at American Express.

Normally, Rumana was restrained in her reaction to Sumon's nighttime complaints and ramblings. But she couldn't help herself when he suddenly declared, "Your parents don't love you."

"Why would you say that?" Her parents' love was the bedrock of her identity.

"Because your father didn't pay me anything for you. They needed to find someone to hand you over to, to take over responsibility for you. Your dad had no money."

Rumana was speechless.

"Do you think your father is a king? Why are you so proud? I could understand if your father was filthy rich. You should be happy you're married to a rich family."

The contrast between the status of Sumon's father and her own laid bare, Rumana saw her marriage in a different light. Perhaps Sumon was paying the price of his parents allowing him, in marrying for love, to marry beneath him. Ruby had boasted to her about how marriageable her son had been, that many families had wanted to make a match of their daughters with him, including a family who lived in their building. "They had a lot of money and their daughter was very pretty. The father was a cardiologist. We told your dad this." Weeks into the marriage, during Eid al-Adha, Ruby spoke admiringly to her of a family friend who sent the new in-laws of their daughter a bull for sacrifice and, a few years later, gave them a new car. Then, pointedly, "Other families get so many things from the fathers of their daughters-in-law."

Had the Kabirs always known that her father did not understand the language of money? A week after the wedding, Ruby was showing her around the Paribagh apartment, and she asked what her tastes were so that she could tell the cook. Rumana replied that her mother had to tell the cook to add less spice for the family's portion. Her mother-in-law was wide-eyed. "You ate the same thing? No wonder your father didn't have money."

And then there was the day that Ruby first saw how she was dressed for school. She looked askance at her daughter-in-law: "How can you wear that? People will think badly of us." Sumon answered his mother: "If she wants to dress like a beggar, let her. She will always do something to insult our family."

A crack began to spread in the edifice of pride Rumana had for her family.

What good was the prestige of her father's name and his reputation as Major Monzur in his army career, or his success in the engineering business, when he'd diminished his stature with his failure in the garment industry and years of losing money? Perhaps her faults, her shortcomings as a wife, could be traced to the family of her birth.

Sumon stood barring the way.

Rumana's terror of him had compelled her, if she could get out the door first, to flee the apartment. Her screams of "Save me! Save me!" together with Sumon's screaming at her, had brought her mother-in-law scurrying to the foyer. Sumon had given chase, overtaken Rumana, and thrown himself against the front door, preventing her from leaving. At the sight of his mother, he roared. "I'll kill her!"

Ruby's reply was stern. "You don't know her father. He will kill you if anything happens to her."

Sumon stood aside.

Fear and adrenalin propelled Rumana out the door, down the elevator to the street level. She hailed a rickshaw and told the wallah to head for Dhanmondi.

As the rickshaw bumped and rattled along the streets, she calmed her racing heart. She scrambled to think of what to say to her mother and grandmother, who would be surprised to see her, alone and after dark. Hopefully, they'd assume that she had come with the permission of her husband and her in-laws. Rumana directed the wallah to the gate at the top of the alley to her parents' building, then past a side garden of neem trees to their front door. When her mother opened the door to her, Rumana put on her brightest voice. "I was missing you, so I came!"

Her mother and her grandmother acted as if her appearance were perfectly natural. Rumana said she'd stay on for dinner for the chance to see her father. When he came home, Rumana looked for anything unusual in his demeanour that would indicate the Kabirs had contacted him. Nothing. After dinner, with still neither a phone call from Ruby nor a ring of the doorbell, Rumana decided she could push her luck. She told her mother she'd sleep over in her former bedroom. For old times' sake.

After breakfast the next morning, Ruby called the house. From what Rumana could overhear of her mother's side of the exchange, it was perfectly sociable. Her mother passed the telephone to her.

Ruby cajoled her, "Hema, come back. It doesn't look good." Indeed, a married daughter who went home to her birth parents too soon after she married brought shame upon not only herself but both her parents and her in-laws.

Rumana had her father drop her off on his way to work. On stepping back into the apartment, Rumana closely observed her mother-in-law and Sumon. She knew she was in the wrong. She'd been gone overnight, and even though it had been obvious to Ruby where she had gone, she had not communicated her whereabouts to her or Sumon. Her in-laws were responsible for her security. She was obligated to tell them where she was going, and when she would return—except for school; Sumon had her schedule of classes.

Rumana braced herself: Had Ruby told Sumon's father of the altercation between her and Sumon? That she'd fled the apartment? When she saw Ruby and Sumon talking together as if nothing were out of the ordinary, she breathed a sigh of relief.

The next time Sumon became so enraged that Rumana feared something worse than a beating lay in store, Ruby was away, visiting her sister in Chittagong. Rumana again fled to Dhanmondi. As before, her grandmother and mother suspected nothing untoward from her sudden appearance or her staying through lunch, dinner and then the night. She had made no decision about when she'd return to Paribagh, since Ruby was away. The maid found a private moment with her. She told her that yesterday she'd gone on a shopping errand for the cook and that she'd spotted Sumon standing outside the main gate. He looked distressed. When she returned, he was still standing there.

Rumana was unswayed.

She let the thought of divorce alight in her mind. But just as quickly shook it off. She could just hear the gossip: "Rumana Monzur, who was just married? Who had the love marriage? She's divorced?" If it came to that, Rumana knew she wouldn't have the strength to hold up under the shame and the talk. She'd have to drop out of university. The embarrassment to her parents—the thought of it was too much to contemplate.

That afternoon, the phone rang and it was Sumon. He pleaded with Rumana: "Come home, Hema. So that we can talk. If you don't like what I say, then you can go back to your parents, and then you can decide yourself what you are going to do. I won't stop you. But please, just hear me out, then decide."

Thinking his proposal reasonable, and hearing how dejected he sounded, Rumana told him to send the driver. The guards, all of whom exchanged a friendly word with her when she was coming and going, had seen her the day before frantically hail a rickshaw. She wanted them to see the Kabirs' driver leave and then return with her in the car. With Ruby still away, she wanted someone to see that she had not come back of her own accord.

Sumon said he felt terrible that he'd frightened her to run from him again. As the hours lengthened without her, he'd missed her more and more. Finally, unable to bear her absence, he'd gone to her parents' house to wait for her to come out so they could go home together. Night fell. Still she did not appear. Then the skies opened, pelting down rain. Still he was determined to wait. But hours later, soaked, chilled and tired, he went home. "Hema, remember one thing. I can't live without you. If you leave me, I'll kill myself."

Rumana was horrified to hear him speak in such a dire way. She couldn't live with herself if someone killed themselves on her account. Feeling the strain of the last couple days and pressed because she had a test tomorrow for which she hadn't studied enough, she got to the point. "I can't live like this. I can't live constantly in fear. I'm doing my best to not interfere with your life, to not disturb you, but you have to do the same for me." She begged off discussion for now, telling him she had to study.

Sumon relented. Her studies came first, he said.

—

With Sumon's mother returned from Chittagong, he seemed back on an even keel. He was in a good mood day and night, his surly side nowhere in evidence. The familiar routine of several days of regular study calmed Rumana. She felt no urgent need to return to the conversation she and Sumon had begun.

Some days later, the maid set the dining table early for the evening meal. Rumana normally worked there after school if her husband was in the bedroom, because the rustling of her papers irritated him. With no choice, she went to the bedroom. He was at his desktop computer—he'd had a small tabletop built into a nook next to the closet to accommodate it—and was playing *Civilization*, in which players build a virtual empire with the goal of taking over the world. A single game can take days to complete.

Abruptly, Sumon rose from his chair. He issued a stern order to Rumana. "You cannot leave this room." Then he walked out, closing the door behind him. Rumana heard a key turn in the lock. Alarmed, she went to the door and tried the handle. Sumon had locked her inside. (Rooms also locked from the outside, should a family need to keep what was inside away from children or as a signal to the help that whatever was inside was not their business.) Rumana heard a jangle of keys. Thinking Sumon was taunting her, she pounded on the door. "Let me out! Let me out!"

She heard nothing. Had he left?

She pressed her ear against the door. The television was on in the lounge. Hopefully, her mother-in-law was there. Rumana screamed out for Ruby, several times.

No one came.

Time ticked on, broken only by Rumana now and again calling her mother-in-law's name. She lay on her bed, distraught, her books abandoned. She had no interest in watching television. The room's one window offered no distraction; it looked out over the rooftop terrace of a neighbouring building, on which was nothing but a rusty bathtub and other garbage.

Her throat felt parched. She'd emptied her water bottle. The water from the bathroom taps was not potable.

Finally, after a couple hours, she heard the key in the door. Sumon entered. In a voice dripping with sarcasm, he said, "When are you planning again to go to your parents?"

Rumana understood his meaning.

She lost count of her confinements. Captive in her room for hours, Rumana would sort her closet and shelves, rearrange what was on the hangers, take out her jewellery, look at the pieces. She prayed when it was time for one of the five daily prayers. Once, Sumon stayed in the room with her. He took a chair and sat with his back against the door. He warned her: "Don't create a scene. Do you want to create drama? Do you know how capable I am of creating drama?"

After every confinement, a more diminished Rumana emerged.

By the time the confinements stopped, when Sumon decided he'd made his point, her enthusiasm for her studies had waned. She had missed classes and had to borrow notes to study. She lost interest in what was being taught. Deadlines came and went. Soon she couldn't rouse herself to attend her classes. She decided to look to exams; students who faltered during the year could make up for it on the all-important finals.

In Rumana's year-end marks for the second year of her program, a lone B stood in a field of C pluses. She had expected her marks to slip from her first-class standing in first year, but this was a disaster. If she didn't do something to reverse the steep slide in her marks, her education would be in jeopardy. She'd destroy a chance at a career. How could she face her parents, who had made completion of her education a condition of marriage?

To fail at either her education or at her marriage would be to fail at both.

She knew what she had to do: rededicate herself to her school work and lower her expectations of marriage. Just to survive her marriage would have to be enough.

She no longer cared what Sumon intended to do with his education. He told his parents that he made it to the interview stage of the admission process for the MBA program but no further. Taking his son's interest in business at his word, Kabir called on a family friend with a large construction company, who, as a favour, agreed to partner with Sumon in a brick-making operation.

The infrastructure for making bricks, which remained the dominant building material in Dhaka, was so basic that thousands of kilns had sprouted in the city's outskirts, where poor farmers were willing to sell clay-rich soil and had space for a kiln, storing materials and drying bricks in the sun. Sumon's obligation to oversee the operation—brick-making was possible only in the dry season—required little more than checking that the pug mill and the kiln were up and running. In every other step of brick-making, labourers toiled by hand, from digging out the clay soil and kneading the clay once tempered to setting it in brick forms and, once the bricks were dried, loading them into the kiln for firing. Once or twice a week Sumon had the driver take him out to have a look around and settle accounts.

Rumana felt obliged, having taken a course on environmental degradation, to point out to Sumon that brick-making eroded the soil and threatened food security, that the smoke and coal soot spewing from the towering chimneys of the kilns polluted the air and made those living nearby sick. He snapped back: "Will the environment feed you when you don't have any money?"

Rumana's return in earnest to her studies paid off. More time at the university meant less time at home and less exposure to Sumon, and thus, fewer chances to trigger his anger. The beatings didn't end, but in an almost magical turn, her intense concentration on her studies seemed to numb her to Sumon's blows.

When her parents offered to take her and Sumon to her favourite Chinese restaurant for her twenty-fourth birthday, Rumana looked forward to it. Chinese food was a top choice among Bangladeshis for dining out. Both cuisines shared a passion for fish.

For Rumana to do anything social for herself was rare. Once she married, her outings with cousins or friends came to an abrupt halt. The few occasions she'd made plans to meet someone, Sumon pouted: "Oh, so they're more important than me?" Or, as she dressed to leave, denigrated her. Or started a quarrel. Miserable to the point of tears, she knew that she wouldn't be good company, better that she stay home. Sumon also seemed to have lost touch with his friends. Some weeks after the wedding, two engineering friends came by, but they never came back. Rumana could understand why: Sumon had been sullen the entire time of their visit. Their only social life now was with family. She and Sumon went to gatherings with his side of the family, but they soon missed more with her family than they attended. Or Sumon could be planning to join Rumana, but at the last minute change his mind. Rumana became skilled at making excuses for why she was cancelling or appearing alone. She preferred to go alone; it irked her to see Sumon putting on the charm for her family.

A couple hours before Rumana's father and mother were to pick them up, Sumon, as Rumana could have predicted, started mumbling about not wanting them to go out. Tired of making excuses for why they couldn't attend, she began to protest, saying she was keen to go.

What came next, she didn't see coming. She crumpled to the floor. Sumon's vicious kick had landed on the left side of her back.

Rumana moaned and struggled to catch her breath. She started to cry. This was pain she could not ignore.

"Don't be such a drama queen." Sumon turned his back on her and walked out of the bedroom, slamming the door behind him.

Eventually, the pain subsided enough that Rumana felt she could get off the cold floor. But weighed down by self-pity, she stayed where she had fallen.

At the sound of the bedroom door opening, she renewed her crying, louder now. Sumon stood over her. "Stop pretending. Get up." He held out the portable phone. "Call your mother. Cancel the dinner." Rumana rolled onto all fours and, with enormous effort, pushed herself up. She told her mother that she had a major assignment due that she hadn't finished and, therefore, they couldn't make dinner.

An hour or so later, Sumon came back to the bedroom with painkillers and told her to take two pills every four hours. That he'd gone to the trouble of going to the pharmacy, especially after dark without her to accompany him, told Rumana that what he had done to her had scared him.

For the next three days, Rumana stayed home. She thought the kick had bruised her left kidney. Neither Sumon's mother nor brother inquired why she walked about the apartment with a limp, favouring her left side. On the fourth day, she felt well enough to resume classes.

On her return, Sumon grilled her. "Did you go to the doctor?"

She shook her head.

"I'll find out if you do go."

Going to see Seddiqi had been the furthest thing from her mind. He'd have asked questions about her pain. She'd have had to lie, he'd suspect something and gossip could start. The possibility of going to the doctor married to Ruby's sister had not occurred to her. She liked the fatherly Dr. Hafiz Rahman. A pediatrician, he was the only person at family events who engaged her in conversation. But if she did go see him, word would certainly get back to Sumon; his wife and Ruby were particularly close.

Rumana resigned herself to the sorry state of her marriage and her standing as a wife. Sumon was not going to change.

After the kick, Sumon no longer closed their bedroom door when he berated Rumana or beat her. He grew more emboldened. He chastised Rumana right under the nose of his mother, sometimes accompanying his hectoring of her with a jab or a shove. Afterwards, he and his mother would pick up their conversation where it had left off, as if Rumana suffered in a parallel universe.

But then came a day when he shoved Rumana so hard that she pitched into a dining room chair. The chair jammed under the table, driving the back of the chair into her ribs. The chair clattered to the floor and Rumana fell with it. Sumon stomped off. At the slam of the bedroom door—so violent it was a wonder it didn't fall off its hinges—Ruby beetled for the lounge and turned on the television.

Rumana picked up herself and the chair.

Thinking she'd best avoid her husband, she followed Ruby to the lounge. The two sat side by side on the couch, their eyes forward. Ruby kept up a stream of chatter about whatever was on the television screen. She means well, Rumana told herself. At least she tries to distract me.

Sumon gave no argument when Rumana told him that on days her classes finished earlier, she would stop by Dhanmondi on her way home. She had worried how these visits to her parents, without her husband, would look to the neighbours, if it would invite speculation about trouble in her marriage that could then get back to her parents. But then she decided that she was safe, that the neighbours would tell each other she was young and probably still attached to her mother.

To be at Dhanmondi, and especially to be in the presence of Grandmother Momena, buoyed Rumana's spirits. It resuscitated her former self, the smiling, laughing, bubbly Rumana, replacing the downcast, quiet Rumana at Paribagh. She also made use of the visits to surreptitiously stock her former bedroom with a toothbrush and hairbrush, undergarments and a shalwar kameez, in case she had to flee Sumon again.

Trouble came from a source Rumana did not expect—her grandmother. As Rumana was preparing to leave for her in-laws', Grandmother Momena asked where Sumon was. "He doesn't have a job, why doesn't he come to pick you up?"

"He's busy."

The old lady was persistent. "Where's Sumon?"

Her grandmother's questioning became less question than comment. Rumana turned more evasive. "I don't know. He's busy or something."

The brick-making operation had folded. His parents argued over who was at fault. Ruby argued blame lay with the partner for diverting resources to his construction enterprise, while Kabir was inclined to blame Sumon for shirking responsibility and not paying enough attention to the business. He was insisting that Sumon repay, with interest, what he'd loaned him to fund his share of the operation. Rumana asked Sumon if he'd consider taking a job. She took his reply—"I can't, because of my eyes"—as an excuse. After all, he could sit for hours in front of his computer playing *Civilization*.

Kabir subsequently set Sumon up as owner of a half-dozen CNGs, small three-wheeled taxis that ran on compressed natural gas. His drivers picked up and returned the vehicles each day to a space he rented in a nearby garage. For Sumon, it was but dabbling; owners with a going concern had fleets of thirty or more. His only obligation was to meet them at street level two or three mornings a week to collect his share of their fees. Rumana's father strictly forbade the family to use the CNGs, deeming them unsafe (the passenger compartment was essentially a metal box with a door cut into it, and roofed in resin) and their drivers reckless. Scooter riders and motorcyclists thought the same, throwing curses at them, "Naked son of a dog." "Child of a cow." "Son of a pig." As a business, CNGs were considered shady and exploitative, where both owner and driver expected the other to be trying to cheat them. For drivers, the money was paltry, and the thick exhaust and noise of traffic took a toll on their health. Sumon's business was not a subject to be brought up in polite company.

Rumana worried her repeated non-answers would invite more questions from her grandmother. So that she could be forthright when asked, she changed her Dhanmondi visits to weekend mornings. The first time she showed up, she explained the change before her grandmother could ask. "On weekends, the Kabirs sleep in."

Still, unease chewed at Rumana. What if her grandmother detected something in her granddaughter's manner? What if she pinned it to her marriage and asked more probing questions? Rumana did not want any of her family, least of all her grandmother, anywhere near the disgrace of her failings and humiliations. So she stopped her solo visits, and decided as further precaution to attend events on her side of the family either as a couple or not at all.

Seddiqi asked his wife, did she think it odd that Rumana and Sumon showed up ever more infrequently at family events.

In Seddiqi's family, he and his seven siblings had long since drifted apart; no one so much as remembered a sibling's birthday. When he married into Shoma's family, he marvelled at how they came together in solidarity. Her relations, close and distant, found no end of reasons to gather—birthdays, anniversaries, graduations, new jobs, new babies. Likewise, moving through life like a murmuration of starlings, in tight, fluid formation, they rushed to someone's side if anyone was having problems or unwell.

Shoma said the absence of her cousin and Sumon bewildered her too. If it had to do with Sumon, it didn't make sense; he had to be comfortable with the family—most had known him since he was a boy.

Seddiqi took to cornering Rahima and Monzur at family events. "Where's Hema?"

"She's a bit busy."

Couldn't Hema take one evening off? Seddiqi had a full schedule between his shifts at Labaid hospital and his own practice, but he made every effort to attend every family event. "Busy at what?"

"I think she's with Sumon."

Seddiqi wagered that the party he planned for his wife's fortieth birthday would be the one occasion, out of respect for the senior cousin, that Rumana and Sumon would attend, or at least Rumana.

Though disappointed when they didn't show, Shoma wasn't surprised.

She thought about times her younger cousin had asked her questions at family events that sounded like more than naive curiosity. "What are marriages like at the beginning?" Another time, "What are men like at first, how do they behave?" It had crossed

Shoma's mind that her cousin might not be completely happy. "All relationships can be difficult at times, but they don't have to be," she replied, trying to leave the door ajar should Rumana want to divulge more.

She didn't.

Shoma didn't want her own speculation to spark gossip. It would be deeply hurtful and cruel to Rumana. Instead, she resolved to suggest activities so they could spend time together. But every time she called, she discerned a disinterest on Rumana's part. As a mother of three—two of them twins—with only so much time to try, Shoma didn't push it.

In the third year of her program, Rumana drew the notice of one of her teachers, Amena Mohsin. Seeing her as smart, curious and inquisitive, she offered Rumana a job as one of her two research assistants at an institute affiliated with the university. Rumana asked her father-in-law's permission, and he gave his approval.

Rumana finished the third year of her program ranked 10th of the 130 students in her cohort. She was not satisfied. If she was going to do better in her fourth and final year, she had to figure out why, despite her renewed focus, she had failed to bring her work to her own high standard. She combed over her performance of the past year. She saw a pattern she had missed: Sumon's outbursts had routinely preceded her assignment deadlines and upcoming exams—when she was most under pressure.

Now going into her final year, besides a strategy of keeping a laser focus on improving her marks, she settled on how to insulate herself from Sumon: she would not let anything disparaging that he said register with her. Not his cursing, name calling, disapproving comments, or his insults.

It did not take long for Sumon to notice his verbal attacks losing effect. He dangled disaster in her face. "If you weren't so good in bed, I would leave you for another woman." The threat bounced off Rumana. Cheating takes effort.

She knew her strategy was working when he changed tack. "I am your destiny. What would you do if you left me? No one would respect you. Your life would be miserable without me."

In her final year, Rumana went the extra mile in every course and with every assignment. When given an assignment to present a topic in a twenty-minute oral presentation, she decided to enhance her talk on theories of post-modernism by accompanying it with visuals. She took over the floor of the living room where there was space enough to lay out bristol boards end to end.

Ruby looked on, perplexed. "Does everybody do that?"

"No, I'm making a special effort."

"What's the point of studying? You are married and we have money."

Coming up to her graduation, Rumana began to think about her next move. When she first was accepted at Dhaka University and mentioned to her father about a possible goal of working in the foreign service, he said she'd have to take the civil service exam. Uncertain what work outside the home her in-laws would permit her to do, she'd tested her father-in-law by saying she was thinking of writing that exam. His response made clear where he stood: "The civil service is no place for a lady. For ladies, the teaching profession is best." Since a career in teaching required a master's degree, Rumana asked a senior teacher how she could pave her way to being accepted in the graduate program. Given the advice that it was a publish-or-perish world, she contacted an editor of a journal, and polished for publication an undergraduate paper on the Kosovo War.

When final fourth-year results came in, Rumana had come to within one place of topping her graduating class. She shared her achievement with Sumon and his mother and told them that the department had accepted her straightaway into the one-year master's program.

They said nothing, but the look of surprise on their faces had been unmistakable.

five

ADVISED BY DOCTORS TO CURTAIL HIS ACTIVITY BECAUSE of his worsening coronary artery disease, Kabir, at sixty-one, retired and reunited with his family in Dhaka. He traded his work wardrobe for the pristine white loose pants and long shirt of the Panjabi, attire that signified a man of high standing who did no physical labour. He remained a striking figure, still handsome, still hiding the grey in his hair with henna. Except for a short walk to keep his weight in check, his devotion to his faith governed his day.

Though now part of each other's daily life, Rumana and Kabir were no less formal with each other. Their exchanges, ever respectful and unfailingly polite, remained limited. He had his strict schedule of prayer at the nearby mosque and her master's program was demanding, all the more because she had resolved to be extra conscientious from day one, by conducting additional research and making every assignment and presentation stand out.

She spent long hours at the university library, in part because dial-up internet service made slow work of accessing and downloading articles from online journals using a dial-up internet service.

For the first time since she married, someone greeted Rumana on her return from the university at the end of the day by asking how her classes had gone. Then in the evenings, she and her father-in-law convened in the lounge to catch the day's news in Bangla, on the popular Ekushey (ETV) channel. Kabir first poured himself a drink—his health scare had prompted him to give up cigarettes but not alcohol. "It relieves my stress," he told his daughter-in-law, as if feeling the need to explain himself, since Islamic law forbade drinking.

Kabir, who talked the least of his family, seemed even quieter now. His liveliness and humour revived only when a neighbour or friend visited. However, his presence seemed to ignite arguments between his sons. The brothers took to fighting openly over what family assets each deserved to inherit. Once, in frustration, Kabir hollered at his sons, "Get out of my house! Get out!" only to have one of them snipe back that the house didn't belong to him. When he lectured them on right and wrong, one huffed that he had no business pronouncing, since he had engaged in corruption. Kabir would have none of it. He said that he had never done anything so grievous as build something unsafe. Without payoffs, he insisted, projects simply wouldn't get done.

Rumana did her best to stay out of the fray. But when Kabir denied his oldest son's request for money—Sumon worried his brother would inherit more than his share of money and property—Sumon took it out on her. "Marrying you was my biggest mistake.

All my luck disappeared. My parents don't listen to me anymore. It's all your fault."

Rumana's master's program proved gruelling. Of ninety-one students who began the program, by year end, ten had dropped out. As final exams approached, Rumana feared she wouldn't be able to study effectively in the tempestuous environment of the Kabir household.

She went to her father-in-law. She told him that she needed to focus and eliminate distractions during the two weeks before exams and the two weeks of the exam period itself. She said that for those four weeks she would like to live with her parents. Kabir agreed that would be best for her studies.

Rumana's father had recently moved the household to another part of Dhanmondi. The family's new address was an apartment on the fourth floor of a relatively new five-storey building. As ever, Monzur's priority was security. He'd looked to rent in a building with few units: with only two units per floor, the building's families would know who was coming and going. The property had no gate at the top of its long narrow driveway, but a building in front obscured it from the street, and a guard-cum-caretaker could be found in a little room off the entrance to the garage. Security aside, what particularly appealed about the new location was Dhanmondi Lake Park, a thirty-five-hectare swath of parkland set aside when Dhanmondi was first developed. It was practically next door, across only two short blocks of light traffic.

Life in the new home took on a more relaxed pace. Monzur had accepted that the time had finally come to bow out of the garment industry. He'd hung on, unprepared to shutter the factory. He'd always felt he had a responsibility to the disadvantaged; when his engineering business was doing well, he brought impoverished boys and men from the village and placed them with his contacts to train them as gardeners, construction workers and drivers. The workers in his garment factory were almost all women and girls, whose only alternative employment would be lower-paying domestic service. Losing their jobs in his factory could be a catastrophe for the families left behind in their villages. But Bangladesh's textile industry, and Monzur, faced a day of reckoning. The end of 2004, just one year away, would see the expiration of thirty-year-old quotas, agreed upon by members of the World Trade Organization, of fixed market shares for textile and clothing from developing countries like Bangladesh. The local industry, distorted by its supply of cheap labour, had never broken out of low-value casual wear. Seeing no prospect for ever turning a profit, Monzur relinquished his investment to the building's owner and returned to where he first found success when he retired from the army. He and an associate set up an engineering business, working out of an office in Dhaka.

Leaving behind the tumult of the Kabir household paid off for Rumana. In June, the department of international relations published final exam results and standings of the master's students. Rumana ranked atop the merit list.

When Amena Mohsin, now serving as chair of the department, saw Rumana's stellar marks, she pegged her former research assistant and student as a possible new recruit. The department was looking to hire three junior lecturers. Amena had twice had Rumana as a student, in an undergraduate course on feminism and post-feminism, and in a graduate course on security and gender. To avoid an appearance of conflict, she had a colleague suggest to Rumana that she apply.

Amena was one of the founding members of the university's department of women and gender studies, inaugurated in 2000. In the early 1990s, along with two women colleagues, she had faced pushback in the department before it finally agreed to offer a course on gender and international issues. Amena's father was the first to open her eyes to gender disparities. She was eight years old when she and her father and an uncle were trudging home to the village and they came upon a roadside fish seller. Her father stopped her uncle from buying some: "Do not. It will be dark by the time we get home, and it is the women who would have to clean them." By the time Amena was a teen, she had learned to question men's expectations of women. Sitting in the cinema watching Pakistani films, she grew exasperated at the women on screen always asking men for forgiveness.

Rumana had set her sights on a career as a teacher, but she'd not expected to go from her master's straight to teaching at Dhaka University. The university's teachers were the country's leading intellectuals. Instead, she had been thinking of her father's advice, that to build a sound foundation for a career she should consider doing a second master's, ideally abroad.

Knowing she would need her in-laws' permission no matter which career path she chose, Rumana went to Sumon for his opinion about the lecturer position. From what she heard, to get any job at Dhaka University, one had to have political connections. She didn't think she stood a chance.

Sumon's response surprised her: "Don't listen to those people."

But she didn't see how she could measure up against other candidates. She was not a member of the student wing of any party. She had not joined any student organizations nor served on any committees. Nor had she participated in any activism on campus.

What Rumana had heard about connections was true. Politics permeated Dhaka University. The success of the 1952 language movement turned the university into the nerve centre for all subsequent political protests and movements. When the ruling Pakistanis sought to crush the independence movement by unleashing Operation Searchlight, their primary target was the university, to cripple any effort at nation-building. After independence, the university became ever more synonymous with the state. The institution was so deeply rooted in the politics of the young country that, by law, student organizations had to be affiliated with a political party. All committees had to have representation from both the ruling and opposition parties. When it came to hirings, an applicant's political affiliation could have as much bearing as their merit.

Sumon acknowledged the politics of Dhaka University, but argued that Rumana had attributes other candidates would not have. At only twenty-six, she was a contemporary of the students and, in what had to be unusual for a newly graduated master's student, she'd had two papers published. And more unusual yet, she had published the first during her undergraduate years.

Rumana submitted an application.

During her interview with the three-person selection panel, the dean of the faculty of social sciences asked the inevitable question: "What are your politics?"

"Do you really think my politics would affect how I would teach?" Rumana answered.

The dean would later disclose to Rumana that he'd been impressed to have a candidate prepared to rely on marks alone. He added that he'd recognized her as the student who, three weeks before, had come to his office to purchase copies of a book he'd authored as gifts for speakers at a workshop. Any other student in her position, he said, would have used that opportunity to lobby him for the lecturer position.

Rumana did rely on merit alone, and she was hired, becoming the youngest faculty member of the international relations department. The other two positions went to men: a fellow student in the master's program; and an applicant with two master's degrees and a PhD underway at an Australian university.

Kabir came to Rumana privately to congratulate her and to bestow Allah's blessings. To celebrate her appointment, Rumana held a small dinner at her in-laws' with her parents and Sumon's, plus Ruby's sister and her pediatrician husband. Rumana kept the celebration low-key, thinking that Sumon's mother would not be happy to see such attention paid to her daughter-in-law in front of her son. She celebrated separately by going out to dinner with a few of her new colleagues. She chose not to invite Sumon or his parents, knowing she'd have difficulty explaining what he did and thinking that her mother-in-law's lack of sophistication and education—she'd gone only to tenth grade—would reflect badly on her.

Ruby had an idea what ought to come next for her daughter-in-law and her son. "Why don't you two have a child?"

Rumana and Sumon had not discussed children.

He was quick to dismiss the idea. "Who wants that responsibility. A child is a lot of work."

"Not now," Rumana said. "I've just joined the department." She was sure her father-in-law would want her to use her talents.

How strange it felt to go from a student knocking at the office doors of one's teachers, Rumana confided to Sumon, to spending one's days in an office alongside them.

"Oh, wow," he said, "I'd never have thought that Dhaka University gave teachers their own offices."

Rumana explained. Only full professors had an office to themselves; assistant professors and junior lecturers shared offices. Her office mate was Tanzimuddin Khan, the more senior of the other two newly hired lecturers. Sumon was decidedly not happy to hear Rumana was sharing an office with a man, even if he was married; he told Rumana to tell her department that she would only share with another female teacher. She ignored him.

Rumana and Tanzim Bhai—she addressed her colleague with the honorific for a brother—got along from the start. Both were energetic; she was effervescent, he was gregarious and good-natured. It amused Tanzim that she immediately declared that the placement of their two wooden desks required symmetry, and the office, with its dreary faded green paint on the walls, needed decoration. He asked only to keep his poster of the Bengali Nobel laureate Rabindranath Tagore. Rumana realigned the desks and put paperweights on each—a dragon for his, a head of a lion for hers. On one wall she hung a clay artifact of a farmer and his wife. Across the length of the wall opposite, she applied decals of maple boughs with red and yellow leaves in full autumn splendour.

Rumana shared with Sumon that she was finding it hard to stop thinking of herself as a student and of her colleagues as her teachers. She found departmental politics a challenge, doubly so as a woman and complicated by her youth. Again, Sumon dismissed her concerns. Set aside worry about passing probation, about earning promotions and making a life's work at Dhaka University, he told her. Keep in mind that there would be teaching options at other universities.

Three months in, Rumana saw a notice for a week-long conference for young South Asian scholars in Kathmandu, Nepal. She asked Amena for a letter of recommendation. When she was accepted to attend, she gave Sumon the dates she would be away. His response served as reminder that decisions about how she could advance her career were not solely hers to make. Sumon was vexed. A young married woman spending nights away from her husband looked bad, he said. She should not have applied without first asking his permission.

Rumana went to her father-in-law in hopes of getting his blessing for her to attend. She explained that she had applied because she wanted to become a better teacher. She told him that Amena Mohsin—a name he knew because Rumana had needed his approval to work for her as a research assistant—was also attending and was a speaker at the conference.

Kabir voiced no objection. Rumana did not tell him that Amena was flying in and out the same day. Nor on Rumana's return did she share with Sumon that the conference organizers included in the programming day trips for the scholars, that they'd taken them hiking and whitewater rafting.

Soon after Rumana's return from Nepal, ETV—Bangladesh's first private television channel, popular for innovative programming and promotion of youthful voices—invited her to come on as an expert from Dhaka University to comment on American-Pakistani relations in the wake of the intention of the US and India to cooperate in civilian nuclear activities. Rumana asked her father-in-law if he'd help her prepare. He happily obliged.

Rumana was in the bedroom marking papers when Sumon asked if he could interrupt. He asked politely. Ever since she had joined the faculty at the university, he had seemed to show a measure of deference to her new standing. He said that he had something he wanted to tell her.

Rumana put down her pencil and gave him her full attention. He asked her to hear him out.

He divulged that he suffered from an addiction to Phensedyl.

Rumana could never have expected this.

What little she knew about the codeine-laced Indian-brand cough syrup came from the news. Phensedyl, banned in Bangladesh, was legally manufactured in India and much sought after by addicts hooked on the narcotic in it. In Dhaka, the syrup fetched up to ten times the store price in India. So lucrative was the black market for it in Bangladesh that factories operated just over the Indian side of the border. Seizures of massive quantities of the contraband by Bangladeshi police were a daily occurrence; packing the syrup in juice bottles was one of the more popular ways to conceal it.

Rumana was puzzled. She'd seen no bottles or other evidence of the cough syrup, concealed or not, in their bedroom or bathroom.

"What does Phensedyl do when you take it?"

"It's a bit stronger than usual cough syrup. When you're down and you take it, it makes you feel better."

Sumon said that he was telling her this now because he wanted to face up to his misdeeds as a husband. "I tried to quit before we married, but I couldn't. Now I feel I can."

That her husband's addictions had haunted their marriage made sense to Rumana. His ill temperament once they'd married had not fit with his behaviour before. It was out of character for someone so smart, sophisticated and cultured. She felt enormous relief to learn of Sumon's addiction now rather than at the start of their marriage. Better at this stage, when she had the maturity to deal with it.

Rumana didn't want to be the kind of person who refused a person a second chance. If this was an opportunity to make their marriage better, she had to take it.

But, in this moment of openness, why not push Sumon further? She reminded him that early in their marriage, she'd told him that she didn't like him smoking. She had never actually seen him smoke, but she'd come home to Paribagh to the residual odour of smoke in their bedroom. He had said he would quit. But then, after a time, the odour would be back.

"I'll try to quit. I'm trying to change. Please help me, Hema."

He's suffering, she told herself.

Sumon said he had a friend he would ask for help to overcome his addictions.

When Rumana saw him perform one of the ritual prayers of the day, something he had previously ridiculed her for doing—"Your creator put you in this situation that you aren't happy with, why do you still pray to him?"—she took it as a sign that he might truly be repenting.

Life brightened. Sumon's aggression disappeared. He didn't curse or use harsh words. He accepted that she could clean the bathroom on her schedule. If she didn't get to it, he accepted her reasons—obligations at the university or fatigue. When he called for her, he didn't expect her to immediately drop what she was doing. Rumana allowed herself to believe that, if he really was attempting to change and this progress continued, maybe they really could love each other.

Occasionally, Rumana would inquire gingerly of Sumon whether he had called on the friend he had mentioned for help. "It's my problem, Hema, I'll deal with it," he'd say. "You don't have to get involved."

After the 2004/5 academic year, Rumana's first year of teaching, Sumon surprised her with a romantic suggestion. He proposed a five-day getaway for the two of them to the Kuakata Sea beach. The dark marbled sand, stretching eighteen kilometres along the Bay of Bengal, was famous for its panoramic view. Still uneasy about being totally alone with Sumon so far from family in Dhaka, Rumana suggested they invite her cousin Rana. Sumon was entirely enthusiastic.

Rana hesitated. He'd not forgotten an unsettling encounter with Sumon. He and Rumana had had a longstanding custom of exchanging birthday presents, and on Rumana's first birthday after her wedding, he'd dropped by Paribagh. Only Sumon had been home. He invited Rana in, but didn't offer him even a glass of water. After ten uncomfortable minutes of Sumon staring at him with no effort to make polite conversation, Rana left.

Rana asked Rumana if he could bring along two school chums from university. Sumon agreed, again with enthusiasm.

The trip to Kuakata beach was a pleasant diversion: overnight on a steamer, with cabin accommodations, and then a privately hired van and driver. Kuakata was a division of the Sundarbans, the world's largest tidal mangrove forest. At low tide, at points along the beach where stands of mangrove trees reached across the sand into the surf, tiny iridescent ruby-red crabs emerged from their holes amid the exposed roots. Rumana rolled up the cuff of her shalwar to wade into the shallows; the others ventured deeper. Having researched the history of the area, she also wanted to visit a nearby temple housing an eleven-metre-high statue of Buddha (erected by the Rakhine people, who sailed in from Burma in the 1880s), the largest Gautama Buddha statue in South Asia. The road there was nearly impassable, but Sumon mollified the driver, telling him a visit there was important to his wife.

A highlight of the trip was the seafood—especially the giant freshwater shrimp, too expensive at home to be an everyday dish. Sumon paid for everything: the transport, the hotel, the meals. Especially considerate, Rumana thought, as Rana and his young friends were students, living frugally.

Rumana found her husband to be exceptionally good company. Conversation among the five was always animated, interesting and filled with laughter. Rumana told herself that this was the Sumon of before, the one who adored and loved her, who was considerate and kind. He's normal again.

—

Rumana knew as soon as her period was late.

She was eager to share the news with her husband. The timing was right to have a child. A child would finally secure the marriage, would repair all that had gone wrong.

"You weren't taking your birth control pills?"

"I'd forgotten to."

On a day that Rumana returned home from an ultrasound, during dinner with the family Ruby asked whether the baby was a boy or a girl.

At word it was a girl, silence fell over the table.

Normally Kabir, who said little at any time, was even quieter at mealtimes. He looked at Rumana, finally. "You know, having a daughter like you is way better than the two sons I have."

One week later, Sumon came to Rumana. She looked up from preparing a lecture. It was obvious that whatever it was he wanted to say wasn't coming easily.

"You've just joined the department. Having a baby to look after will make it hard for you to keep up your responsibilities at the university."

Rumana grew suspicious. Of course she could juggle motherhood and a career.

He continued. "A girl is not what I want. I would prefer a son over a daughter." He told Rumana he wanted her to have an abortion.

She returned to her notes.

At early spotting, Rumana hastened to the doctor. Ordered to take three months' bed rest, she moved to Dhanmondi so that her mother could care for her. For all her husband's stated indifference, he paid regular visits to her during the confinement. Knowing that lychees were her favourite fruit, he spoiled her one day with the Bedana variety, considered the best in Bangladesh and available only in late June.

The bed rest was effective. Rumana went back to work. She had given notice that she would take a four-month maternity leave, beginning two weeks before her due date. She read every book she could in the university library about pregnancy, baby care and parenting. Thinking that isolating herself from Sumon for a time would help her build her strength and new identity as a mother, she wanted to go again to her parents. But how to explain this desire to her mother-in-law? She told Ruby that she wanted to live with her own mother before she became one, for a period of six weeks before the birth, but in addition, she'd like to stay on six weeks after the birth. Fine, said Ruby.

Sumon came now and again to visit, staying a night or two.

Grandmother Momena started again with her questions, laden with disapproval. "Why does Sumon stay in the bedroom all day?" "Why does he insist on you two dining alone, instead of sitting with your parents and me?"

As Rumana neared full term, she would need to get out of bed often to pee, and her heavy belly made it nearly impossible to sleep comfortably. One night, as she tossed and turned, Sumon growled: "Get *out!*" Thereafter, when her husband was staying over, Rumana returned to the familiar routine of decamping for the couch in the lounge and making sure to creep back to the bedroom before anyone woke for the day.

Rumana booked a hospital stay that began one week before her due date, to guard against likely traffic tie-ups she'd face when labour actually began. On her second day in residence, Rumana's waters broke, and her obstetrician opted to do a Caesarean. She was alone in the recovery room when family saw the newborn. Kabir leaned into the baby's right ear and whispered the first words that a newborn Muslim baby should hear: "God is great, there is no God but Allah. Muhammad is the messenger of Allah. Come to prayer."

Sumon's first reaction to seeing his daughter was disappointment that her skin wasn't more fair—a hallmark of beauty in Bangladeshi women.

Rumana had a name ready for her daughter. She'd searched girls' names online at the university. She'd printed out lists, studied them at home and chosen the name Anusheh, the Persian word for "fortunate."

Research told Rumana that a mother could expect postpartum mood swings, but she experienced only bliss at the knowledge that here was a human being who could not survive without her.

Whenever the baby was awake, Rumana held her close. She allowed no one else to care for her or even handle anything related to the baby. Seeing her daughter's growing fatigue combined with a troublesome recovery from a C-section, Rahima didn't see why someone else couldn't sterilize bottles, clean the baby's bathtub, and wash, fold and iron the baby's clothes. "Why don't you take help from the maid?"

"I can't be confident of her personal hygiene." By doing everything herself, Rumana reasoned, she could avoid worry about anyone doing it incorrectly. If she entrusted her baby to someone else, and they did something untoward to her, how would she know?

Once back at Paribagh, Rumana's continued possessiveness elicited no comment. It did not seem to occur to anyone in either family that there could be a deeper reason for Rumana's behaviour.

Sumon's singular preoccupation concerning his daughter's care was to insist that family and visitors use hand sanitizer before touching her. Otherwise, his disregard for quiet around her naptimes perturbed Rumana. He didn't turn down the volume on the television when she was trying to put the baby down or keep it low when she was already asleep.

Feeling the need for time alone with her child, Rumana strapped her baby seat into the back of her father's Toyota, which she'd borrowed, and took long drives toward the airport, a route with few stops and starts. Her father was right that a woman needed a thick skin to take to the road. At taunts from male drivers—"Daughter of a slut!" "Child of a cow!"—Rumana just rolled up the windows and turned on the air conditioning.

As the end of Rumana's maternity leave approached, Ruby returned to a familiar refrain. "Why do you have to work? We have money."

Rumana adjusted her morning teaching schedule so that she left the house while the baby was napping and returned when she needed to be nursed. Once Anusheh's changing routine made that no longer feasible, Rumana taught classes with her daughter strapped in a carrier to her chest.

There came a day, finally, when Sumon asserted himself as a parent. He came home carrying a large bag of fruit, which he did from time to time to treat the family. He declared that his daughter, now six months and having started on solid foods, ought to taste the king of fruits. He'd bought the prized Langra variety of mango, desired for its floral scent and slightly sour taste. Available in late July, the Langra's ideal ripeness lasts only hours. If eaten too green, an allergic reaction will swell the tongue; if too ripe, its flesh will have gone to mush. Rumana realized her husband's gesture had to have taken some thought—he had to time it precisely. Within the hour, Anusheh's rapid-fire farting, an encore to how much she had enjoyed the fruit, brought the household to gales of laughter. It struck Rumana for the first time that Anusheh was not hers alone.

Anusheh's whimpering stirred Rumana from sleep. She looked at the clock. It was three in the morning. Anusheh, at eight months, was still not sleeping well. Rumana picked her up from the bedside crib and tried to nurse her. Anusheh was uninterested and now wide awake.

Rumana contemplated taking her to the lounge. But no, it would be stifling hot there. In August, it can take until morning for the outside temperature to drop even one degree. Besides, moving the baby back and forth from air conditioning might cause her to catch a draft.

Suddenly, the bed jolted violently. Anusheh jerked in her arms, wailed and began to cry. By Sumon's rigid posture beside her, Rumana knew he was feigning sleep. They both knew what he had done. Rumana felt a wave of disgust: Why did I have a child with this person?

By the light of morning, she had made up her mind. Sumon's kick had glanced off Anusheh's diapered buttocks, but she had to protect her daughter. She told Sumon that she and Anusheh were leaving Paribagh that morning for Dhanmondi. When Sumon said he'd join them, Rumana did not argue; Sumon would not dare misbehave with her father at hand.

Both sets of parents accepted Rumana's explanation of why she and Sumon and the baby were moving homes. Her work was piling up at the university and she needed her mother's help with the baby. The part about her work was true; on top of her teaching, she was up against a deadline to finish a paper slated for publication in a Sri Lankan journal about global security and underdevelopment in failed states.

In their second month at Dhanmondi, Sumon began pestering Rumana for them to return to Paribagh. "My parents deserve to see their granddaughter grow up." Four months in, he demanded that they leave.

Rumana told her mother they were returning to her in-laws the next day. Upset at the suddenness, Rahima asked why.

"Sumon's having problems with his business."

"What kind of problems?"

Rumana pleaded ignorance. Better that than say more and appear to be hiding something.

The three had barely settled back in at Paribagh when Rumana's father called one morning. Her mother had fallen in the

park and gashed her nose. He'd taken her to a clinic where she'd
had stitches, but now he needed to get to work. Could Rumana
come stay with her mother?

Over breakfast together, Rahima told Rumana that she and a
neighbour had met to take their regular walk, each at their own
pace, in Dhanmondi Lake Park. Trying to keep the faster neighbour within sight, Rahima tripped. A few steps later, she tripped
again. She fell hard, breaking her glasses and bloodying her nose.

After breakfast, Rahima napped. An hour later, she woke and
threw up blood. Rumana called Seddiqi, who had Labaid hospital
send an ambulance. When magnetic resonance imaging revealed a
massive brain hemorrhage, doctors rushed Rahima into surgery.
Two days later, because blood continued to pool in her brain, doctors operated a second time. Doctors told Monzur brain bleeds
were likely fatal, and to expect a clinical death soon. Against their
advice, he moved his unconscious wife to the private Metropolitan
Hospital, which had a neurosurgery unit.

For two days, Rahima hovered between life and death. On the
fourth day, she stabilized.

Apart from the exhaustion of travelling daily from Paribagh
to the hospital and back with Anusheh, Rumana wearied of
Sumon repeatedly calling her cell phone when he expected her
to have arrived home. "Why are you staying so late?" When she
finally returned, as the car was pulling through the gates of their
building, Rumana's heart would begin to race. As she rode the
elevator up, she felt almost sick to her stomach. She had to will
herself to open the door of the apartment. She thought about telling her father that she was unhappy, that she didn't like living

with her in-laws. It would be a first to divulge something personal to him, but her mother's crisis had brought them closer.

She put it out of mind. Her father had just had a huge shock. It wouldn't be fair to burden him.

A lucky reprieve came. Her father, also feeling the strain of shuttling back and forth daily, rented a room at the hospital, and Rumana and Anusheh joined him there.

Rumana took note of who came to the hospital to keep her father company. Family on the Monzurs' side had rushed to the first hospital and diverted to the second when Rahima was transferred. Of the many friends of her father, Kabir was the most devoted, visiting several times and sitting at length with him.

On Rahima's discharge, doctors advised Monzur that his wife was facing a long and uncertain recovery. Brain surgery carried risk; she would have permanent problems with speech and vision as well as concentration, memory and balance. They recommended she be surrounded by familiar faces. Rumana seized the opportunity. When she told Sumon she and Anusheh were moving to Dhanmondi to help her mother, he again said he'd join them. She told him to come only occasionally, but when he saw that she'd loaded up all the baby gear and all her clothes except for her formal saris, he gathered some of his belongings and joined her anyway.

It would be six months before Rahima regained a measure of physical strength, but by then their stay had taken on a sense of permanence. Now and again Sumon slept at his parents', and Rumana returned when Ruby asked for her help, usually with packing before she and Kabir went on a trip. Rumana had left her telephone number in the faculty directory as the Kabirs' landline, and her mother-in-law dutifully relayed messages that students left for Rumana Madame.

The Kabir household had its own consuming issues. Shawon had returned from Canada, where he'd gone a year and a half ago to begin a bachelor's program at the University of Waterloo. On account of his failing grades, the university expelled him. Rumana told her young brother-in-law that he could start over, but she backed off when she saw him caught in a running argument between his father, who blamed his laziness, and his mother, who told him the university was at fault.

The conflict came to a head on a day Rumana was at Paribagh and about to leave for the university for a meeting of the academic council; attendance was mandatory. Panicked shrieks from Ruby brought her running. Shawon lay bloodied on the living room floor. A shard of glass protruded from his arm; he had punched through the glass of the buffet. Rumana called for an ambulance from Labaid and sent Sumon to the mosque to fetch his father. Then she called the university, to say she wouldn't be at the meeting. Sumon stayed with his mother while Kabir and Rumana followed the ambulance carrying Shawon.

Sitting at the hospital, Rumana worried what the department would make of her absence. It had already once formally warned her that she wasn't fulfilling her professional duties. She'd half expected it. To align her teaching with baby Anusheh's feeding, she'd repeatedly cancelled or rescheduled classes. Called to account, she'd cited her mother's unresolved health issues and, therefore, her inability to help mind her daughter. Thankfully, the department assumed that her husband worked and was unavailable. Recognizing that she was a popular teacher and well liked by her students, the department temporarily reduced her teaching load.

Would they be so accommodating now, and accept her explanation that there had been a family emergency?

Doctors told Kabir his son was lucky. He'd come close to severing a major artery and could have bled to death.

Back on track, Rumana was soon promoted to assistant professor. Sumon had Rumana's teaching schedule. Why was he calling her during class? "Where are you now?" "Have you left?" A few minutes later, he called again. "Haven't you left yet?"

Once she was in the car with the Monzurs' driver, Sumon kept calling. "Now where are you? Exactly where?"

Rumana had to ask the driver, though she didn't want to distract him. Dhaka had become frustratingly congested, and driving required concentration. In any traffic tie-up, buses, cars and CNGs lurched forward to claim even an inch of space. Drivers also had to make quick decisions about alternate routes.

It seemed Sumon was tracking her progress. "Why aren't you here by now?" The accusations started. "You're not coming straight home, are you? You're going on a date with Tanzim, aren't you?" He was forever dragging in the name of her office mate.

The driver, an older man who'd been with the family for the last two years, looked up at his rear-view mirror to catch Rumana's eye. "How do you tolerate him?"

As she did every time before stepping through the door at Dhanmondi, Rumana took a moment to don a mask: the cheerful, smiling Rumana her parents and grandmother expected to see. She felt a greater need than ever to bear her unhappiness alone. Her father's worries toggled between his wife and his mother, whose respiratory problems were worsening. She was on twenty-four-hour oxygen, and calling ambulances for her had become a recurring event.

He did not need to worry about Rumana as well.

On an evening when business at the university had kept Rumana late, her mother hurried to meet her when she came through the door. She looked upset, unusual for her. She said Sumon had locked Anusheh in the bathroom. Rumana rushed to the bedroom to free her. That their daughter, almost two years old and long since toilet-trained, had soiled her pants led Rumana to believe she must have been terrified. Rahima explained that the maid had alerted her that she could hear the child crying in Sumon's bathroom. Rahima had gone to get her granddaughter, but at the door to the bedroom, Sumon had given her a push, then shut the door to her. Rumana saw a rare anxiety in her mother's face. Clearly, Sumon had frightened her.

Sumon told Rumana that Anusheh had been "bothering" him.

From that day on, Rumana took Anusheh with her to the university. Her mother couldn't do double duty caring for Monzur's mother and her granddaughter. When Rumana had a class to teach, she parked Anusheh in a chair next to the lectern and gave her Kraft Singles to occupy her. When she saw that students were finding her daughter more interesting than her lesson, Rumana moved her to the back of the room.

Just short of Anusheh's second birthday, Grandmother Momena took a turn for the worse. She could sleep only sitting up, propped between pillows. When she could find no relief from the pain in her swollen and blackened ankles, Monzur consulted Seddiqi. He said he could administer medication to dilate her veins, but whatever broke loose of the clot in her leg could migrate upwards and lodge in her lungs, bringing on sudden death. Monzur saw no option. His mother lasted a month.

It fell to Monzur as the only son in Bangladesh to organize his mother's funeral and burial and three days of mourning. Rumana thought, surely, this was one time that Sumon would step forward to shoulder some of his father-in-law's burden. He did not. She thought back to her mother's brain hemorrhage, how relatives came daily to keep company with her father. Sumon came only twice, each time staying briefly.

A subversive thought resurfaced. She could divorce Sumon. But then, her mind landed on the fallout. She taught at the country's most prestigious university. What would her colleagues think? And her students? It was always the woman's fault. She'd be a subject of gossip. Everyone would stare at her. She'd be scorned. And what about Anusheh? She'd be teased, whispered about as the girl from a broken home, without a father in her life.

Rumana buried the thought.

One day, Ruby came to Dhanmondi for a visit with her granddaughter. She showed up, as always, with a treat for the girl. Sometimes a toy or an outfit. Sometimes a pot of yogourt, an import from Australia. Today, it was Anusheh's favourite, fresh strawberries, an import from Turkey that was not easy to find in Dhaka.

The visit over, Sumon as usual rose to escort his mother to the garage where the Kabirs' driver was waiting. As a courtesy,

Rumana accompanied them to the elevator—always slow to come—to take them downstairs.

She was calling the elevator when Ruby and Sumon, who were standing behind her, began to grouse at each other. By Ruby's complaining tone—"Oh, you always listen to her, that's why you say those things to me"—Rumana could only conclude that she herself played some unknown part in their squabble.

Suddenly, Ruby screamed.

Rumana whirled round. "What happened?"

"He hit me!" Then, to her son, "How could you do that?"

That Sumon could be so cowardly as to hit his own mother dislodged Rumana's fear of her husband.

"You're not paying attention!"

Sumon was asking Rumana to fill out a form and a cheque for him to sign, which she was then to drop off at the brokerage. Sumon had joined a stampede into the country's two stock markets, both on a tear after the Awami League's landslide electoral win in 2008—the first national election in seven years—had promised a period of political and economic stability. When his stocks paid dividends, he dispatched Rumana to the brokerage to pick up a cheque. Then he insisted she go with him to the bank. Yet once there, he just stood over her shoulder, while she conducted his business on his behalf with the teller.

Rumana had to admit, sometimes Sumon's voice didn't even register with her. It was the inevitable progression of her latest adjustments to surviving her marriage—ignoring her husband as much as possible, and communicating with him only as necessary. No longer did Rumana volunteer anything about her life at the university. She used to. But now she shared nothing, out of fear of how Sumon would react if he learned about anything she had not disclosed. Now some days the only words Rumana spoke to Sumon were to announce a meal was about to be served.

Sumon revived his cursing. He called her *khanki*. If labelling her a whore were not base enough to demean her, he called her *khanki magi*, a prostitute in a brothel. He impugned all her intentions as only vulgar. At the bank, he scorned her as they walked away. "Why are people so nice to you? Is it because you flirt with them?" He would listen to her end of a call with a colleague and demand she change the tone of her voice. He'd see her well dressed and coiffed to go to the university and, in a mocking voice, ask, "Oh, are you going on a date with Tanzim?"

Let him think whatever he thinks, Rumana told herself. It was all so ridiculous, almost laughable were it not so tiresome.

Sumon's renewed verbal abuse proved a harbinger of another return. Rumana had deluded herself to think that living under her parents' roof would be deterrent enough. But at least Sumon restrained his beatings beyond slapping her face. He seemed careful to avoid breaking her nose; that would be impossible to disguise. Since he took his anger out on her in the evenings, any swelling had usually calmed by morning. Camouflaging the marks he left on her face was never difficult. Face powder, mixed to get the colour right to cover the degree of redness, did the job.

Rumana was confident that her parents heard nothing. Their bedroom and her parents' bedroom were at opposite ends of the apartment, with walls in between of concrete. She felt grateful their daughter was not often a witness to the physical altercations. When she was, Anusheh cried. Rumana was careful to not show that she was in pain. If blood dripped from her nose, she waited until Sumon left their bedroom before cleaning it up, and she did so in silence. Recognizing that a young child looks to her mother for explanation, and counting on her intuition that a mother has to manage a difficult person, she'd tell Anusheh, "The way your father is sometimes is not the way you want to be." Afterwards, she'd gather Anusheh in her arms, tell her a story, sing a song, distract her.

Since their appointments to the faculty, Tanzim had tried to nudge Rumana toward incorporating activism into her teaching: "We're teachers in a university. We ought to be socially aware. We face students in the classroom every day. Moral positions are very important." The first of Tanzim's publications took the government to task for allowing food to be adulterated for profit (for example, adding urea fertilizer to whiten rice and lead chromate to turmeric to dye it a brighter yellow). His PhD work questioning the government's support for a survey in a protected national park by the US multinational Chevron brought him a devoted student following. Seeing him as unafraid to challenge the government on controversies of the day earned Tanzim the respect of teachers from across the university.

When Tanzim saw little interest from Rumana, he assumed her limited social conscience came from her having an elite background, and her naïveté from a cosseted upbringing.

Still, he kept trying to provoke her. When he saw her suddenly start a routine of beginning her work day by reading the Qur'an, he couldn't help himself. "Are you going to teach your students the Qur'an? Why are you reading it?"

Rumana gave an enigmatic smile. "It makes me feel peaceful, Tanzim Bhai."

How could she claim to be on moral ground, open to her colleague's awareness of and concern for social issues, while staying silent about the indignities of her marriage and her struggles to break free from her husband's control?

In the fall of 2009, her fifth year of teaching, Rumana, determined to continue an upward climb in her career, followed the example of Tanzim's career progression. She applied for and won a UNESCO / Keizo Obuchi two-year research fellowship for scholars under forty, which Tanzim had won three years before. She won the fellowship with a proposal to examine the role of women in a sustainable peace in Sri Lanka, a country emerging from twenty-five years of civil war (the defeated rebel Tamil Tigers had been fighting for an independent homeland). And she decided it time to pursue a second master's degree and, as her father had advised, to do it abroad.

Rumana informed the department that she would take a study leave in the fall of 2010. She planned to apply to a master's program at one of the top-ranked schools for global affairs, Georgetown University in Washington, DC. The department was happy to pay the fee for her to take the Graduate Record Examination, a requirement of applicants to graduate schools in the US. She told the department that if accepted, she would apply for a Fulbright award for foreign students studying in the US.

When Rumana told her parents not to mention anything to Sumon—"He might try to stop me from filling out the application"—and that she'd tell him only once she had a confirmed GRE test date, Monzur understood why. Kabir had conservative views and his son probably shared them. He'd see a young married woman going abroad alone to study as highly unusual. Monzur and Rahima had themselves grown more relaxed about the right of their children to make their own choices. A year before, they'd visited Mashrur, and he'd introduced them to a fellow university student, Tara Stowe, who could trace her family's lineage to a crew member on the *Mayflower*. "Get used to it," Mashrur had told his parents. "I'm going to marry her." Monzur had voiced his concern about conflict in a cross-cultural marriage over how to raise children, but within days Tara's outgoing personality won him over.

Once Rumana had a test date of December—three months away—she told Sumon she would be going abroad next fall to study.

He took a hard line: "You can't. You have to do whatever you can from here. You have to listen to what I say."

When Sumon saw her retreat to the third bedroom—unoccupied after her grandmother's passing—to study, and her stack there of numerous GRE guides and practice books, he stopped moving between Dhanmondi and Paribagh and planted himself at her parents'.

Rumana devised a new routine for her evenings: get Anusheh to bed by eight, then retreat to the third bedroom and divide her time for the rest of the evening between preparing her lectures and marking papers, and studying for the Graduate Record

Examination. She was precise in allocating her study time, allowing time for each section of the GRE and taking practice exams within the prescribed time limits. Worried that her skills in English might pull down her score, she allotted extra time to study antonyms, synonyms and analogies.

From the start, Rumana would barely have sat down to work when Sumon would barge in. He'd rant at her. She was a terrible wife. She was unfaithful. She flirted shamelessly. She was a bad daughter-in-law. She didn't appreciate what his family did for her. He plumbed the past for her failings, rhymed off the occasions when she didn't do as he asked, didn't ask his permission, didn't obtain his consent.

Already run ragged between a full-time job and motherhood, Rumana slipped. Demoralized by Sumon's harangues, she began to lose focus and started to forget what she had been reading.

If only someone would throw Sumon out of the house.

Fifteen days before the test date in December, Rumana, with a heavy heart, knew that Sumon had defeated her, that she was unprepared, that she wouldn't meet the minimum score to be competitive to be admitted to Georgetown. She saw no alternative but to cancel her sitting for the exam. She had the awkward task of telling her department that she would not be taking the GRE—for which the department would receive only a partial refund—and that she would therefore not be applying to Georgetown.

Rumana was despondent. She knew she had lost face. She had forfeited an opportunity to go abroad to study and maybe stymied the advancement of her career at Dhaka University.

The abandoned pile of study materials did not escape Sumon's notice. "Oh, you aren't studying for the GRE? Now I know for sure you are a complete loser." He went back to living at Paribagh, with his parents.

Over the days that followed, Rumana's familiar ambition returned and beat back her despair: an assistant professorship was not where her drive to achieve stopped. Freed of Sumon's hovering, she could think again. She plunked herself in front of her father's desktop and dialed up the internet—her father wasn't tech savvy but he was an early subscriber to internet access—to search master's programs abroad.

She saw that Canadian universities did not require GRE scores. She narrowed her choices to the political science programs at the University of British Columbia and McGill University, and the global affairs program at the University of Toronto. Rumana was euphoric when in early March, two offers arrived. The first was from UBC, where she'd be in a class of twenty and be done in ten months, less than half the time she'd spend in a class of forty at her second option, U of T. She looked up both campuses on Google Earth. The leafy campus of UBC was perched on a peninsula that looked out to the Pacific Ocean. She was smitten.

As a late applicant for international graduate student housing, Rumana's only option at UBC was St. John's College. In her application, she referenced the college's mission to "inspire a global vision" and to "cultivate lasting friendships," and wrote of her desire to acquire knowledge in different ways and to learn about other cultures. Rumana secured a place. Because the college did not accept children, her parents happily agreed to look after Anusheh. "Sumon wouldn't know how to look after a child," Rumana told them.

The next time Sumon appeared at Dhanmondi, Rumana casually dropped her news. "For your information, I've received admission offers from two universities in Canada. I've accepted the offer from the University of British Columbia."

Sumon stared at her. Finally, "You didn't tell me? What, I'm a nobody? I don't have the right to know beforehand?"

Feeling in control, she turned the tables on him. She was defiant: "You didn't let me write the GRE. You deliberately made it impossible for me to study for it. At some point, I saw why. I saw the kind of person you really are. You do not have respect for my career, and my career is what's important to me."

She knew Sumon had expected her to whimper and apologize.

It took him several moments to find his voice. "Oh, what's the point of letting me know. I already look like a complete idiot. You will do what you want."

Later that evening, Rumana telephoned her in-laws to tell them that she'd been accepted into a one-year master's program at the University of British Columbia. Her tone made it clear: there was no going back in her decision.

"What does Sumon have to say about it?" Ruby sounded stunned by her news.

"I didn't ask him."

Kabir interjected. "I'm so happy for you. You always make me so proud."

A couple days later, Sumon appeared at Dhanmondi. He glowered at Rumana. "So, you are going to go to Canada. You will take all kinds of liberties and I won't know anything."

"You will know. Because your sister and your cousin in America are my friends on Facebook."

"How will they know what whoring you are up to."

Rumana just wanted him to leave. "I'll give you my password; I have nothing to hide."

Not since she was a young girl had Rumana owned a Western wardrobe for wearing in public. There was a limited market in Bangladesh for westernized clothing; the garment factories manufactured clothes for export. Rahima accompanied Rumana to some stores that sold factory rejects and through a couple of malls before they finally assembled an array of long skirts, tights, leggings, yoga pants, denim and corduroy jeans, and long-sleeved blouses. In her packing for Canada, Rumana added a few saris from her closet. According to the college's handbook, the college held several formal dinners over the year.

When Rumana gave Sumon the details of the residence, he was upset to hear that it was coed. "You don't know the people there. You don't know what they are thinking." He ordered her to wear a head covering: "It will tell everyone that you are a modest, married woman." Rumana asked a favour. In her absence, would he come every few days from Paribagh to Dhanmondi to set up Anusheh on Skype on Monzur's desktop? Sumon agreed.

On the eve of his daughter's departure, Monzur asked her to visit her in-laws to say goodbye. Rumana took Anusheh with

her. She told the Kabirs that she couldn't stay long; it was almost
Anusheh's bedtime and she still had packing to do. Kabir said he
was happy for her and wished her well. Ruby echoed her husband,
but Rumana interpreted her sideways glances and raised eyebrows
as surprise that her son was permitting her to go.

Back at home, Rumana updated her status on Facebook to let
friends know she would be studying in Canada as of September. A
reply popped up from an Agrani friend, Zana Shammi. Some years
before, Zana, newly married, had gone alone to Canada to start
her master's at the University of Toronto, with her husband joining a year later once he sorted out his visa. Zana hoped they could
get together while both in Canada. Maybe Rumana could come to
Toronto, since their friend Farzana Morshed also lived there.

The next day Monzur, joined by Rahima and Anusheh, drove
Rumana to the airport. Sumon had declined to come. When the
time came for Rumana to say goodbye, she held Anusheh tight,
told her that they'd be able to see each other and talk to each other
on Skype, that she was not really that far away. Tears streaming
down her face, Rumana struggled to let go of her daughter, but if
she was going to get through security in time to make her flight,
she had no choice. As she looked behind at Anusheh waving to her,
she felt the pull of motherhood as never before.

SIX

RUMANA FOUND EVEN THE AUGUST TEMPERATURES IN Vancouver a shock. While out walking, she took pains to avoid the chilly shade. September brought another surprise: the sight of buff students clad in workout gear. She thought to herself how unfit she must look in contrast. She considered a coed yoga class on offer by a fellow student at St. John's College, but deciding it crossed the boundary of decorum for her, she opted instead for long, brisk walks.

One day a student from China heading out from the college for a run suggested Rumana join her sometime. She did, and soon Rumana was dedicated enough to buy trainers and a sports bra— she hadn't known such a garment existed. Now that she broke a sweat from exertion, she relished the cooler temperatures. By the time November rolled around—a month that Vancouverites call the worst month, when a moody overcast sky tucks in as tight as a fitted sheet, and chilly rain slashes the ground day after day—she would appreciate the climate even more. She kept up her running routine, three or four mornings a week, setting out along Marine Drive, past old growth Douglas fir trees standing sentry on the steep cliffs above the Pacific Ocean, past the Nitobe Memorial Garden, which was beautiful in all seasons, and UBC's Museum of Anthropology, to a stretch of road where the view opened up to a panorama of the North Shore mountains and the Strait of Georgia. Half an hour later, in a heavy sweat but exhilarated, she was back in her room.

Among residents, motherhood distinguished Rumana from her peers. On move-in day, fellow students had been amused to see her walking around the college with her laptop and talking on Skype. She explained to them later that she had been giving a tour to her young daughter in Bangladesh.

Rumana had been keen to share her new surroundings with Anusheh. She began in the great dining hall with its cathedral ceiling—where she took breakfast and dinner from Mondays to Thursdays—then showed her the three lounges. Each had a fire-place, one had a grand piano, another a billiards and a foosball table. Then Rumana's tour continued to what was on each of the three floors of residents' rooms, a communal kitchen and a dedi-cated room for reading and studying, and another for watching television. On the top floor, she showed off the expansive patio—a prime spot to sight bald eagles—and to hear the screech of seagulls so that Anusheh understood how close the ocean was. Finally, she showed her daughter her own room on the second floor, with its view to the treed and grassy quadrangle of a courtyard below.

Everyone was soon able to predict the moment at dinner in the dining hall when Rumana would abruptly excuse herself— "I have to Skype my daughter!" Many of them juggled time differences when communicating with family. None asked or even thought much about who back home was caring for her daughter, but in hindsight, they realized they had just assumed that it was her husband, the child's father.

This year, 160 students came to St. John's from forty-five countries spread over five continents. Besides being the sole student from Bangladesh, Rumana stood out in several other ways, beginning with her polished appearance. Curious students, on first seeing her hair shiny and coiffed, her makeup perfectly applied, and her outfit accessorized with a colourful scarf, would ask, "Are you going out?"—only to realize that this was how she presented herself even coming to breakfast. She was also one of two older students that year. At thirty-two, she had as much as a decade on those fresh out of their undergraduate degrees. The other was Mohsen Seddigh, pursuing a doctorate in law. Out of Iran for the first time, he had worked for a couple years as a journalist before taking further graduate studies. He and Rumana bonded immediately over the name Anusheh, bringing to mind for him Anousheh Ansari, the Iranian American engineer who joined a 2006 *Soyuz* flight to the International Space Station to become the first Muslim woman in space.

The principal had encouraged all students to populate the two-metre-long tables in the dining hall seat by seat during orientation week. Rumana's warmth won over her first tablemate, Isabel Andrade, from Ecuador. Soon, one habitually collected the other when heading to the dining hall. A month later, the pair become a trio. Sotonye Godwin-Hart, a Nigerian student, transferred to St. John's from another graduate residence on campus because it wasn't wheelchair accessible. Rumana watched the new arrival make her selection at the cafeteria, and, one hand alternately balancing her food tray on her lap and the other wheeling her chair, head toward her room. Rumana hurried after her. At Rumana's insistence, Sotonye returned to the dining hall and joined her and Isabel at their table, as she would do routinely from that day on.

The three fast friends fell in as part of a wider circle of a dozen students, among them, Mohsen and three other Iranians. The four men enjoyed the ease of speaking Persian and cooking familiar cuisine together, and could often be seen tossing a football back and forth in the courtyard. Various combinations from the dozen would gather to prepare a meal on Fridays and Saturdays, when residents had to fend for themselves. When taking time off from studying, they would link up to go on outings. As luck had it, one of Mohsen's friends had a car, and so did a friend of their's who lived off campus, allowing them to make the most of what, for many, was limited time in Canada.

Before Rumana left Dhaka for Vancouver, her father suggested that she be the one to call home, rather than the other way round: "Your study time should take priority." She agreed. In that way, if her parents did call, she'd know it was important. As for Sumon, let him be the one to call her; she had nothing to say to him.

Rumana lived by two clocks in Vancouver: local time and Dhaka's. On any given day, she had two narrow windows in which to Skype her daughter. One was before breakfast, which allowed her to catch Anusheh before her mother readied her for a shower and bed. But that left Rumana pressed to get to breakfast and class. Instead, her preference was to call after her dinner and before her father had to drive Anusheh to school.

From her first class at UBC, Rumana had to adjust to a different method of teaching than she was used to. In Bangladesh, communication went one way, from teacher to student. Here, professors gave out long lists of required readings and expected students to engage both with the professors and each other; graduate seminars were three hours long.

With her days taken up by her classes and meetings with her thesis supervisor—the requirement to write and defend a thesis was another difference from her first master's degree—Rumana's evenings were consumed with study, assignments, and grading papers for a teaching assistantship she'd taken on. In addition, she wanted to make the most of the university's twenty-four-hour high-speed internet to access academic journals from around the world.

If Rumana was going to do well in her studies and stay woven into her daughter's life, she would need to manage her time rigorously.

"You talk non-stop about Anusheh!"

Isabel and Sotonye were astonished how much a mother could miss her child.

Anusheh was as much a part of their lives as her mother's. She made a new friend. She learned to dance. She had her hair cut (if

Rumana were there, she'd have kept it shorter). She added "book" and "bed" to the English words she could spell (two more objects that Rumana had taught her by holding them up to the camera or pointing to them in her room). She finished her clown painting (at her mother's suggestion, she held the jars of various paint colours beside the clown's hair to see which colour went best with the red she'd already chosen for the nose). She improved her drawing of the Bangladesh flag ("Put the red circle inside the flag, but not in the centre," Rumana directed her. "Think of it as being close to the flagpole. . . "). On it went.

With their friend already a university professor, the two younger women saw Rumana as leagues ahead of them in life. Isabel, emotionally volatile, often felt as if she were at sea; uncertain of her decision to study adult education and to pursue her degree so far from home. Both she and Sotonye had boyfriends, but neither saw these men in their futures. Isabel's Ecuadorian boyfriend was at a culinary school in France, but she was leaning toward breaking up. Sotonye, who had a purposeful matter-of-fact manner, had a boyfriend in Nigeria, but they weren't serious.

Yet as mature as she perceived her friend to be, Sotonye also found her a contradiction. To let off steam from the intensity of their programs, the three friends would engage in foolery: someone might start a spitball war or a water fight. But no matter who started it, Rumana, given to childish abandon, extended the antics until Sotonye called it to a halt. "For Pete's sake, can we do something else?"

But when talk turned to boyfriends, Rumana appeared disinterested, every bit the older, contented, married woman.

—

Initially, Rumana had been confounded that Sumon called her repeatedly when she was in class. He had her schedule; he knew her phone would be off and that she hadn't purchased a voicemail option on her cell phone plan.

Then it struck her; he didn't trust that she was where she was supposed to be.

Rumana could be walking to or from class, in the library, or meeting her supervisor, and he'd call. She didn't answer and didn't return his call until she was back in her room. By then, he would have barraged her with angry texts: "WHERE ARE YOU? WHY AREN'T YOU PICKING UP MY CALL?"

He'd only keep calling and texting until she did call back.

"Where were you?" was the first thing he'd say. She told herself she didn't answer to him: he'd sabotaged her studying for the GRE, and she hadn't asked for his permission to study abroad.

Sumon next started calling at all hours. He'd call after dinner, interrupting her study time. She could be deep asleep and he'd call. He'd call in the early morning, intruding on time she needed to ready herself for the day.

To add to Rumana's frustration—and Sumon's—cell service frequently dropped in the middle of a conversation, the price of having signed with the cheapest cell phone service provider. When calls dropped, Sumon expected Rumana to leave her room to find a better signal, which because of the low placement of the college, meant going outside. If late at night or in the early morning, she worried about disturbing sleeping residents as she pushed through the corridor's successive heavy doors and they clanged shut behind her. Once outside, she sometimes had to walk to a parking lot a hundred metres uphill to get any reception. Standing there alone in the dark, she'd fret about her safety; the university had recently warned students about the daytime murder of a woman jogging in the provincial park adjacent to campus.

Sumon never asked about her studies. He interrogated her only about her personal life. How many friends did she have? He wanted names, female and male.

"I have many friends."

"I knew it. You're having a blast there, aren't you? That's why you wanted to go abroad."

Rumana told herself that he was spewing nonsense.

Sumon was back. Monzur and Rahima asked themselves why he felt the need to live with them again. Other than watching a DVD with Anusheh or bringing home a toy for her, he showed little inclination to parent. He kept to his routine of sleeping in and left it to Monzur to take her to and from school. Thinking it fortunate that Anusheh was too young to realize her father was not making much time for her, Rahima and Monzur compensated by taking her on frequent outings and buying her treats. They also wanted Rumana, who they knew would be missing her daughter, to see on Skype that the girl was happy.

It became clear in Rumana's absence how much she had been running interference for her husband. More than once, the dinner already served, Sumon had summoned the cook and declared neither of the curries to his liking. He demanded something else.

The replacement never satisfied. Too salty, not salty enough. Not enough chili, too much chili. Once, in a fit of pique, he'd splashed water from his glass in the maid's face. Another time, swept the offending dish onto the floor.

Monzur and Rahima noted to each other their son-in-law's idleness. They saw no evidence of what, if any, business he was engaged in. There was no mention of brick-making or of CNGs.

Monzur prodded Sumon, suggesting that he make use of his education. "Why don't you try to get an engineering job? Electrical engineers are much in demand." He offered to call on his and his partner's connections.

"I cannot work as an engineer because of the strain on my eyes."

"Electrical engineers don't have to go out to the field. You can get a desk job, do research."

Getting nowhere, Monzur dropped the subject.

Rahima remarked to Monzur that she thought it curious that Sumon squirrelled away in his room. Sometimes she had to knock two, three times just to get him to come out for a meal. "Could Sumon really be on the computer for hours and hours? Why doesn't he go out, mix with friends?"

Monzur agreed. "For a man to sit around the house all day is very unusual."

From what they could glean, the only company their son-in-law kept was on the phone, and from what they overheard, his daily calls were limited to his mother and Rumana.

Monzur, who felt vested in his daughter's education abroad, could not rein in his exasperation at the inconvenient hour and length of Sumon's calls. He wondered, What arrangements had she made that Sumon should call at any hour? Mindful of the pressures on her time, he and Rahima waited for her to call them.

Monzur finally spoke up. "Why are you calling Hema now? Now is not a good time."

Sumon said nothing.

The next time Monzur was speaking to Rumana, despite his and Rahima's belief that once their children married, any interference on their part in their married lives was overstepping, he couldn't restrain himself.

"Why don't you tell Sumon not to call at those times? Even if you're not studying, you could be resting."

"I'll tell him. I've already told him. I'll tell him again."

Many at the college were prolific users of Facebook, regularly posting and commenting on their own pages and the college's, which was public and visible to anyone. After Rumana's initial posting on the college's page to promote her country—she posted two links: one to Beautiful Bangladesh, the government's tourism website, and a second looking ahead to the opening ceremony of the 2011 Cricket World Cup, to be co-hosted by Bangladesh, India and Sri Lanka—she deliberately restricted her time on social media. In any event, her basic phone had such a poor-quality camera that it wasn't worth taking pictures, so she didn't have any photographs to post.

However, when she did see photos that others posted and that she was tagged in, she was grateful that they served as a record of new friends and of the college as a home away from home, and that they captured the spontaneity and spirit of life there. One of the most special moments was the day Vancouver got its first blast of winter. For many, it was their first experience of snow. Everyone rushed out to the courtyard to make snow angels, and soon enough, a snowball fight broke out.

Sumon's calls took on a new tone of accusation. "Who are the guys standing next to you? What are their names?" Rumana could just see him poring over photos she was tagged in on her Facebook profile.

"They are just my friends."

He chastised her for a neckline he'd seen her wear. He said it was too low. "You bitch, you are forgetting that you are a wife and a mother!"

Rumana didn't need him to police her. She policed herself, and in more than how she dressed. She always wore a scarf because she always felt the cold, and for the same reason always covered her arms to her wrists. At formal dinners, she put a long-sleeved blouse under her sari, foregoing the traditional bared midriff and arms. At those dinners, she drank only sparkling water and made sure to leave before the others' drinking led to any perturbing behaviour. One morning after a party, she'd overhead a student joking with another, "Was I bad last night? Did I say anything bad?" and thought how risky to drink to the point where you didn't remember what you said or did.

Sumon's needling became ludicrous.

"How many men did you date today?"

"Who did you flirt with today?"

"Who are you having an affair with now?"

When Sumon's interrogations and insults petered out, he'd complain about her family. Her father didn't have a good attitude toward him. Her father protested his smoking. Her father dishonoured him as a son-in-law. Anusheh was growing up to be stubborn. Why can't he find anything good to say?

One day Rumana took Sotonye and Isabel by surprise, their conversation going where it never had before.

"My husband wants another child," she said, adding quickly, "I don't want to."

This was Rumana's first mention of her husband, though both friends had just assumed that they were in regular contact. Sotonye knew she and her friend shared the disadvantage of having signed up with a cheap wireless carrier, providing an unreliable signal. Every Saturday morning at seven, Sotonye made her weekly call to her family in Lagos. She'd make her way to the front door of the college. Without fail, she'd find Rumana there on the bench inside the foyer or standing outside on the cement pad and talking, she presumed, in Bangla and to her family in Bangladesh. Ten or fifteen minutes later, Sotonye ended her call. Always, she'd leave her friend still talking.

Rumana made this comment so casually that it had the opposite effect.

Sotonye and Isabel jumped to take the side of her husband. "Why not? When you've got a guy who's so supportive of you, who's so forward thinking, who let you come here, who's willing to take care of your daughter."

"Which is amazing, considering the culture you come from."

Rumana said nothing in reply.

"What's the big deal? You should think about it."

The conversation moved on.

Later, the two friends discussed how it was that Rumana spoke so often of missing her daughter but had not said the same of her husband. They told each other that just because she didn't mention it didn't mean she didn't miss him. Of course she missed him.

Sotonye made for Rumana's room to give her a stern warning: she did not want them to be late for the formal dinner that evening. At the last formal dinner, residents had been invited to exchange traditional attire with each other in keeping with the theme of the dinner: international cuisine from five continents. Having lent her formal saris to a couple of friends, Rumana had to help each one wrap, fold, pleat and drape them. Sotonye had waited impatiently as they then fussed over their makeup. As a result, they'd all missed the reception before dinner.

Sotonye rapped on Rumana's door and pushed it open. She saw that she had interrupted a Skype call. On the screen of Rumana's computer was the face of a curly bob-haired child who looked like Rumana—it had to be Anusheh. Standing behind the girl, a well-dressed man. Sotonye assumed he was Rumana's husband.

She introduced herself to him.

He replied only "Hi." That was the extent of their exchange. Sotonye decided to leave. Anusheh seemed to be having a tantrum of sorts and Rumana was trying to calm her.

Rumana had not been expecting the call. But Sumon had texted her that Anusheh said she wanted to speak with her mother. Because it was long past her daughter's bedtime, it had Rumana worried. If it was important, why hadn't her parents called her? Or did they call Sumon instead and ask him to come from Paribagh?

As Sumon positioned a tired and cranky Anusheh in front of the computer, the real reason he had set up the call soon became apparent. He told Rumana that he did not want her to attend that evening's formal dinner. She went anyway.

Over the break for Christmas and the New Year, Rumana was among a dozen or so students who stayed at the college. A holiday tradition new to many of them, they cooked turkey with all the trimmings and gathered after dinner around the piano to sing Christmas carols.

Rumana had two missions during the Boxing Day sales. A good single-lens reflex camera was essential for her upcoming thesis research. She could also record her own memories of life at the college in the second term. The other was gifts to take home in the summer to both her family and the Kabirs. For the two mothers, she bought perfume and a Guess purse; for the fathers, cologne and Tommy Hilfiger sports shirts in fine cotton; and for Sumon and his brother, Tommy Hilfiger dress shirts in the colour and style each preferred. Despite her differences with Sumon, Rumana thought she'd best stay on her in-laws' good side.

As Rumana began second term, alarm bells rang when she felt her concentration erode and her ability slip to absorb what she was learning. She realized the reason was Sumon's insistent texting and calling. His calls after dinner stole her study time; his calls late into the night cost her sleep. And because of his early-morning calls, she'd had to set her alarm earlier to give her time to get ready and make it to class.

She hit on a solution. The next time he called, she took the call, then lay her phone down on her bed and carried on with her work.

His voice droned on but only as background noise. Until, that is, his voice jumped up from the bed cover. "What did I just say?"

She picked up her phone. "I was doing my chores."

"You bitch."

Rumana changed tactics. Once a call went longer than she could tolerate, she disconnected in mid-sentence—to make him think it was a network failure. Of course he'd call back. She'd have to pick up.

Tiring of the charade, she stopped answering. Sumon was not to be outsmarted. He called from her parents' landline. Seeing the number appear, Rumana always picked up.

She had never imagined how his attempts to control her would escalate. Sumon threatened her: "If you don't stay on the line, I'll take Anusheh from your parents to mine."

Rumana felt at once terrified and deflated. If he took their daughter there, on her return from Canada, she'd have no choice but to leave her parents and go back to living with her in-laws.

Hostage to Sumon's threat and not daring to anger him further, she gave in to another of his demands and shared the password to her Yahoo email account. She didn't see how her Yahoo account, which she'd used exclusively for her academic dealings, would interest him. Many teachers at the university set up accounts because of the slowness of the university's server.

Between Skype calls with Anusheh, Rumana felt as if she were holding her breath. Sumon's parents did not have internet access, so a Skype call from Dhanmondi confirmed to Rumana that her daughter was still there.

Sumon took to looming in front of the webcam. "What, you don't want to talk to me?"

In February, Rumana relaxed. That month Ruby and Kabir left for Austin to visit their daughter, Sabira, and Rumana would be back in Dhaka before their return.

In March, Sabira called Rumana on Skype. Rumana had had no communication with her in-laws since the night before she'd left Dhaka. Sabira asked what her room was like. Rumana carried her laptop around to show her the desk, the small refrigerator and sink and counter area, large closets, and the private bathroom. And best of all, the view of the courtyard below where the first blush of pink blossoms had appeared on the cherry trees. Sabira was impressed. She asked about the food at the college, asked if she had friends, said that she liked all the photographs she'd seen on Facebook.

Sabira put her parents on.

Rumana found her in-laws to be as friendly and respectful with her as ever. They asked little more than how things were going in her program and studies, to which she answered that all was fine and going well. They said they were returning to Dhaka in late June. Both sides signed off with the anticipation of seeing each other back at home.

Rumana heard nothing in the call to suggest either Sabira or her parents knew anything of the fraught communications between her and Sumon.

With two months to go before her coursework ended, it was time to embark on a thesis. Rumana began discussions with her supervisor to hone her topic. When first accepted at UBC, she had checked the areas of expertise of the political science faculty and emailed Peter Dauvergne, a scholar in global environmental politics and head of

UBC's Liu Institute for Global Issues to ask if he would supervise her thesis. She explained her interest in the effects of climate change on the coastal population of Bangladesh, and he agreed to take her on. Having grown up in the 1970s in a fishing village on Canada's east coast, where the slow disappearance of cod stocks led to lost jobs, fish plant closures and devastated communities, Peter could appreciate Rumana's homegrown concern about climate change.

In subsequent face-to-face meetings, they had discussed her proposal to posit climate change as a security threat, if rising sea levels turned catastrophic for coastal human settlement. If so, the crises of refugees on the move, loss of cultivable land, food shortages and destruction of infrastructure would render borders with neighbouring states meaningless. Peter said it was a powerful, even unique, perspective, but he cautioned that characterizing climate change in that way could lead states to react to the resulting crises in draconian ways.

As the clock ran down for those whose programs were ending, conversations around the dining hall tables turned to the next steps in their futures, either academically or in the work world. Should they go home, or should they enrol for further studies abroad? Or should they apply for permanent residency, and keep open the option of living and working in Canada?

Privately, Rumana thought about the person she had become in Vancouver. She made independent decisions. Moved about the city without first having to seek approval, unaccompanied and accountable to no one for her whereabouts. She dressed as she chose. Spent money as she liked. She smiled and laughed openly. She expressed herself freely. She forged close friendships, female and male, on equal footing. With greater freedom to be out and about in the world, she was more confident. She had more experience and was more sure of herself.

She evaluated what had allowed for her success at UBC.

For sure, it was the distance from Sumon. The realization was like a beacon, guiding her along a path to a different future. Rumana saw how she could both solidify her career at Dhaka University and extricate herself and Anusheh from the marriage. UBC permitted master's students with a first-class standing who showed research ability or potential to apply to transfer directly into the doctorate program. To go directly from her master's to a doctorate abroad would give Rumana another five or six years away from Dhaka.

Her supervisor was supportive when Rumana asked his opinion about continuing her studies in Canada. Peter, who had a boyish enthusiasm, regarded her as a star candidate in the master's program and had been impressed to see her include field work in her thesis proposal. She had mentioned that she was returning to Bangladesh for the summer—often she spoke of how much she missed her young daughter—and would take that opportunity to travel to the coast to do research.

Rumana saw a way ahead. The first step: inform herself on the process to file for divorce. She had someone she could call once back in Dhaka to connect her with a lawyer. She had stayed in touch with a fellow international relations student over their shared love of cricket; after graduation he worked for the Bangladeshi telecommunications company Grameenphone, which sponsored the national team. As the only son in his family, he'd had to engage a lawyer to sort out the family's business and property after his father's death.

When Rumana's students came to her with legal problems, she'd ask him for names of lawyers who could help them out.

She planned to contact him under the pretext that one of her students needed a family lawyer.

Rumana booked a flight home to arrive in Dhaka on May 11, 2011.

Her friends noticed how teary-eyed Rumana became as her departure date approached. The depth of her sadness baffled them. "Rumana, we've created beautiful memories here. It's not like you're leaving forever. You'll be back to defend your thesis."

One young friend, Sarah Meli, a master's student from Malta whose volunteer job at the college required her to become acquainted with each and every resident, teased her, trying to turn her mood. "Let's go buy you some sexy lingerie." Rumana's smile did not reappear.

Residents who were not returning traditionally received a farewell gift of a large Canadian flag, signed by their fellow residents. A different gift awaited Rumana, a collaboration between Somaye Hooshmand, so committed to the college's mission statement that she added a Farsi translation of it to its website, and Navid Tahirdin, one of the brotherhood of four Iranian students. The two canvassed for photographs from students and asked each to handwrite Rumana a message. Somaye used a computer program to lay out the best of the photographs on one side of a poster and the messages on the other. Navid then had the poster professionally printed and laminated.

In the same week that Rumana was leaving for Dhaka, Navid was leaving for Canada's far north, where he'd taken a permanent engineering job with a mining company. Their group of friends held a joint send-off potluck dessert party on the scenic third-floor patio. Mohsen offered the toast to Rumana and Somaye presented her with the large, scroll-like poster. Rumana was thrilled. Somaye suggested that once Rumana was back in Dhaka, she have the poster framed between two sheets of glass, so that she could choose between displaying the photographs or the signatures. When time came for the requisite souvenir photographs, the friends posed in turn with Rumana and Navid, then, hamming it up, took a second photo with hands joined and leaning in opposite directions. In every instance, Navid, tall and gangly, was awkward. The others teased: "Relax! You're so stiff!"

While packing up, Rumana asked Sotonye if she could store a box of clothing, mostly turtlenecks and trousers suited to cooler weather, until her return; she expected to be back in the fall to complete the writing of her thesis and to defend it. In return, Sotonye asked a favour: Could Rumana bring her a scarf? Other friends who'd admired her scarves asked for the same.

On her last afternoon, Rumana stood for several long minutes at the window of her room. She would miss the view of the courtyard. The last blooms had faded on the cherry trees, but the maples were coming into glorious full leaf. She picked out a corner under a maple tree. Then, she took from the freezer of the small refrigerator in her room a parcel tiny enough to hide in her palm. She went outside and in the spot she'd chosen, pushed it into the soft dark earth.

Rumana's grandmother Momena would have appreciated that she had finally fulfilled the rest of a promise. On the seventh day following Anusheh's birth, as her grandmother asked, Rumana had shaved the baby's head—the weight of the hair must be offered in equivalent silver to the poor—and done a first cutting of her nails to show the baby to be a servant of Allah. And she had preserved a piece of the umbilical cord, which custom had should be buried in the earth, anchored to a place beneficial to the child's future.

For years, Rumana had kept the remnant, until now.

Rahima was the first to spot Rumana among the arriving passengers. "Oh! She's so-oh pretty."

"She's changed," Sumon said, as if a censure of his wife.

Faced with greeting her husband after so many months apart, Rumana avoided eye contact. She said only, "Hi, how are you?"

Initially shy with her mother, on the drive home Anusheh snuggled on her lap. She began a running patter as she pulled items from her mother's tote bag: her camera, wallet, lip gloss, a package of rainbow gummy bears. At Dhanmondi, Rumana presented her daughter with the first of several gifts: a basket of fresh strawberries, purchased the morning before her flight at the Save-On-Foods grocery store near campus and carefully rewrapped so that it would survive the trip.

Only when dinner was announced a couple hours later did Rumana give anyone else her attention. During the meal, Sumon asked about the conclusion of her program, if all went as she'd expected. His voice was sweet and caring. What, she wondered, is going on in his head? She answered politely.

After dinner, Rumana watched Sumon go to the lounge, heard him turn on the television. She didn't understand. He was acting as if he lived here. She took Anusheh to the bedroom to play, and when it was her bedtime, showered her and put her in nightclothes. She had just finished reading her a bedtime story when the door opened and Sumon walked in.

She was surprised that he still hadn't left for Paribagh.

Sumon narrowed his eyes. "Why are you not paying any attention to me? You are completely neglecting me."

Rumana looked at him coldly.

Sumon settled on the bed beside Anusheh, picked up the remote and turned on the television. The girl leaned against her father. To see the two of them behave as if this were perfectly natural, Rumana was confused. While she was abroad, had Sumon been coming to Dhanmondi more often than just Anusheh's Skype calls? The few times she did see him during the calls, he was neatly groomed and dressed smartly as he was when in public, not in the casual clothes one wore at home.

Exhausted from her long day of travel, Rumana retired to the third bedroom and left Sumon and her daughter watching television.

The next morning, she observed her parents' casualness to the closed door of the bedroom indicating Sumon was sleeping in. Rumana's first thought was that if, as it appeared, he was back to living with her parents at Dhanmondi, it was going to make it difficult to tell him privately of her intentions. She pushed the logistics from her mind. Now was not the time to think about that.

The cook spoiled Rumana with a crisp and flaky paratha wrapping a fried egg along with a creamy mango lassi for breakfast. Rumana told her parents and Anusheh how she had been longing for the fresh juice and fruit of home. At the breakfast buffet at the college, the juice options came in boxes, and the fresh fruit was limited to apples, oranges or bananas. But cooler temperatures had their advantage; they would be amazed at how long foods could be kept out before going bad.

After breakfast, Rumana doled out her gifts. For Anusheh: a jar of artisanal strawberry jam, two sets of cuddly nesting pillows shaped like a ladybug and a turtle, a stuffed baby dinosaur—a character from one of her favourite animated series, *The Land before Time*—and two bathing suits. For the young house girl whom her mother had hired to help with Anusheh, Rumana had a skirt and a top, and the same assortment of bangles, earrings and hair clips that she'd bought for Anusheh. The girl was soon to leave, not only because of Rumana's return but because her mother had found her a husband. For the cook and the maid, she brought a variety of Canadian souvenirs in the shape of a maple leaf. She'd also purchased for her household and the Kabirs stroopwafels, for which she'd first acquired a taste during the family's travel in Europe.

As she asked, Sumon took her gifts for his family to Paribagh. Even though his parents weren't due back from the US for another month, Rumana knew his mother would call to ask Sumon what gifts she had brought them. Knowing Ruby's expensive tastes, she had made sure he could recite only designer labels to her.

As it happened, Rumana's arrival coincided with a business trip to Dhaka from her uncle Moynul. He invited the extended family to join him at the Jharna Grill, built in the style of Mughal architecture, at the glittering five-star Pan Pacific Hotel Sonargaon.

Sumon said he would not go, but on the day, the third since Rumana's return, he changed his mind. Rumana chose from her closet one of her dressier silk shalwar kameez. The off-white tunic was delicately striped with gold threads and trimmed in white and gold sequins, the mustard yellow in the neckline picking up the mustard yellow of the trousers. She noticed that it fit loosely on her.

Twenty-five family members, adults and children, gathered to enjoy Moynul's hospitality. After a year of becoming accustomed to exchanging hugs in greeting with female friends, Rumana threw her arms around each of her female relatives. Ordinarily, she'd have only touched an arm or put a hand around a shoulder. All evening, she was bright-eyed and bubbly, smiling and laughing, taking an interest in everyone and everything.

She heard the same compliment many times over. "Hema, you look beautiful. Hema, you've lost weight!" She explained she hadn't aimed to drop weight, but seeing how active people in Vancouver were, she'd become conscious of keeping fit and eating more healthily.

On their return to Dhanmondi, Sumon rounded on her. "Why did you try to lose weight? Who are you trying to impress?"

The next morning, he left for Paribagh.

For the next week, the Monzurs' home was a hive of activity, with relatives coming and going and gathering for meals, and conversations that continued late into the night. Family came to visit Moynul and catch up with Rumana.

All were eager to hear of her time in Vancouver. Conveniently, she could use Somaye's poster to illustrate. Again and again, Rumana unrolled it. At the poster's centre, a photo of students with their gifts in the Secret Santa exchange. Arrayed around it:

Rumana dressed for Halloween as a Barbie doll—complete with a platinum blonde wig—alongside a witch, a mermaid and an angel. Rumana making a snow angel. Rumana on ice skates. Rumana doing yoga. Rumana and her friends mugging for the camera in a mock spat of too many cooks in the kitchen. Rumana and her friends at the formal dinners. And one of her favourite outings off campus, on Cypress Mountain on Vancouver's North Shore, posing against a bird's-eye view of the city below and the waters of the Strait of Georgia.

No one was keener to hear about her time in Vancouver than her uncle. Moynul told Rumana that he hoped that her time abroad would be as life-changing as his had been. At the end of the War of Independence and just out of high school, he had left for London, England. He'd worked as a porter, a cleaner and a waiter to pay for university. He was waiting tables at a Wimpy restaurant when a Danish girl came in and caught his eye. In time, he and Anne Marie Oestergaard married. To his native Bangla and his fluency in English, he added Danish. He went on to earn two master's degrees. He turned to business, built a company with an international reach, and added a fourth language, German.

Moynul asked Rumana about her academic work and the friends she'd made. He told her, "I'm so proud of you, Hema. This shows how vibrant your life was in Vancouver and how diverse your many friends were."

Once Moynul left, the Monzur house fell quiet.

Rumana's mother told her that during the past week, Sumon had been to the house several times, and that each time he'd waited to talk with her. Finding no opportunity, he had left. Rumana had seen him out of the corner of her eye, hovering nearby. She did not interrupt her conversation with visiting family to even acknowledge him.

Rumana heard back from her friend at Grameenphone. He had the name of a family court lawyer she could pass along to the student.

Rumana called the lawyer. She asked about the process by which a wife initiates divorce. He said that as long as the contract of the Nikahnama was registered with the City of Dhaka, divorce could happen in as soon as ninety days. It was a three-step process. Whoever is seeking the divorce—the wife or the husband—sends the written notice of divorce to the spouse by registered post. Within thirty days of the spouse's receipt of it, an arbitration council calls the couple before it to try to bring about a reconciliation. After a separation of ninety days (to account for three menstrual cycles; if the woman becomes pregnant, the divorce action is cancelled), if the council deems reconciliation not possible, it issues a divorce certificate.

Rumana told the lawyer she was particularly concerned about child custody; she and her husband had a five-year-old daughter. The lawyer said that with a child as young as five, the courts could be expected to rule in favour of the mother.

He offered to send Rumana the papers to initiate the process.

"No. Don't send them. When I'm ready, I'll pick them up." She did not want an envelope from a lawyer's office arriving at her parents' house when she wasn't there to intercept it.

Rumana had already decided she had other more urgent obligations, that initiating a divorce could wait until fall, when she and Anusheh were leaving for Canada.

seven

MIDDAY, SUMON SHOWED UP AT DHANMONDI, TELLING
Rumana that he had come to see Anusheh. He called his daughter
to him. She unwrapped her arms from around her mother's thighs
and ran to him. Sumon swung her up in his arms, hugged her and
gave her a kiss.

No one else was home.

Relieved now of Anusheh's care, Monzur and Rahima were visiting a travel agency to finalize arrangements for a trip that had been
two decades in the making. In the early 1990s, when on business
in Dubai, Monzur had made a side trip to Mecca. At the time, he
resolved that when he did finally perform Hajj—what every able-
bodied Muslim, financial circumstances permitting, must do once
in their lifetime—he would do it with Rahima, since females were
required to be accompanied by a male guardian. Because the Saudi
government assigned a limited number of annual Hajj visas, he had

applied in 2009, two years ahead. The trip to Saudi Arabia for the pilgrimage in November would be the couple's second trip in 2011. In August, Monzur and Rahima would travel to Pennsylvania for the wedding of their son to Tara. Sumon was the only family member not going; he'd told Monzur he had no interest in attending.

Rumana did not want Sumon to linger at Dhanmondi, but as it was nearing lunchtime, it would be rude not to invite him to join her and Anusheh for lunch. From the moment they sat down at the table, Sumon was oddly attentive. He immediately reached for the water pitcher and filled Anusheh's glass, then Rumana's, then his. Ordinarily, if the maid didn't fill his, he'd have left it to Rumana. He also served himself, not expecting Rumana to fill his plate.

During lunch, his pointed attention to their daughter and to the dishes the cook had prepared—as it happened, her curried fish was a favourite for both Sumon and Anusheh—gave Rumana reason to avoid speaking to him directly. Anusheh, a quiet child, focused on her food, as ever, careful not to let a single grain of rice slip from her fingers. Still, Sumon elicited answers from her. Which of the dishes, the curried fish or the dahl, did she like better? Did she like the spinach in the palong shaak the way it was—at room temperature—or did she like it better hot?

Rumana's mind drifted elsewhere. It occurred to her that with both her parents out of the house and not expected home for some time, an opportunity had presented itself for her to tell Sumon her intentions. Until now, she'd only considered telling him in the fall, timing it for when she was on the brink of returning to UBC. Why not tell him today, while he was here? But what to say to him? And a bigger question, how would he take it?

Lunch over, Anusheh went off to play.

Rumana stood up from the table and went to her bedroom.

Sumon followed. "What are your plans?"

To give herself time to gather her thoughts, Rumana eased into a reply. She spoke of her academic obligations, beginning with what he'd known before she left for Vancouver, that she had to make a research trip to Sri Lanka for the UNESCO fellowship and that she would take Anusheh along; UNESCO had generous provisions for child care expenses. She said that in addition, she had to fit in a trip for her thesis to the coast of Bangladesh. Again, she'd take Anusheh.

A sense of her coming freedom overcame Rumana. Any caution of foresight forgotten, her words now came tumbling out.

After wrapping up the fellowship, she'd start writing her thesis, then she'd return to UBC to finish it and defend it. Then stay on to do a doctorate.

Sumon's eyes widened. Before he had a chance to respond, she took the plunge: "I am going to file for divorce."

Rumana waited for what she'd said to sink in.

Sumon stood fixed to the spot, seeming to search for words that did not come.

She took his stillness as invitation to go on.

"You deserve to be with someone who loves you. I tried to love you, but I could not."

For a long moment, Sumon remained silent. Finally: "I love you. I still love you."

"No, you do not love me!"

Rumana's vehemence surprised her, but she pushed on. "If you did, you would never have done what you did to me on the very first night of our marriage. If I'd known that was how you'd be as a husband, I would never have married you."

Sumon reacted with a dead calm. He did not act contrite, or apologize, or beg forgiveness. "Think about your family," he said. "What would people say."

Rumana wasn't going to relinquish the upper hand she had now.

"It's not fair for you to live with someone who does not love you. That's why I think we should get a divorce."

"You know that I cannot live without you. What can I do to change your decision?"

"I have never loved you, and I will never be able to love you."

To Rumana's mind, the conversation was over. She had expected Sumon to yell and curse, but he had remained composed—she'd go so far as to say he'd handled her news maturely. Had she misjudged him? Maybe he really had changed.

"Just remember, Hema, I cannot live without you."

Rumana felt a flicker of pity for her husband. "This is better for both of us. We can still be friends if that's what you want."

Sumon said he wanted to talk to Anusheh. Rumana called their daughter to the bedroom. He knelt down to her. "You will not see me again." With that, he stood up and walked out.

Confused, Anusheh looked to her mother. Her father had not said *Ashi*—the equivalent, in English, of "See you later" for someone you expect to see again soon.

"Your father said that because you and I are not going to live with him anymore. You will stay with me."

Too young to grasp that she'd just been told of her parents' separation, the little girl understood only that life had returned to normal. Her father, as before, would come and go. Now her mother, who'd been away for a while, would again be the constant in her life.

After Rumana put Anusheh to bed, she felt herself relax, as if she'd exhaled stress and breathed in renewed hope. She had made the right decision.

She took out her laptop. Her father had signed up for cable internet access, a welcome change from the slow and unreliable dial-up of before. She logged onto Facebook, scrolled down to the Relationship section, clicked Edit Info. Moved the cursor down the options and clicked Single.

Then, Save.

Minutes later, a private message popped up, from Sumon's cousin in California. The eldest son of Ruby's sister and Dr. Rahman, Shujan was a year older than Sumon. Rumana had met him at family events of the Kabirs. Shujan had done his undergraduate studies in India and had gone on to do a master's degree in California and found employment there.

"What's happened?" he wrote.

Rumana did not reply.

A day later, Sumon appeared at Dhanmondi again.

Rumana told herself that if he'd come to persuade her not to file for divorce, she wasn't going to give him an opening.

He said he'd come to visit Anusheh.

Father and daughter snuggled on the bed and watched a DVD from Anusheh's collection.

At lunch, Sumon took his usual spot at the table with Rumana and Anusheh and Rahima. After lunch, he hung around.

Rumana was puzzled: he's acting as if yesterday never happened.

Afternoon turned to evening. Rumana's father returned from work and everyone sat down to dinner. Conversation at the table was agreeable and pleasant. Rumana felt as if she and Sumon were putting on some kind of show for her parents. Surely he was going to leave after dinner.

He did not. He went to the lounge. Her parents retired to their bedroom, and he remained there, watching television.

Rumana took Anusheh to the bedroom to play before bed. Because she'd left the door open, she heard the ring of Sumon's cell phone and heard him greet his cousin who lived in California. She looked through the open doorway and saw Sumon leave the lounge and go across to the apartment's main bathroom. He closed the door, presumably to take the call in private.

Some minutes later Sumon burst into Rumana's bedroom. His face bore a dark scowl. "Did you change your Facebook relationship status?"

Rumana said nothing.

"Change it back to married!" He was yelling. "Change it right now!"

Upset that Sumon should carry on like this in front of their daughter, Rumana appeased him. "I will. I will change it," she said. She made no move toward her laptop.

"I am asking you, do it right now!"

Rumana stood her ground. "No. I will not."

At the standoff, Sumon left the room.

Rumana closed the door behind him and resumed her bedtime routine with Anusheh. She showered her daughter, brushed her hair, rubbed body moisturizer on her, put her in her night-clothes, read her a story, pulled the covers over her and kissed her goodnight.

She decided she ought to do some unpacking. What with the visitors and bustle of the last while, Rumana had hardly had a chance to even unzip her suitcases. Still feeling the effects of jet lag, she wasn't ready to go to bed.

Rumana was still awake when Sumon barged into the bedroom. She'd assumed he'd let himself out of the apartment hours ago.

"Where is your camera?"

It sat in plain sight, on her desk.

She picked up the camera only to have Sumon snatch it from her. He began to click through the photos. "Who is this guy?" "Who is this guy?" "Why do you look so happy? Were you sleeping with them?"

Just get out of my life.

Worried the commotion would wake Anusheh, she scrambled to think of how to get him to follow her out of the bedroom. She changed her mind; better that they stay in the bedroom so that her parents wouldn't overhear.

"Don't look at me like that. Don't look at me as if you haven't done something, you bitch." Sumon tossed the camera aside. "Get in the bathroom!"

At least in the bathroom, we won't wake Anusheh.

Sumon grabbed Rumana by a wrist and pulled her to the closet. He reached in and took out an extension section of a clothes hanging rod. Then he yanked her into the bathroom and locked the two of them inside.

His hand blazed across her cheek. He raised the metal rod: "I'm going to teach you a lesson." He lashed her arms, left and right. She tried to fend off the blows, but her bare feet slipped on the tiled floor, still wet from Anusheh's shower. As she fell, the rod dealt a glancing blow on her right cheek.

Suddenly Sumon stopped. He unlocked the bathroom door and walked out. He returned with her poster from her friends at St. John's and a pair of scissors.

He stood over Rumana and began to cut the poster. He handed her the scissors: "Keep cutting." Scared, Rumana worked the scissors, shredding the images of the smiling faces and memories of her time at the college.

Sumon scooped pieces off the floor, flung them out the bathroom window, then left the bedroom.

The thud of the heavy front door told Rumana that he was gone.

Her tears started. Her arms felt weak. Her cheek stung; blood trickled from her nose, spotting the white tiles red. She didn't want to get up off the wet floor.

But then she panicked. Had Sumon taken Anusheh? She leapt to her feet. Their daughter lay sound asleep. Afraid Sumon might return, she ran to the front door and slid the deadbolt across. Then, to doubly secure it, she lifted the levered handle to cinch the locking rod into the top and bottom of the door frame.

Rumana returned to the bathroom and faced herself in the mirror. Welts flecked with blood had erupted on both her arms. She leaned in close. A red streak and scratches marred her right cheek. She wiped her nose clean of blood. She told herself, tolerate Sumon a little while longer. He'll be out of your life soon enough.

In the pre-dawn, before the cook and maid had stirred, Rumana crept to the front door and returned it to its unlocked position. Her parents only ever locked the door if they were going out of town and had given the help the time off.

Hardly had Rumana stepped back into her bedroom when Sumon appeared behind her. She hadn't heard him enter the apartment. He told her to get Anusheh. Unnerved, and fearful of waking her parents, she roused her daughter, took the sleepy child in her arms and followed Sumon outside. In the shadows, a rickshaw waited.

At the hour when Sumon could be certain his mother-in-law would be up, he called the Dhanmondi apartment from the Kabirs' home in Paribagh and told her that he had thought it would be a good idea for him, Rumana and Anusheh to get away for a few days. He said they were in Bandarban, that they'd left early that morning.

Rahima reached Monzur at work. She was worried about the variable weather in Bandarban at this time of year. One of the three hill districts in the Chittagong Hill Tracts and home to the country's three highest peaks, Bandarban was a climb of some thirteen hundred metres above Dhaka. Come late May, tourists avoided the region unless looking for cheap hotel rates; the warmer weather and the approaching monsoons could trigger landslides and strand travellers for days.

Monzur immediately called his son-in-law. He aired his displeasure that Sumon had left on a trip with Rumana and Anusheh without informing him and Rahima beforehand. "How can you decide that without telling us? You can't just leave; that was irresponsible of you." He berated him; travel into the hills at this time of year was unsafe.

Monzur demanded that he put Rumana on the phone.

Rumana told her father that they'd left so early in the morning they hadn't had a chance to tell him or her mother, as they were both sleeping.

"What kind of nonsense is that?"

Sumon hissed at Rumana. "Tell him you have to go, you have to hang up."

In the dead of the third night after stealing his wife and daughter away from Dhanmondi, Sumon woke them up and delivered them back to the home of his in-laws.

Hours later, Rahima rose, relieved to see her daughter and granddaughter safely home. Mindful of keeping her injuries from view, Rumana had dressed in long sleeves. She was as careful to speak to her mother from a distance. She told Rahima that she had much work to catch up on, that she'd already let the maid know that for the next few days, she and Anusheh would take their meals in her room.

Two days later, Sumon strode into Rumana's bedroom. "Give me your camera. Give it to me. *Now.*"

Fearful that she might be in for another beating, Rumana got out of the room as quickly as she could. She rushed past him and made for the dining room. If, as she expected, she found the maid, she'd tell her that on this morning she and Anusheh would take their breakfast there.

Monzur appeared. Normally at ten in the morning, he was already at the office. "Oh, Hema. I picked up Anusheh's passport. Why don't I give it back to you."

Rumana had mentioned to her father that Anusheh's passport needed to be renewed, and he'd said he'd take care of it, that he had a contact in the ministry of home affairs. To walk in off the street and expect service at a government office was wishful thinking; it would not be an exaggeration to say that a client would be lucky if a clerk so much as lifted their head.

How opportune that her father not only showed up at this moment, but that he had business with her. She followed him to her parents' bedroom.

The shower was running; her mother was up.

Rumana sat waiting on the bed.

Monzur was looking in a drawer in his desk. He turned, and with Anusheh's passport in hand, came toward Rumana. He stopped cold. He leaned in, his brow furrowed. "What happened to your face? And to your arms?"

In her haste to get away from Sumon, Rumana had completely forgotten that she was still in her nightclothes, which left her arms exposed. She had also not remembered to keep her head tilted to the left, so that her long hair fell like a drawn curtain. Instead, as her father had come toward her, she had lifted her face to him.

Unable to lie, Rumana began to sob. "Abbu, Sumon is responsible."

The blood drained from Monzur's face.

Once the tears started, Rumana could not stop them.

Her father turned grave. "Hema. If a man has done this once, what will he do next? A husband is supposed to be his wife's most reliable, most dependable person. Once he takes a hand to his wife, he is not a man.

"You must stay away from Sumon. I will bar him from this house. Your mother and I will take care of this; I will speak to his parents today."

Monzur assumed a military briskness. He instructed Rumana to stay put in the bedroom. When he opened the door to exit, Sumon nearly tumbled into the room. He must have had his ear pressed to the door.

Monzur restrained an urge to thrash his son-in-law right there and then. "Follow me."

In the lounge, he stood close enough to Sumon to make him uncomfortable. "Did you beat Hema?"

Cowering before his father-in-law, Sumon said nothing.

The seconds ticked by, like soil slipping down the sides of a newly dug grave.

"That is your answer, then. I am going to speak to your parents. You are to leave, and you are not to return to this house."

The leisurely shower her mother was taking gave Rumana time to debate how much to tell. She decided she'd spare her parents the details. For sure, leave out the metal rod. Say nothing of Sumon having beaten her before. Her father had been shocked enough as it was; there was no need to make it worse for her parents.

Suddenly she was scurrying from her parents' bedroom to her own—she found Anusheh playing. She combed the apartment, going from room to room. She found no sign of Sumon, nor of her father.

Then she remembered her digital camera.

Sure enough, it was missing from her bedroom.

As morning would be dawning in Texas, Monzur, having wrapped up his day in the office, called Sabira and said he wished to speak to her father and mother. He told Kabir and Ruby what their son had done. "We cannot even conceive that a husband could beat his wife. A husband's role is to give his wife shelter. The most trusted place for her must be with her husband." He told Sumon's parents he had barred their son from the house.

An upset Kabir repeatedly said he was sorry.

Monzur said that he wanted their two families, now, on the telephone, to settle the terms of the marriage between their children. He would insist on one point: from now on, Sumon and Hema must live apart. "The question of Hema living together with such a man does not even arise."

The Kabirs resisted agreeing to anything over the phone. They were scheduled to return in less than a month. "Let's not do anything in haste out of hostility. Please, wait for our arrival before you take any decisions. As soon as we get home, we will work something out."

Monzur yielded, for now. To wait a short time seemed reasonable. He was sure the two families could reach an arrangement amicably.

Rumana was on her laptop browsing online articles for the most recent scholarship on climate change and security, to add to the bibliography of her thesis.

Her cell rang. The caller ID said Sabira. Rumana answered. Ruby was on the line.

Her mother-in-law was her usual friendly self. She asked after Anusheh. What was it like being back with her? She must seem so grown up. Rumana played along, biding her time to see where the conversation was headed.

Ruby asked, now that she was done her program what were her plans?

Rumana burned with frustration that her mother-in-law couldn't come right out and speak of what Sumon had done.

She answered, speaking only of her academic obligations and deadlines.

"I heard you want to make a separation from Sumon."

Rumana's anger erupted. "Yes. After what he did to me? I'm hardly back from Vancouver, we didn't even have an argument. What kind of person does that kind of thing?"

Never before had she spoken with anything but respect to her mother-in-law.

Ruby's geniality evaporated. "You have to forgive him. He just did it because he was angry. I told you that things like that happen. It's part of marriage!"

Rumana repeated what she'd told Sumon. "I am going to file for divorce."

Ruby shrieked over the line. "How can you make such a decision? Don't you remember, you have a daughter. Think about her!"

"I am thinking about my daughter."

Ruby changed tactics. Her tone softened. "Hema, if you leave Sumon, he will die. He can't live without you. You know how much he loves you. He loves you more than he loves me."

Rumana rolled her eyes. The call was a complete waste of time. "I'm not going to change my mind."

An exasperated Ruby put her daughter on.

Rumana was prepared to give Sabira her say. More than once when Sabira and her husband were visiting Bangladesh, she had defended Rumana against her mother's criticisms. One time when Rumana had left the room—not wanting to be part of an audience to Sumon mocking some visitor who'd just left—she heard her mother-in-law gripe to Sabira that as a wife, Rumana should stay by her husband's side. "She probably has something that has to be done," Sabira said.

Sabira took the same line with Rumana as her mother. "Sumon is madly in love with you. He'd die if you were to leave him."

So they planned this, Rumana thought to herself. They think they are going to walk me through this, talk me into going back to Sumon.

She shot back, "What would you do if this had happened to you? If it was your husband?"

It was a subdued Sabira who answered. "You don't want to give it a second thought?"

"I don't have to think twice about it."

Rumana kept from her parents that Ruby had called her. She didn't want them to know that she'd been impolite, belligerent even, in parrying her mother-in-law's defence of her son.

Her mother-in-law and sister-in-law would call a second time, trotting out the same lines.

Shawon sounded worried. He told Rumana that he was calling her instead of his parents, because it was only five in the morning in Texas. The previous evening, he'd heard his brother come in, long past midnight. Usually, when up late, by two or three in the afternoon he'd emerge looking for something to eat. At four o'clock, when Sumon still wasn't up, Shawon knocked on his bedroom door.

There was no answer. "He usually mumbles something." Shawon had tried the door; it was locked. He didn't know what to do.

"Get the spare key," Rumana told him. "Open the door and call me back."

Shawon called back in a panic. He'd found Sumon lying semi-conscious on the bathroom floor. He'd managed to get him back in bed.

Rumana's father was home. He reached Sumon's uncle, Dr. Rahman, a pediatrician, and the two men agreed to meet at the Kabirs' home in Paribagh.

Monzur and Rumana, the first to arrive, found a dozen or so empty blister strips on Sumon's bedside table. The only pills Rumana had known Sumon to take were vitamin E—because he worried about hair loss—and multi-vitamins.

Monzur called Seddiqi.

"Check the strips. See if it's diazepam," Seddiqi said. "It can become habit-forming. If you really think he's in danger, I can send an ambulance."

When Dr. Rahman arrived, he and Monzur agreed that an ambulance was advisable.

In a waiting room outside the emergency ward at Labaid, there came a moment when both Monzur and Shawon had stepped out, leaving Dr. Rahman and Rumana waiting alone to hear of Sumon's condition.

"Hema, the swelling and marks on your face? What happened?"

Rumana pulled up one sleeve, then the other, and held out her arms for Sumon's uncle to see. Her voice flattened of emotion, she said, "Sumon beat me with a metal rod."

Concern clouded Dr. Rahman's face. He reached into his black bag. "You need to take these. You might find yourself in a lot of pain if there is infection."

"It looks worse than it feels." But, wanting to acknowledge Dr. Rahman's kindness, Rumana accepted the pills and put them in her purse.

Sumon did not need to have his stomach pumped but was admitted to a ward for observation. Everybody went home.

Having broken her silence to Sumon's uncle on what Rumana had intended to withhold from her parents, she felt freer to share now with her father.

Monzur leaned on his army training. A leader is not immobilized by shock; he absorbs it and takes action. That Sumon had been physically violent with Rumana in itself was unthinkable, that he'd taken a weapon against her was unforgivable. "Hema. You must now decide. A man who can do this is not a human being. He is not reliable. Enough is enough. You must never go back to living with him. If you do, he will kill you someday."

For the briefest moment, Rumana thought of telling her father that she had no desire to live with Sumon, ever again. But a daughter could not just say such things to her father. If only her father would ask about her feelings, she could tell him that, in fact, her wish was to have the finality of divorce.

The moment passed.

Late that evening, Rumana got a call from Sumon's uncle. She still had his bottle of pills, untouched. She thought he was calling to ask if she had any pain.

Instead, he asked something else. "Hema, is anything going on, do you want to say anything?"

She was quick to answer no.

Maybe she and Anusheh might want to stay somewhere else? Would she like to stay awhile with him and his wife?

Rumana told him she had no need.

The call ended there. Rumana felt she'd said enough already tonight.

Rahima and Rumana took Anusheh to the rooftop terrace in the early morning to ride her bicycle around the smooth cement before the sun rose higher and baked the concrete. They watched her while also keeping an eye skyward for wild parakeets circling, before the heat drove them into the canopy of trees in Dhanmondi Lake Park.

Sitting at the rail with her mother, in the serenity of the morning and with the terrace to themselves, Rumana decided to come right out with it.

"Ma, I want to divorce Sumon."

Divorce was a step further than her father was contemplating; she hoped that if she could obtain the backing of her mother, Rahima could help persuade her father.

"Go ahead."

Her mother's response surprised Rumana. After all, it would be her parents, living in Bangladesh, who'd have to endure rumour and vicious gossip about her as a divorcee. If her plans came through to continue on in a doctorate at UBC, she and Anusheh would be far away in Canada, insulated from the fallout.

Rumana said nothing more except to ask her mother to relay her wishes to her father.

Her father came directly to her. "Hema, whatever you decide, we will not oppose you. The decision is yours. Your mother and I will give you our full support."

Monzur breathed easier; his daughter's position gave clarity to the discussions to be had with Kabir and Ruby on their return to Dhaka. Much of the process of divorce was governed by law. There was the matter of custody of Anusheh, but judging from what he and Rahima had observed of Sumon as a father, he'd see their daughter as primarily Rumana's responsibility. Regardless, Monzur felt sorrow that Rumana's decision to end her marriage would mean that she would have a broken family.

The Kabirs called from Texas to thank Monzur for stepping in with their son's emergency, then again two days later to thank him for delivering him home from the hospital. Knowing that the Kabirs had given their driver the time off while they were abroad, Monzur had thought it the only decent thing to do. He also settled the bill for the ambulance and the hospital care, seeing it as his responsibility because Sumon had been living most of the time under his roof.

One day later, despite having been ordered to stay away, Sumon came again to Dhanmondi.

Monzur was polite. "Are you feeling better?"

Sumon asked to speak with him.

Monzur took him into his and Rahima's bedroom and closed the door.

Sumon wept. "I'm sorry. I won't do it again."

The gall of the boy: Did he really expect to be forgiven? To be taken back when Hema's face and arms were still red and swollen?

"You are not to come back to this house until after your parents have returned from abroad and we have made an arrangement."

Sumon asked if he could retrieve some belongings from the bedroom.

"Make it quick." Monzur was brusque. "Take your things and get out."

He walked Sumon to the bedroom and stood waiting by the open doorway, as Rumana was inside. For the last few days, he had been turning over in his mind a failing of his own: neither during Rumana's time in Vancouver nor since her return had he thought to monitor the comings and goings of Sumon or his movements inside the house.

Rumana had only one thing to say to Sumon. "Do you have my camera?"

"You're not getting it back," he said.

Rumana made a note to make sure her father asked the Kabirs about the camera once they were back from the US. He was to demand its return and to be firm about it. She had not yet downloaded the memory card, which contained the photographs she took at St. John's and, once back in Dhaka, of Anusheh. Most critically, she needed her camera for her summer research.

Seddiqi remained troubled by whatever had landed Sumon in emergency. As an internist, he had treated many gastrointestinal issues, from diseases and infections to poisonings and overdoses. "Some will overdose on pills to gain sympathy," he told his wife. "I can see Sumon—if he did take the pills, my view is he faked it—doing it with deleterious motives."

On Sumon's second day in hospital, Seddiqi had called Monzur. He told him that his son-in-law's blood work did not match the quantity of pills he'd told doctors he'd taken. "I've seen cases where a patient will say, 'I took the entire package or bottle of thirty pills.' In reality, they've taken ten pills and flushed the rest down the toilet. Sumon did not take any more than ten pills. His life was never in danger."

Seddiqi wondered aloud to Shoma, could Hema be holding back something that might help explain the attempted overdose?

The doctor's routine when working at Labaid had been to join Rahima for lunch—Dhanmondi was a five-minute rickshaw ride from the hospital. Any time Rumana and Sumon had been home, the two would emerge from their room to greet him, then excuse themselves and retreat back to their room. Then, Rumana's behaviour had bothered Seddiqi. Now, he didn't know, was she trying to protect her husband?

Shoma knew her husband took a dislike to Rumana's husband from the start. "You shouldn't feel that way," she'd say. "Sumon is family." During Rumana's time abroad, Seddiqi continued his lunchtime routine with Rahima until the day that he badgered Sumon to join them. Sumon tried to beg off, saying he'd already eaten, but Seddiqi insisted—to his regret. He explained to Shoma that Sumon's demeanour had made him uncomfortable: "The whole time, he sat there, arms folded. Not relaxed at all." Besides, Rahima had once told him how petulant Sumon could be, that he once threw a dish he didn't like onto the floor. "What if Sumon did something in front of me? I'd have to say something, or just sit there seething."

If there was more than this recent episode troubling Rumana, Seddiqi said he couldn't see her opening up about it to Monzur or Rahima. "Hema is scared of her elders. That's how we were raised—to be scared of them."

Shoma accepted her husband's suggestion that someone in the family ought to go to Monzur. But who? And how to broach their unease and suspicions about his daughter's marriage without being hurtful to him and Rahima? Shoma thought her mother, Jolly, the eldest sibling in the family and close to Rumana since birth, was the logical one to approach Monzur.

Not only did Jolly refuse to talk to Monzur about it, she discouraged her daughter from getting involved, telling her that they would be interfering where they should not.

Seddiqi was unwilling to let the matter drop.

Shoma said they could seek the opinion of her brother Rashed about what, if any, course to take. Family of her mother's generation universally respected her brother, not least because of how he had ably stepped into his role as the eldest male of the next generation, but because presented with a problem, he homed in on a solution.

Seddiqi and Shoma asked Rashed how Rumana appeared to him of late. He said he didn't get much chance to talk to her at Moynul's party, but he thought she looked radiant, that she was jubilant about being home. Beyond that, Shoma's brother couldn't offer much. He and his family had only weeks earlier returned from a three-year posting with Citigroup in Jakarta. Between taking up his new job as head of its operations in Bangladesh and settling Samia and their two young daughters back into Dhaka, he hadn't yet visited Dhanmondi.

He agreed, however, that Rumana had been distancing herself from her side of the family since marrying Sumon. Her attendance at family events had fallen off. She didn't join in Shoma's fortieth birthday party. She came to the Gaye holud for Javeed, Rashed and Shoma's younger brother, but not the wedding. When she did come to events, with Sumon or alone, she always left early—just as she had done from Moynul's party. Rashed recalled a party he and Samia had hosted just before they left for Jakarta for their youngest daughter's third birthday. In the hour Rumana was there, Sumon called her cell three or four times. "The moment the knife sliced into the cake, she and Anusheh left."

The three didn't know: Was Rumana's behaviour by choice or in acquiescence to Sumon's wishes? Rashed acknowledged that in the days before Sumon and Rumana married and he used to come from his hostel at BUET to family events, he and Samia had enjoyed his company. But in the years since, they'd both soured on the way he hovered over Rumana, as if he wanted to hear everything she was saying, and how he looked at them all sideways, as if he suspected them of something.

In the end, Seddiqi bowed to the opinion of the two siblings to abide by Jolly's instruction. It came down to their respect for Monzur: "Why create chaos in his household? Leave them in peace."

Shoma told her husband that if it made him feel any better, he should know that years before she had tried to reach out to her younger cousin and been rebuffed. "Hema doesn't like others getting into what she sees as her own matters."

As if each of the Monzurs had pushed a reset button, the family made an effort to put the drama of the past week behind them—at least until the Kabirs' return to Dhaka, when tension was sure to flood back into their lives.

For some time, Monzur and Rahima had talked about fitting in their annual four- or five-day visit to her family's ancestral village before they performed Hajj in the fall. A visit with Rahima's birth family would parallel the spirit of the Hajj, strengthening the bonds of brotherhood and sisterhood. Unfortunately, Monzur couldn't spare time off from work. He and his associate were in the midst of laying thirty kilometres of gas pipeline in a hilly area of Chittagong. Weekly, Monzur had to make an inspection on site, then return to the office in Dhaka to calculate what materials to order, purchase and ship. It was imperative that they make progress ahead of the monsoon season, as rain and flooding can play havoc on excavation sites, clogging pipes and choking drainage.

Monzur suggested to Rahima that she invite his sister Molly to go in his stead, and that they take advantage of the lull before the return of the Kabirs. Molly was keen on the idea of getting away for a few days with her sister-in-law. On Saturday, June 4, Monzur drove the two to the bus terminal. In Rahima's days as a student at Dhaka University, the village was an arduous overnight journey from Dhaka; now it could be reached in under seven hours, most of them spent travelling paved highway in the comfort of an air-conditioned coach. She and Molly would call to let Monzur and Haque know what bus they would take back.

As it happened, Monzur ended up weighing whether he should go to work on Sunday, the start of the work week. The opposition Bangladesh Nationalist Party had called for a twenty-four hour hartal beginning at dawn. The Awami League's decisive victory in 2008 had quieted the opposition, who'd been restrained in their calls for collective strike action. However, since this past May, public anger about rising prices had brought people out in protest. That month, for the second time in four months, the state-run petroleum agency had hiked its still-heavily-subsidized price for domestic petroleum products. Before this increase, the last price hike had been almost three years ago, but spiralling record world oil prices had forced the agency's hand. Overnight, fuel prices jumped. In a domino effect, so, too, did the cost of electricity and the price of food.

Though only the sixth hartal in this government's term, Sunday's would be the second in eight days. On hartal days, supporters and hired hands of the opposition party, readily recruited among slum dwellers, came out in force to join rallies, torch public buses and ransack cars, hurl grenades and petrol bombs at police barricades, and detonate explosives on roadways. Monzur evaluated the risk of being caught in street violence against the loss of valuable time on the pipe-laying project if he stayed home. He conferred with his associate. They agreed that they could not afford to lose a single day of work.

Her father gone to work and her mother away visiting her family, Rumana relished having the house to herself and Anusheh for the next few days. As anxious as she was to make progress on her academic commitments, Rumana was determined to give equal priority to Anusheh. She wanted to prepare her for the travel in the coming months, the long sojourn abroad, and ultimately for life as the child of a divorced mother.

At St. John's College, when Sotonye's cell rang and Rumana's name popped up, she was in one of the communal kitchens talking with Mohsen. The two students were making coffee and taking a snack from their individual stores of food in the fridge.

Sotonye was surprised to hear from Rumana; it had been barely three weeks since her friend had left Vancouver. She wasn't expecting to hear from her until fall.

She put Mohsen on to say hello.

Later, Sotonye shared with Isabel that she'd heard from Rumana. And that something she'd said had struck Sotonye as odd. "She said, 'My husband isn't letting me be. When I come back, I'll tell you the whole story.' Isa, what do you think this is about?"

Isabel was as perplexed as Sotonye. She could only speculate. "I'm thinking this has to be about having another baby."

Sotonye nodded. That had to be it.

eight

ALMOST OVERNIGHT IN DHAKA, JUNE BROUGHT OPPRESSIVE heat, downpours and thunderstorms, ushering in the monsoon season. It was important that Rumana get an early start to her day while conditions were still tolerable.

She elected to work in her parents' room, so that if the phone rang she wouldn't have to run to answer it. She settled her daughter on the floor. As long as she had her dolls and colouring books and a store of pencils, crayons and markers and paper, Anusheh would keep herself occupied. Rumana set herself up with her laptop and papers on the bed, under the ceiling fan and facing the window air conditioning unit.

Sitting cross-legged and comfortable, Rumana paused to order her priorities and devise a schedule so that she'd have something to measure her progress against. She had obligations on three fronts: UBC, Dhaka University, and UNESCO—the fellowship had to be wrapped up this year.

UBC required master's students with a thesis in progress to keep in frequent touch with their supervisor. Rumana set a goal for the end of day: send an email to Peter Dauvergne updating her thesis plan so he'd have it in his inbox by Monday morning his time.

Rumana felt remiss not only with Peter, but also with her chair Delwar Hossain at Dhaka University. The university expected teachers on study leave to notify administration and to attend administrative meetings if they returned to Dhaka for any length of time. She ought to make an appearance soon at Dhaka University and call on Delwar to report on her academic progress. He'd be pleased to hear of her intention to begin a doctorate at UBC. Rumana made a note to apply for a renewal of her study leave; the university granted leave one year at a time. She also had yet to reply to an email from her colleague Amena Mohsin asking when she was returning to Dhaka.

In mapping out her summer, Rumana put off setting a date for her thesis research trip to coastal Bangladesh until she'd settled the timing of her trip to Sri Lanka for her fellowship. She was flexible on the former, but on the latter she was at the mercy of the Sri Lankan High Commission, which would need to grant her a visa.

Rumana allocated the rest of the morning to getting a start on what was required in support of the visa application. It was extensive: written confirmation of her fellowship, an explanation of the purpose of the trip and an itinerary, and an attestation that she had no political ties to the rebel Tamil Tigers.

By the time the maid knocked on the door to tell her lunch was about to be served, Rumana had sketched the broad outlines of a trip: one week in the capital, Colombo, and a second week in the northeast, the former rebel stronghold, to interview Tamil women in a refugee camp. And she had elaborated on the support she'd need: an interpreter and a research assistant to help draw up and translate questionnaires. She'd make a second trip for the fellowship research if necessary.

Rumana devoted the afternoon to elaborating her approach to field work for her master's thesis. She began by delineating the research into two parts, on the mainland and from the water. She'd interview former dwellers of the two largest islands in the Meghna River estuary, who had been forced onto the mainland because parts of the islands had become submerged or because the dry season had become shortened or eliminated. In addition, she'd visit flood control offices to collect data on changes to the salinity of groundwater, expecting to see a correlation with refugee numbers at emergency shelters. She'd hire a boat from which to observe the mangrove forest of the Sundarbans (disembarkation was not permitted because of the sensitive ecology and habitats—including of the Bengal tiger). And she would assess the forest's function, to act as a buffer zone and preserve biodiversity, which was vital to the woodcutters, honey collectors, fishermen and oyster harvesters who lived on the tidal shores and islands.

By mid-afternoon, satisfied that she had enough to report, Rumana started an email to Peter. She sent greetings from Bangladesh—he had never been to the country—and wrote of her joy at being reunited with her daughter. She then addressed the timing of her field trip and began a detailed explanation of her thinking thus far on the scope and methodology of her research.

She hoped to demonstrate that she was already thinking of avenues for further original research should she be accepted into the doctorate program.

After a couple of hours, Rumana found herself surrendering to the heat, the hottest day since her return. The window air conditioner, already working at its maximum capacity, was no match for the outside temperature, which by noon had already reached the daytime high of thirty-three degrees. Rivulets of sweat trickled down under Rumana's shalwar kameez. With the air so humid and laden with moisture, even perspiration could not easily evaporate.

She checked the time on her laptop; not quite three. She lifted up the heavy weight of her long hair to bare her neck.

She decided a cool shower would help clear her head.

Anusheh was content, used to the close heat. Rumana turned on the television beside the bed. Her daughter was soon engrossed in *The New Adventures of Winnie the Pooh*. Despite the series being in English, she knew all the characters in the Hundred Acre Wood by name.

Rumana retrieved a fresh shalwar kameez from her bedroom and returned to her parents' room.

In the shower, she let the water cascade over her head, drenching her thick hair and flowing down her back. Refreshed, she turned off the tap. She towelled off, dressed and combed out her long hair. She inspected her right cheek in the mirror. The injury from the rod had not healed; a red streak was still visible.

Re-energized, Rumana opened her laptop and returned to the email. With her hair still damp, she felt a slight—welcome—shiver.

—

Over the groaning motor of the AC unit and the *click click* of her parents' wobbly ceiling fan, Rumana did not hear the bedroom door open. Nor the turn of a key locking the door from the inside. The television volume suddenly blared. Odd, she thought. She swept to the side with one hand, searching on the bed covers for the remote.

In an instant, Sumon had her by the hair. He yanked her violently backward, flat to the bed. With an efficiency as if practised, he straddled her, pinned her arms to the bed and sat heavy on her chest. His face wore a mask of cold rage.

He locked his eyes on her.

A low hiss slithered out of him. "I'm going to kill you. I wanted to kill you with acid. Lucky for you, I couldn't find any."

"Anusheh, run away! Run!" Rumana could see her daughter standing frozen by the bed.

She appealed to Sumon: "Why are you doing this to me?! Let me go. Let me go." She pleaded. "Please."

"No. I won't let you go."

Rumana flailed with her feet, trying to wriggle free.

Sumon released his grip on her arms, only to clamp his hands round her neck. "If you are not with me, I will not let you be anybody else's."

He began to squeeze.

Rumana tried to pull his hands off. She saw her daughter's small hands tugging at Sumon's T-shirt. "Don't hurt Mamma. Why are you doing that to Mamma?!"

Think, think, you have to save yourself.

Rumana swiped, uselessly, at Sumon. She heard Anusheh: "You are doing such a bad thing!"

Losing consciousness, Rumana tethered herself to the fading voice of her daughter. "Don't do that! Don't hurt Mamma! Go away from her. . . "

Sumon released his grip.

As Rumana gasped for breath, he grabbed her arms and pinned them above her head. Then he bent toward her and bit deeply into the flesh of her right forearm.

He freed her arms, but with one arm limp with pain, Rumana could hardly fight back. Sumon's palms loomed suddenly over her face and his fleshy hands obliterated her view. He forced his thumbs into her eyes.

Rumana's world went to black.

If she screamed, she didn't hear herself. He bored left and right, left and right, deeper and deeper into her eyes.

She felt hot breath on her face, then the cold, hard lens of his glasses digging into her cheeks. Then came the shock of his teeth gripping her upper lip. He pulled at it, tearing her flesh.

He wasn't done.

He bit down hard on her nose and gnawed at it.

Hot blood ran into her mouth, so much that she gagged. More spilled down the sides of her face, pooled in her ears, in her hair.

Suddenly the weight of Sumon's body was off her.

Rumana felt him grab her by her hair, so hard she feared it would come out by the roots or lift part of her scalp off. She was being dragged backward, tangled in wet, slippery bed covers. She fell hard off the bed, slamming her back to the ground.

Objects clattered onto the floor.

Something struck her, something blunt against her temple.

Then she was struck again, on her arm, this time with something sharp.

She had no idea how to avoid Sumon, didn't know where he was. "Save me, save me!" Her voice was raspy and weak from Sumon strangling her. She could only hope the cook and the maid were nearby.

Where are they?

She told herself to get to her feet and get out of the room. But how to find the door? She tried to feel for the flow of cool air from the AC unit; the door was almost directly opposite it. She tried to push herself up, with the use of only her left arm. She couldn't lift herself to standing; the floor was impossibly slick with blood.

The cook and maid had remarked that it was strange to hear the bedroom television over the sound of their show in the lounge. They raised their heads again at the sudden chaotic dull thuds from down the hall.

At Rumana's unmistakable cries for help, the two women rushed from the lounge. The bedroom door was locked. There was a set of spare keys in the glass-fronted dining room cupboard, where the family stored the good plates and glasses.

In their nervousness, the women fumbled with the keys before finally opening the door. The cook began to scream hysterically. Rumana lay on the floor, whimpering, her face a sea of blood.

Anusheh, wide-eyed and spattered with blood, stood in silence.
Rahima and Monzur's possessions lay broken and strewn across
the floor. The bed was askew, the sheet and cover only half on
the bed.

The maid yelled at Sumon: "What have you done? What have
you done?"

Sumon, also bloody, rushed to the door. "Nothing has happened. Nothing. Everything is fine." He tried with one hand to
push the two women out of the room and the other to close the
door, but they resisted.

He abruptly let go. He went back to Rumana. "I will find you
wherever you are. I will kill you, you bitch. I'll shoot you. Or I'll
throw acid at you. Don't think this is the end."

Then he was out of the room and gone.

Rumana cried out to the cook and the maid, "Get my father
on the phone."

The maid held the phone to Rumana's ear. "Abbu! That bastard
attacked me!"

Monzur paced outside the intensive care unit of Labaid hospital.
Doctors told him they had to get the bleeding under control before
he could see his daughter.

As he waited, the maid phoned him. The building's guard had
called to say he'd heard a man yelling on the rooftop terrace and
saw that it was Sumon. The maid had told the guard that Sumon
had attacked Rumana. The guard was asking, should he detain
him? What should she say?

"Tell him, let him go," Monzur said.

Finally, he was allowed in to see Rumana. At the sight of her, he had to fight to keep his legs under him. She lay on a gurney, in a blue hospital gown. Her eyes were closed, seeping blood and swollen grotesquely. Gauze bandages covered what appeared to be a hole in her nose and holes in the side of one cheek and temple. Her lip was torn and ragged; her hair, matted with dark blood, looked like seaweed tossed up on the beach after a storm.

Monzur clasped Rumana's uninjured hand. Her other arm, bandaged, lay limp at her side. "Hema, everything will be okay." He had to try his utmost to stop his voice from wavering. "Inshallah, we will take care of everything."

Alerted by Monzur, Seddiqi arrived just as an orderly was returning Rumana from the operating room to have her lips stitched. The sight of her gutted him. Early in his career, Seddiqi had worked in remote rural public clinics, where he would hear doctors tell of cases where husbands had severely beaten—even killed—their wives. He struggled to comprehend what his eyes were seeing now: it was if a mad dog had mutilated Rumana. For a human being to have done this—without even the intent to kill? What kind of mentality did that take?

Seddiqi called his wife. Go immediately to Dhanmondi and fetch Anusheh, he told her, and take her to our home. Then track down Niaz Rahman: tell him Seddiqi wants him to come to emergency to see his niece.

Seddiqi then went to find Monzur. He wanted to hear it directly from his mouth.

"Who did this? Where is he?"

Monzur was slow to lift his head. This was not the Monzur

that Seddiqi knew. His eyes were vacant. "I don't know what I'm supposed to do."

Rashed turned the car around for Labaid hospital. He and Samia had been on their way to a nursery to buy potted plants for the balcony of their new home when Molly called. Word was racing through the family: "Sumon has injured Hema." Molly and Rahima were catching the next bus back to Dhaka.

At Labaid, Rashed found Monzur outside the ICU, sitting in a chair, slouched over, hanging his head in his hands.

With few exceptions, the ICU allowed no visitors. Rashed insisted with the nurses that they ask Rumana if she'd permit him to see her. She said yes.

Rashed found his cousin agitated. "Hema. . . "

"He's destroyed me, Rashed. He's completely destroyed me. I want him behind bars. Rashed, don't let him get away."

Rashed went back to Monzur. He spoke firmly to his uncle. "You have to go to the police. Any delay and Sumon will be long gone."

His uncle stared blankly at him.

"The assault happened in your home; you are the father of the victim. You have to be the one to go."

Finally, something seemed to register with Monzur. He shook his head. "What happened does not concern the police. It's the responsibility of the two families to make things right, no one else's."

Soon Molly's husband Haque arrived. Rashed appealed to him to help persuade Monzur: time was passing, the attack happened more than three hours ago. To his surprise, Haque, who held the rank of colonel after a lifelong career in the army, sympathized with Monzur. "Rashed, this is a good family; they don't have run-ins with the police."

The family's urgent concerns, Haque said, should be to support Monzur by being at his side, protect Rahima, because of her precarious health, and ensure Anusheh's safety.

Rashed phoned a lawyer whom he and Samia had met years before when she'd handled a messy divorce case on Samia's side of the family. Alena Khan's work since included several high-profile cases of human rights abuses. The first step to triggering a police investigation into the attack by the husband, she told Rashed, was for someone to file a General Diary with the Dhanmondi police station. She explained: every police station kept a General Diary daily log in which the duty officer recorded all transactions in the station, as well as any offences, incidents, complaints or problems noted by police or reported by the general public. She said it was critical to go to the station to lodge a GD before eight the next morning, when the diary for June 5 closed. When Rashed told her of his uncle's intransigence, she asked to speak with him. Alena lectured Monzur: "As long as the husband is out there, your daughter and granddaughter are not safe. If you don't go to the police, then what? You yourself are obstructing justice."

Monzur would not bend.

Frustrated, Rashed issued an ultimatum to his uncle. "Someone has to go to the police. If you won't, I will. I'm leaving. *Now.*"

Only then did Monzur relent.

It was after one in the morning when Monzur finally went home. For the past several hours, he and Rashed had taken to a corner of the spacious marble-floored hospital lobby to draft a General Diary, which Monzur could review with fresh eyes in the morning. Alena advised that it had to be concise, yet detailed, and that the police had the discretion to accept a GD or not.

As soon as Monzur entered the apartment, the metallic stench of blood hit him. He nudged open the door to the bedroom he shared with Rahima. Smears and streaks, sprays and flecks of blood mingled with bits of flesh everywhere, on the door, the floor, the walls. The blood-stained bedsheets and cover had been dragged off the end of the bed. Twisted up in them, Rumana's laptop and papers. By the side of the bed, Anusheh's colouring supplies and dolls, arrayed as if ready to be played with.

Rahima's dressing table was swept bare. Scattered about on the floor, her Qur'an, her cosmetics, oils and soap nut powder, her perfume bottles, hair ornaments and brushes. Monzur's desk, which he liked to keep ordered with his drawing sheets, boards, instruments and pencils, was a shambles.

He gently closed the door.

Hours later, Monzur arrived at the Dhanmondi station with his GD before eight in the morning. He emphasized to the officer that the victim, his daughter, Rumana Monzur, was a teacher at Dhaka University. Noting the address where the incident had happened, the officer remarked that the previous afternoon the station got wind of some commotion there. "But no one came in to file a GD."

Monzur was left to wait for almost two hours. Finally, the officer told him that the station would accept his GD. He stamped it with the seal of the Dhanmondi police station, gave it a registered number, and entered it in the station's General Diary log.

—

In the early morning, Dr. Hafiz Rahman went to the ICU at Labaid. He inquired about Rumana. The nurse told him that the patient had spent a quiet night.

He pulled aside the muslin curtain around Rumana's bedside. "Hema."

Rumana knew by the soft, low voice who stood there. And in the ensuing silence, that Sumon's uncle didn't know what to say. She relieved them both of any pretense of the need for cordiality: "After behaving so well, this is my reward."

As Dr. Rahman left the ICU, he thought back to when he and Rumana had sat in the waiting room outside the emergency department, only days ago, while doctors assessed whether his nephew needed to have his stomach pumped. He had waited for an opportunity for a private moment to ask her about the swelling he noticed on her face. She had rolled up her sleeves and shown him worse.

He'd called her later that evening.

He was a pediatrician, skilled at reading young patients, skilled at engendering trust. Why had he not pressed her to tell him more?

The next afternoon, June 7, Monzur stood by as the Dhanmondi police took photographs of the bedroom and removed Rumana's laptop and bedsheets as evidence.

At Labaid, Rashed asked Monzur whether the police were looking for Sumon. Monzur said the officers had said nothing about him. He and Rashed agreed that Sumon had likely fled to

Chittagong, that he'd taken shelter with the family of his mother's sister there.

Rashed dispatched Monzur back to the station. "Ask why they aren't pursuing the husband. The time wasted is only making it all too convenient for Sumon to make a getaway."

The officer suggested to Monzur that he accompany him to call at the home of Sumon's parents, where they could try to speak to Sumon.

Only the Kabirs' maid was home.

"If he shows up, tell him that the police are looking for him," the officer told her. "He should report to the Dhanmondi police station."

At street level, the officer made a cursory look around. Monzur grew impatient. "He has to have gone to a relative in Chittagong; his uncle is the city's chief public prosecutor."

The officer said that the Dhanmondi police station had sent a circular citing its interest in Syeed Sumon to all police stations and posts in the country.

Whether out of sympathy for Monzur as the father of the victim or his own revulsion at the crime, the officer let slip that the day before, hardly had the station lodged his General Diary when a government minister called to speak to the station's officer in charge. He'd asked how the station could be sure that Syeed Sumon had done this.

Monzur understood the minister's message to the Dhanmondi police: back off. He had met the cousin of Ruby, Hasan Mahmud, who was in Sheikh Hasina's government. Monzur had never taken to him, put off by his propensity for foul language, both in public and private. Steeped since pre-liberation days in Awami League politics as a student at Chittagong University, Hasan had been the spokesperson for Sheikh Hasina in her first term as prime minister. In her second term, when she was elected in 2008, she appointed him minister of environment and forests.

A dejected Monzur told Rashed that there was no point in pressing a police case, that Ruby's family could call on ties more powerful than a chief public prosecutor. It seemed so. Alena Khan, the lawyer, had received a tip that a victim of a beating was being treated at Labaid hospital, and that if the victim's family went to the police, "influential persons" would try to suppress the case from going further.

Seddiqi was angered to see Monzur knuckling under the weight of the Kabirs' political connections. He urged Monzur to share what had happened to Rumana with Dhaka University: "Hema's a teacher there. The whole university should be behind her!" A niece of Monzur, herself a teacher at the university, disagreed. She told her uncle that if word of the attack got out, it would adversely affect the university's relationship with the ruling party, that it was best if Rumana immediately resigned her position.

Seddiqi's tone turned scolding. "Monzur, this is a question of survival. The other side will concoct some case against Hema. Ultimately, all her achievements will be for nothing. I shall be very angry if I hear that you have not gone to the university."

Tanzim was on his way to the university that morning when he received a disturbing text from his research assistant. Sajjad Rahman said to meet him at Labaid hospital, that Rumana Monzur had been admitted there.

Tanzim didn't know that his office mate was back from Canada.

The woman who greeted him and Sajjad at the door of Rumana's private room, Cabin 661, identified herself as Rumana's aunt.

Tanzim reeled at the horror that confronted him. Under Rumana's bruised eyelids, were her eyes even there? He leaned close and asked her what had happened.

"I don't know, Tanzim Bhai. I had an accident."

Tanzim gestured to the aunt for them both to step out of the room.

Sajjad, who was about to join the faculty at Chittagong University, had been a year behind Rumana in the master's program. He had served as a research assistant to Amena Mohsin at the same time as Rumana. Alone with Rumana now, he told her that her Facebook account appeared to have been hacked. Suspecting Sumon, Rumana asked Sajjad to try to disable or delete her account.

In the corridor outside the cabin, the aunt said only two words to Tanzim. "Her husband."

Tanzim was alarmed. "Where's Rumana's daughter? Where is she? Where is she, right now?" Anusheh and his daughter, a year older, had often played together during social events at the university.

The aunt turned nervous, as if she'd already divulged too much.

Tanzim returned home. He was shaking. He told his wife that he had never imagined something like that could happen to a teacher at Dhaka University. And how was it that he saw Rumana almost daily yet had no idea that there was anything amiss with her marriage. It struck him only now that as sociable as she was, she never shared anything personal. Still, had he missed clues to trouble? What of the day she came to work sporting sunglasses?

He'd teased her; sunglasses were a Western fashion. She'd made a joke, said she'd collided with a door at home.

Now that the ophthalmologist, Dr. Niaz Rahman, had MRI results from the patient he'd seen in intensive care, he was ready to give his opinion to her father. Seeing how bereft Monzur looked and defeated by worry and grief, the doctor told himself, give the man a ray of hope.

He told Monzur that his daughter's left eye looked to be permanently damaged, but there was a possibility that the right eye could recover if she could see light once the bleeding subsided and the blood drained away. But, he said, unfortunately Labaid did not have the expertise or facilities to treat such a profound injury. "If she were my daughter, I would take her to Chennai, to the Sankara Nethralaya."

Mention of Chennai shook Monzur from his state of inertia.

His methodical, ordered nature returned. His mission now: apply for Indian visas for the family—Rumana would want Anusheh by her side, and the two would need both him and Rahima—then book flights and a hotel. At home, he looked where Rumana told him he could find the passports for her and Anusheh. He found neither. Suspecting Sumon, he called the Kabirs' home. Shawon answered. A day later, he called to tell Monzur he could pick them up.

Irrespective of Seddiqi's urgings, Monzur had no choice but to go to Dhaka University, to call on the chair of Rumana's department. The application for her visa required a letter confirming her employment status.

He found Delwar Hossain bent over his desk, at work under two ceiling fans that struggled to make a dent in the heat. He introduced himself as Major Monzur, the father of Rumana, and explained the reason he needed a letter.

Certainly he could supply a letter, Delwar said. "But what's happened?"

Monzur teared up. "She's at a private hospital. . . "

Delwar was deeply shocked. When Dhaka University had appointed Rumana as a lecturer, he was in Japan completing his doctorate. On his return, he'd been pleased to see the gentle, friendly former student on the faculty, and also to see the department hire on the basis of merit over political connections. He'd never met Rumana's husband; she always came alone or with her daughter to social events at the university.

Delwar asked a colleague, Akmal Hossain, to join them. A former chair of the department and its most senior member—he'd been a reporter before he joined Dhaka University thirty years before—Akmal was a lifelong human rights activist with a broad network. Most teachers either aligned themselves with a party, gambling that it would come to power, or showed unconditional loyalty to the ruling party, thus securing their future through promotions and sinecures. Akmal remained steadfast, however, about staying out of party politics. He considered himself a "free man," living life as a person of conscience.

His first question of Monzur: "Have the police acted against the husband?"

Monzur said that the police had been notified, but he was adamant that he did not want what had happened to progress to a formal police case or become public. The husband was related to a government minister, and Monzur feared if given any reason to retaliate, the minister might prevent Rumana from going out of the country for treatment.

With the letter of employment in hand, Monzur asked to see Rumana's colleague Amena Mohsin. At the chair's request, she left with Monzur for the hospital to visit Rumana on the department's behalf.

At Rumana's bedside, Amena struggled to connect her colleague at the university with the mutilated woman lying helpless in front of her. Amena could recall only two instances, both on the few occasions they'd shared a rickshaw home from work, when Rumana had made mention of her in-laws. Once, to say that her mother-in-law was fond of her. Another time, that her young brother-in-law was not applying himself to his studies and it was causing his father stress. Amena was confounded: If the family of Rumana's husband was traditional and conservative, of the kind who kept a tight rein on their daughter-in-law, how was it that she had gone for her master's abroad? And alone? What of the time, soon after she joined the faculty, that she'd attended the week-long conference in Nepal? Rumana had asked her to write a letter of recommendation; she said she had spoken to her husband about going, that it was not a problem. Was her young colleague covering up for an abusive husband?

Amena realized she knew so little about Rumana. By appearances alone—her fashionable Western clothes and matching high-heeled shoes, perfectly coiffed hair, meticulously applied makeup—all affectations of the upper middle class—one could easily conclude she was the beautiful young wife of a rich man who left her free to indulge herself. When Rumana was newly appointed as a lecturer, some fellow teachers had huffed to Amena, who was then chair, that if the new recruit was serious about being a teacher she ought to tone down her lipstick and dress in saris and sandals. Amena made one conciliatory gesture to her colleagues. When Rumana was pregnant, Amena suggested that, in her state, flats would be more comfortable than heels.

Rashed badgered Monzur. He and Alena, the lawyer, agreed that since the Dhanmondi police were in no hurry to go after Sumon, the recourse was to go public.

Monzur ignored Rashed. He was preserving his mental energy for what doctors in Chennai would say. If the news was bad, he had to be ready to absorb the shock, not only for himself, but on his wife's behalf.

Yet again making no headway with his uncle, Rashed had the lawyer speak to Monzur. Alena, whose short, compact stature only accentuated her energetic manner, was forceful: "Unless you go to the press, the police will not act quickly." She had no more success than Rashed.

For all Monzur's belief that he could keep the attack out of the public eye, news was spreading.

After a sleepless night, Tanzim rang Delwar Hossain. He was upset to learn that the chair had agreed to abide by Monzur's wishes for media silence. Even more dismaying, that the department's academic council had referred the question of any official stance of the university to the vice-chancellor. Worse yet, not only did the vice-chancellor, Arefin Siddique, want to wait on making a final decision, but his initial opinion was that, since the attack didn't happen on campus, it should be treated as a domestic matter between two families.

Regardless, Delwar told Tanzim, an arrest was in doubt because the husband's family had political connections.

Tanzim rang a research partner, Omar Tarek Chowdhury: "We need to do something to bring the culprit to justice." Omar was director of Bangladesh Nari Progati Sangha, a women's rights organization. He phoned his wife, Gitiara Nasreen, chair of Dhaka University's department of mass communication and journalism, and a long-time activist in the Bangladesh Rural Advancement Committee, the country's largest NGO dedicated to women and rural development. To hear that the university had not stepped up to support one of its own angered Gitiara. "All too typical an attitude toward domestic violence—'Don't get involved, the families have to handle it.'"

Gitiara and Omar invited Tanzim straightaway to their home to brainstorm ways to put pressure on the police, who routinely could be slow to act without a public outcry. The three decided to make use of the growing popularity of social media in Bangladesh, given the new wide availability of cable internet and mobile wireless (until recently, Bangladesh's access to the internet was ahead of only Myanmar, Sierra Leone and North Korea). Omar would build a website, Justice for Rumana, and have it up by the weekend. Tanzim would ask Akmal Hossain, whose network of human rights activists would give the platform a wide reach, to be its convenor. Gitiara would draft press releases for it under her own name.

That same day, at the offices of BanglaVision, a satellite television news channel, Faiham Sharif was busy at work, producing stories on the channel's online portal. A post on Facebook caught his eye. It named a teacher from Dhaka University as a victim of a beating by her husband and revealed that she had been brought to the private Labaid hospital. A year out of his master's in international relations at Dhaka University, Faiham had to look twice at the name.

Rumana Madame was one of his few teachers who remained vividly in Faiham's mind. Other teachers didn't care that he skipped class, but after he didn't show up for one of her in-class exams, she'd taken him aside. "I know what you're doing. You should concentrate more on study and less on outside activities. You have potential." He didn't tell her that he didn't see anything useful in his classes, that he preferred the intellectual stimulation of debate with fellow activists at the university's Madhur Canteen. Faiham and his friends convened at the canteen around the same paint-chipped tables and sat on the same lopsided metal chairs as had many of the country's future leaders—including the father of the nation, Mujib—and, like them, drank bottomless cups of hot milky tea and filled ashtrays with their cigarette butts. Those in Mujib's time discussed how to defend Bengali identity. Faiham and his friends debated the future of their post-colonial society, and the burden of a history of oppression. They were united on one premise: if anybody was going to rouse the population, it would take students and teachers to light a fire under it.

The posting on the thread about the teacher was anonymous.

A news outlet had responded: "Can you verify?"

The thread went no further.

Faiham told a senior editor about the messages. The editor sent a reporter to Labaid hospital. He came back empty-handed.

Not to be deterred, Faiham got permission from his supervisor to leave early and went to the hospital himself.

At the door of Rumana's cabin, a woman who identified herself as Rumana's aunt stopped Faiham. She nodded toward an older man inside. "Her father. He's against the idea of media."

"I'm not media. I'm her student. Please tell him my name. See if Rumana Madame recognizes it."

Monzur came out. Between the young man's unkempt hair, his clothes looking as if he'd slept in them, and the worn canvas satchel over his shoulder, he looked every inch the student. Monzur tapped his watch. "You can have two minutes."

Faiham did not stay even that long. The horror of Rumana's injuries aside, he found it emotionally difficult to see someone who had been his teacher weeping in pain. Even as he left, angry that she lay helpless while her husband was free, he began making calls on his cell phone. "Are you available?" By early evening, international relations students were patrolling the lobby of Labaid to intercept any suspicious-looking man asking for the room number of Rumana Madame.

The next morning, Faiham and his friends met to discuss how to force the police to pursue the husband. They decided on a rally and gave themselves three days to organize it, setting it for Tuesday, June 14, at the Aparajeyo Bangla, the famous monument on campus. Commissioned by students in 1973, the three figures of the sculpture—a farmer and a student bearing rifles, and a nurse carrying a first aid box—depicted the struggle for independence as "unvanquished Bangla."

Faiham found mobilizing support for the rally initially a challenge. Puzzled students asked why he was making a political issue out of a domestic matter. "Take whatever lens to it you want," he replied. "Just come to the rally." When he heard from Delwar Hossain that the department had given in to the father's desire to keep quiet about the attack, he challenged him: "Why wouldn't we go ahead anyway? We don't want to see another such act of violence." Angry students soon accosted Delwar: "Sir, why isn't the department coming out stronger? Why isn't it joining our protest?" Soon enough, Delwar and his colleagues, pledging solidarity with the students, rallied the support of left-leaning members of the teachers' association at the university.

Kabir strode into Rumana's room and went straight to Monzur. The two men had spoken on the phone earlier that day. Monzur had not been surprised to get a call from him, since he had expected Kabir and Ruby to hurry back from the US. Kabir said that he wanted to visit Rumana in the hospital. Monzur had hesitated. "I'm not sure you should."

Monzur put a palm out to ward off Kabir. "Please, go. Hema is upset. You can't see her."

He put a guiding hand behind Kabir's back to steer him out, only to have him brush by. Monzur hurried to fetch a nurse.

Kabir leaned over Rumana. He asked Allah to bless her. He began to sob. "I would give my eyes to you if you could see again... I always knew he wasn't the right person for you. I had to go along because he wanted to marry you. You didn't say no. I've never had confidence in him, but I thought maybe you'd be able to change him."

Rumana heard more self-pity than apology in her father-in-law's rambling.

A male nurse entered with Monzur to remove Kabir. Kabir's tone sharpened abruptly. "I came here to ask for forgiveness. I didn't come here to harm anyone!"

Monzur learned from the cook and the maid that, soon after leaving the hospital, Kabir had shown up at Dhanmondi. When his knock at the door went unanswered, he yelled that he'd come to see Anusheh, that he had strawberries for her. Finally, he left, shouting, "I did not come here to kill anyone! I came to see my granddaughter!"

Alena Khan complained to the Dhanmondi police about Kabir's intrusion. At Monzur's request, they posted a round-the-clock guard outside Rumana's room.

The first of the threatening calls to the landline in Rumana's room began. "Withdraw the complaint or we will kidnap your daughter," the caller told Rumana. "We know where your daughter goes to school."

Petrified, Rumana had Anusheh brought to her hospital room to stay with her there.

The calls kept coming. "We will kidnap your father." "We will kill your dad. We know where he goes." Rumana asked a cousin to accompany her father wherever he went in public, and told her mother to keep the front door double locked.

Rumana's colleague, Amena Mohsin, called a friend in journalism. A noted anthropologist and lecturer, Rahnuma Ahmed was a columnist with *New Age*, a leading English-language daily that branded itself as outspoken. She was married to Shahidul Alam, a renowned photojournalist, teacher and social activist who began his career in the 1980s documenting political and social ferment on Dhaka's streets.

Amena told Rahnuma about the attack and that she'd subsequently called on the parents of the victim at their home. She'd gone to sympathize with a mother's sorrow—she and her husband had known tragedy, illness having taken their only child, a son, at age twenty. Both the victim's parents, she said, looked to be doing poorly. The father stressed the family's desire to keep the incident quiet, saying that if it did become public the husband would concoct something nasty about Rumana to defend himself. Rumana's mother worried that their daughter would be called ugly names.

Amena asked her friend, how could she help the family to keep this out of the press?

Rahnuma came down like a hammer. "We *need* to talk about this. That man is running around. He might harm her. He'll go unpunished. But that's not the issue. The issue is to ask what we can do about this kind of violence."

Rashed decided that if Monzur would not go to the media, Rumana should. He enlisted Amena. She visited the hospital again. "Rumana, I am speaking to you as a woman, as a human being. Please, Rumana, speak up."

Like her father, Rumana's mind was elsewhere. She was focused solely on the treatment in Chennai, and re-evaluating her summer schedule. When her father had to visit the university, she asked him, when speaking to the chair, to apologize on her behalf that she'd not been in earlier to see him, and to tell him that she anticipated that because of what had happened, her work on her master's thesis could be set back by as much as a month.

Rumana had one urgent matter she wanted dealt with before leaving for India; visas were expected on Monday, and the family was booked to fly out Tuesday. She asked Rashed to have the lawyer draw up the notice of divorce and to have it sent to the Kabirs' home in Paribagh, in order that the ninety-day period after which a divorce certificate could be issued start as soon as possible.

Late Saturday evening, June 11, the online edition of the *Daily Star*, the country's largest-circulation English-language daily, ran a late-breaking item, filed by an unnamed Dhaka University correspondent and headlined "Husband beats up DU teacher":

A TEACHER OF DHAKA UNIVERSITY was critically injured and lost an eye as her husband brutally beat her up a few days ago.

The victim, faculty member of the international relations department at DU, was assaulted by her husband Syeed Hasan Sumon on June 5 while staying at her parents' residence in the capital's Dhanmondi area. The name of the victim is not carried in this report on request of the victim's family. The family members also declined to comment on the incident at the moment.

Sources said Sumon, owner of a brick kiln, beat up his wife following a quarrel.

Meanwhile, the husband had threatened to kill their only son if his in-laws moved for legal action. The family, however, lodged a case with Dhanmondi Police Station on June 6.

Sumon is now absconding.

Friend of the victim, Zobaida Nasreen, teacher of DU anthropology department, told The Daily Star that Sumon was bad tempered and used to torture his wife since they got married in 2002.

The victim is now undergoing treatment at LabAid Hospital under police guard. Her family is planning to send her abroad for better treatment, said Zobaida.

Prof Mizanur Rahman, chairman of National Human Rights Commission, visited the victim at the hospital on Friday.

The news report included several factual errors: it described Sumon as the owner of a brick kiln, a partnership with a family friend that had since gone under; it referred to the teacher's son, not daughter; and it misstated the year of their 2001 marriage.

On Sunday, reporters from virtually every media outlet in Dhaka besieged Labaid, seeking information.

When Rashed told Rumana that the story of the attack had broken, and that he'd invited reporters to come to her bedside on Monday for her to speak directly to them, she asked only that he insist reporters not share that her young daughter had witnessed the attack.

Sotonye had just turned out the light in her room at St. John's College when her cell phone rang. It was a fellow resident, worried that something had happened to her friend from Bangladesh. She said she'd seen messages to her from well-wishers on Facebook.

Sotonye had spoken to Rumana on the phone only last weekend, and nothing had seemed out of the ordinary. She wondered, was somebody pranking Rumana? Then came an urgent rap on her door. It was Sarah Meli.

"Something's not right with Rumana. Look on Facebook."

Sure enough: "We are praying for you." "We pray that everything will be fine."

Sarah said that the day before she had received a private Facebook message from someone claiming to have been a student of Rumana's—"Do you know what's happened to her? We have to help her." Sarah thought someone had hacked her account.

The two friends decided they'd call Rumana if they recognized a name among the messages. Finally: Tara Stowe, Rumana's future sister-in-law. Rumana had spoken about being be a bridesmaid later this summer at the wedding of her brother to Tara.

Sotonye dialed Rumana's cell. No answer.

She and Sarah were puzzled. Had Rumana been in a car accident? Had she fallen ill?

Who could they call?

Just then, a private Facebook message came to Sarah from someone identifying himself as a friend of Rumana's, studying in Australia. "Rumana's UBC friends should know that she's been injured in an attack."

But how would this person know? He wasn't in Dhaka.

"Do you think whatever's happened has something to do with her husband?" Sarah answered herself, "Nooo. . . of course not."

Sotonye agreed. "She and her husband have the perfect relationship."

A young
Rahima Khatun.

Syeed Kabir (left) and Monzur
Hossain (right) when they were
roommates with Farruhk Mohsen
and Mustafizir Rahman at the
East Pakistan University of
Engineering and Technology.

Monzur on his commission to the
corps of engineers of the Pakistan
Army, 1970.

Rahima and Monzur's
wedding, September 1974.

Monzur, Rahima and
baby Rumana, 1978.

Rumana's fourth
birthday.

Young Rumana.

Rumana and her
brother, Mashrur.

Grandmother Momena poses with her grandchildren from abroad and Bangladesh (Rumana is to her grandmother's left).

The Monzurs on the beach at Dover, with the English Channel behind them, 1988.

Rumana (far right) and friends on a celebratory day at Agrani School.

Rumana and Mashrur.

Rumana.

Sumon, Rumana
and Anusheh.

Rumana's Facebook
profile picture.

Rumana celebrates
Anusheh's fourth birthday,
January 2010, knowing
she will be in Canada
for her fifth birthday.

Rumana and friends at St. John's College experience snow for the first time.

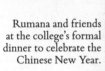

Rumana on ice skates.

Rumana and friends at the college's formal dinner to celebrate the Chinese New Year.

Rumana and her closest friends at the college, 2011.

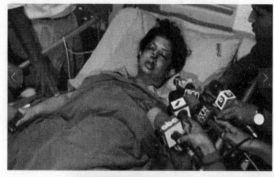

Journalists in Dhaka see the victim for the first time, June 13, 2011, eight days after the attack.

Rumana 17 days after the attack. (*Sk Enamul Haq / The Daily Star*)

Anusheh visits her mother at the hospital. (*Sk Enamul Haq / The Daily Star*)

Students march across the campus of Dhaka University to press police to arrest Rumana's husband, nine days after the attack, June 14, 2011. (*Mahmudul Hoque Moni*)

Rally culminates at the Aparajeyo Bangla. (*Faiham Ebna Sharif*)

Rally organized by students of St. John's College for Rumana in Vancouver, June 26, 2011. (*Mohsen Seddigh*)

A page from the website Hasan Syeed Hotter Biochar Chai (We want Justice for Hasan Syeed's murder).

Rumana defends her master's thesis, June 2013. (*Paul Joseph / UBC Media Relations*)

Rumana at her law convocation, May 2017. (*Paul Joseph / UBC Media Relations*)

Rumana at work at the DL Piper law firm, Vancouver, December 2017. (*Aaron Vincent Elkaim / The New York Times / Redux*)

nine

A FATHER'S ANGUISH WAS STILL FRESH IN THE MINDS OF reporters when they stood, heartbroken, in Rumana's room. When Monzur had addressed them in the hospital lobby, he'd told them that doctors declared her left eye permanently damaged but were unsure about the right one. Then his words tumbled out in a flood of anger and sorrow: "Her husband, he is worse than an animal. He tried to torture and kill an innocent girl, a daughter's mother, a father's child. . . I demand justice! See that he gets the punishment he deserves."

One television channel muted the sound when Rumana's account of the attack came to the point when her husband drilled his thumbs into her eyes and blinded her. Her voice, thin with an eerie vibrato, had left reporters shaken at the horror of the attack. Even without sound, how Rumana shaped her index and middle fingers and held them menacingly above her closed eyes like hooked talons said it all. Hardest to watch was the tight shot of Rumana's face. Her closed eyes, swollen and purple, suggested the injury bored deep below the surface. Where the tip of her nose should have been there was gauze. And appearing helter-skelter— on her temple, her forehead, a cheek, the underside of a forearm— puncture wounds and angry bruises.

Every news story began by identifying the victim as a teacher at Dhaka University. They reported that the attack was provoked by her husband's objection to her going abroad to study, that she had endured torture from her husband from the start of their decade-long marriage, and that she'd kept it a secret because she was afraid for their child's future.

Shock waves rolled across Dhaka that such an act of violence and mutilation should happen to a teacher at Dhaka University, and that it should happen at all in Dhaka. The capital city was home to the educated, professionally accomplished middle and upper classes, people who in their daily lives spoke English, read the English-language dailies, went abroad to study, travelled and were exposed to progressive ideas; wives had careers and did not depend financially on their husbands. If such a violent act did happen in Dhaka, it happened among the *other* class—the labourers, rickshaw wallahs, street sweepers, street vendors who spoke only Bangla, who scrabbled for a daily living, who dressed in lungis, who might never hold a book in their hands. It happened among *them,* not *us.* Or so the narrative went among the city's elite.

Early Tuesday morning, a police car sat outside Labaid hospital, the officers waiting for Rashed to pull in behind it. With Monzur,

Rahima and Anusheh already in his car, Rashed collected his injured cousin and drove the family, under police escort, to Dhaka airport.

At about the same hour, Faiham's friends were preparing for the rally. They climbed the five-metre-high monument of the Aparajeyo Bangla and, in the tradition of protests, gagged its three figures with strips of black cloth. Mid-morning, several hundred assembled behind a wide banner, "Students and Teachers against Repression," and marched in silence across campus to gather at the monument.

From atop its base, speaker after speaker took the microphone to rail against police for allowing Rumana's husband to roam free for eight days. Faculty and students from the international relations department decried as intolerable that, in a department where gender studies were compulsory, one of its own teachers should fall victim to domestic violence. And in a signal to Sheikh Hasina's government and the ruling Awami League that teachers were prepared to challenge lawmakers, the teachers' association, whose elected executive was controlled by a slate of Awami-backed members, issued an ultimatum to police: if Sumon was not arrested within seventy-two hours, teachers would go on strike.

Sayeeda Salim—nicknamed Tulip—first heard the news about her high school friend, Rumana, from an aunt. On her way into Dhaka from the airport after a six-week holiday in the US, Tulip had called the aunt to say hello. The aunt said that Hema had been horribly attacked and blinded. "Her husband did it. It's all over the news." Tulip thought she must be mistaken: "Hema teaches at Dhaka University. She went to Canada to study." When her aunt insisted, Tulip refused to believe it. "That can't be possible. Things like this don't happen."

Tulip called a friend. Indeed, it was true.

She tracked down Monzur's cell number and asked permission to visit. He said no: the family was getting ready to leave for Chennai. She asked, if Rumana did not recover her sight, whether she would stay in Bangladesh or return to Canada. Monzur ignored the question.

It had been four years since Tulip had last seen Rumana, but now in a matter of weeks, twice. At Agrani's fiftieth anniversary, a daylong event followed by an evening concert, Rumana came from the university with her daughter to join her friends. Tulip remembered thinking, What is a teacher doing dressed in a skirt and heels standing in front of a class with nineteen- and twenty-year-old boys? Rumana stayed maybe forty minutes. A few weeks later, Tulip saw her a second time at a going-away lunch for Farzana Morshed, who was moving to Canada. Tulip thought Rumana, who came again with Anusheh, looked sad. Others must have thought the same—"Hema, why aren't you smiling. Why are you so quiet?" That Rumana left early surprised them all; they thought she'd want to catch up with friends whom she hadn't seen in years.

The only time Tulip met Sumon, she didn't have a good feeling about him. She was on a visit home from the UK, where she'd gone for her O levels, when Rumana asked her to go with her to BUET to meet him. Rumana had fussed over what to wear—"I'm not sure what he would like"—finally settling on a long skirt and white top. During that brief meeting, Tulip felt uncomfortable at how Sumon either negated what Rumana said or told her what to think. She blanched when Rumana said she was thinking of cutting her long hair, and he outright said, "You can't." Afterwards, she told Rumana, "Hema, he's very nice, but I find him very dominating. I wouldn't want someone telling me what I can and can't do. You want to think before getting involved with him." Tulip didn't push it. She could see that Rumana was infatuated.

On the other side of the world, at St. John's College, Sotonye got an unexpected call. Monzur asked a favour: "Your friend, my daughter, is in hospital. Could you please go to Dr. Dauvergne and tell him that she has been in an accident?"

When Sotonye hung up, she googled her friend's name. She clicked on a link to a television report. She didn't need to understand Bangla. Why wouldn't Rumana's father have said her husband had attacked her?! She called him back. Could she share the story beyond Rumana's professor? Her father was definitive: "No. You have to understand, these are family friends. They grew up together."

Monzur was too late. Word was already flying around Facebook and in emails. At St. John's, one student messaged the entire community of residents: "We need to talk about this." Some forty students there for the summer converged on the dining hall. Rumana's friend Mohsen aired his concern that she was in danger as long as her husband was free. He proposed that they hold a rally for Rumana to provoke international media attention, as a way to put pressure on the justice system in Bangladesh. Met by a lack of enthusiasm, he didn't pursue the idea. For now, the residents' abiding concern was that Rumana not feel alone. They endorsed residents sending her messages, in their respective languages, in a digital audio file.

Peter Dauvergne reeled at Sotonye's news, and then once again after viewing a Bangladeshi television item online. At home, when his wife, Catherine, a professor in UBC's faculty of law and a scholar in refugee, immigration and citizenship law, returned from work, he shared what had happened to his student. As it happened, Catherine Dauvergne was coming up to the last two weeks of a two-year assignment as special adviser to the university president. She'd seen how the university was quick to offer condolences whenever misfortune or tragedy befell a student. "This is one time," she declared to Peter, "the university has to be able to do more than that."

No doctor at Labaid told Rumana what injury her eyes had sustained, much less explained to her—or her family—that vision interacts with the brain and the inner ear to help control balance and to orient oneself in space and process nearby movement. For Rumana and her parents to contend with her blindness outside the confines of the hospital was to enter a netherworld. Negotiating the most ordinary of activities—avoiding the path of another person, getting through a doorway—was now nerve-racking, perilous and exhausting.

At the airport in Kolkata, where the family had to connect to Chennai, the Monzurs had a standoff with Air India. The personnel at the gate denied Rumana boarding. This in spite of the letter

Monzur produced from Labaid giving her clearance to fly. They insisted on getting the opinion of an airport medic. The family grew upset that the officiousness of an airport employee might deny Rumana the chance for treatment. When the medic eventually arrived, he asked Monzur what had happened. Monzur, having resolved to say little in order to invite fewer questions, was terse: "It was a domestic accident." At his continuing refusal to elaborate, Air India relented.

By the time the Monzurs arrived at their hotel in Chennai, the sheer physical ordeal of getting there, compounded by the brutal heat—Chennai was regularly three or four degrees hotter than Dhaka—left them spent. Still rattled from the confrontation at the Kolkata airport, they were relieved to have made it safely. They rested their hopes on Rumana's appointment the next day at the Sankara Nethralaya, the same renowned facility to which she had accompanied Sumon a decade before.

The young specialist looked with alarm at the injured woman in the wheelchair. He turned to her father: "What happened?"

Rumana answered before her father could.

She had anticipated the question and had resolved to be open in her answer; it wasn't she who deserved shame, it was the person who had done this to her. She told the specialist she was married to a man who tortured her, and when she told him she wanted to pursue her further studies abroad, he attacked her.

The doctor asked after her background. As if in deference to her status as a teacher at Dhaka University, he was frank and forthright. He explained that to use his ophthalmoscope to see through to the back of the eye, he'd have to try to open her eyelids. He apologized in advance if it caused pain. As it happened, the swelling had subsided enough to make the examination tolerable.

The doctor shared his preliminary opinion: unless damaged, the optic nerve should continue to transmit electrical impulses to the visual centres in the brain. That there was no light sensitivity in either of Rumana's eyes suggested that either the retina was not intact or there was injury to the optic nerve.

Damage to the optic nerve, the doctor said, would be irreversible.

Rumana felt the world fall away. This can't be.

Back at the hotel, Monzur told Rahima that Rumana was to return the next day for tests. He added that the doctor was not hopeful. Hardly had the words left his mouth when regret and guilt ambushed him. With the sudden wail of a child unable to hold back tears, he broke down. He turned to Rumana. "I knew he would kill you someday. I knew it. I knew it. What will you do when we are gone?"

Rumana thought her father had gone hysterical. It fell to her mother to restore calm. "Hema, don't worry. If we have to, we will find another doctor."

The burst of media interest in Dhaka appeared to be having some small impact on the justice system. On Wednesday, the day after the rally at Dhaka University, the High Court summoned the three top officers from the Dhanmondi police station and asked them to explain their delay in apprehending the husband.

"We tried hard," they told the court, "but Sumon was untraceable because his cell phone had been turned off."

It wasn't even two hours later that the Detective Branch of the Dhaka Metropolitan Police announced that the Dhanmondi police had arrested Sumon.

Reporters flocked to the branch's headquarters on Minto Road, a wide palm-lined avenue designed by the British for its high offices. Following a tradition of presenting suspects to the public, a Detective Branch officer brought Sumon out to reporters. He was in handcuffs, dressed in jeans and a brown T-shirt with fine red stripes. A puffiness in his unshaven face betrayed a lack of sleep.

Staring blankly through tinted glasses, he unleashed a torrent of self-pity.

"I am the victim of this situation. I loved her."

He levelled an incendiary accusation against his wife: while in Canada, she'd had an extramarital affair with another student. He named an Iranian male, Navid Tahirdin. "She lived for a while with him as if they were husband and wife, while I took care of our daughter. I did not have the slightest idea that all that time she was cheating on me. I informed her parents about it, but in vain.

"A few days after her return, we decided to commit suicide together. We secured one hundred and ninety-two tablets of sedatives. I took one hundred and ten and landed in Labaid hospital in critical condition for two days. She did not live up to the plan."

Sumon turned to what had led to his wife's injuries on June 5. "She was trying to contact that guy. I deleted his name from her Facebook friend list. She saw that and attacked me. She snatched my glasses. I am practically blind without them—eighty percent of my eyesight is gone. I don't quite remember what happened after that. She might have been hurt in our tussle.

"I didn't torture her," he continued. "She tortured me."

Before being led away, he had some last words for reporters. "Please stop harassing me. She did that to herself. That man lives in Canada, and while he was having an affair with my wife, he was keeping two other mistresses." Then, "If you want to find out more about him, check her email."

Later that evening, Rashed called Monzur. Monzur had little to report, only that Rumana would undergo tests tomorrow. Rashed, however, had big news: the Detective Branch was holding Sumon in custody.

According to Dhanmondi police, they'd captured him at the home of a relative in an outer suburb of Dhaka. Rashed was certain the truth was something else. "The police must have told Sumon to leave the home in Chittagong, or else told his uncle there, 'Hand him over and we won't mention anything.'"

More than one newspaper and several columnists had already speculated that while Sumon was "absconding," he had been in Chittagong, where he was being sheltered by his uncle, Kamal Uddin, the city's chief prosecutor. The media's reporting of crime routinely cited influential relations or connections of the perpetrator that might help get them out of trouble.

One newspaper reached Kamal Uddin for comment. He confirmed that Sumon was a relative, but said he was "not on good terms with him."

Rashed's news fell flat with the Monzur family. Their mood was so low, they barely registered it.

—

Residents at St. John's woke up to news that Rumana's husband had been arrested. They were appalled that he had smeared her with false accusations and dragged another student's name into it.

The student and Mohsen had been one-half of the brotherhood of four Iranians during Rumana's year. Fearing for his friend's welfare, Mohsen called him.

Navid sounded frightened.

He told Mohsen that days before he had received profane, threatening texts and emails. The two friends agreed that the husband, to create his fiction, must have scrolled down Rumana's Facebook friend list looking for a man with a Muslim name. He could just as easily have picked any of the four of their brotherhood. Navid considered calling the police, then thought it was best to lie low.

That night in downtown Vancouver—the same day of Sumon's arrest in Dhaka—the Vancouver Canucks of the National Hockey League lost the championship final to the visiting Boston Bruins. Rowdy hockey fans went on a five-hour rampage, breaking store windows, looting and setting police cars on fire. Mohsen shelved his idea of a rally. Who would notice it in the aftermath of the riot? Anyway, his only experience with public protest was as a journalist for an Iranian radio station in 2009, when he covered protests that erupted in Tehran against alleged election fraud, to which police had responded with deadly brutality.

In Dhaka, Tanzim and Omar's next challenge was to pressure the Detective Branch to charge Sumon. The day after his capture, at his court appearance to be formally remanded into custody, a Detective Branch officer told the court that Sumon "admitted to planning to kill his wife" but left room for conjecture, adding that he "did not say how, when and why he wanted to do that." Tanzim, Omar and Gitiara decided to hold a city-wide protest on Friday, June 24, which they would advertise as sponsored by Dhaka University teachers. They set it for five in the afternoon at the central Shaheed Minar. No monument was more politically symbolic to Bengalis. The semi-circle of high, slim white marble columns evoked a grieving mother mourning her four martyred children, representing Bengalis mourning the four students killed by Pakistani police in the language movement. So central was Dhaka's Shaheed Minar to the national identity that expats erected replicas of it in their communities abroad.

Hardly did Tanzim begin to make calls to fellow teachers when anonymous individuals claiming to be from the Awami League menaced him, phoning him and telling him to cancel the rally. His department chair, Delwar, came up against teachers shying away from participating: they said that they didn't know Rumana Monzur personally and didn't know the facts about her husband's charge of infidelity. Delwar had to explain that she was up against political muscle and be forceful in saying that no matter what she was doing in Vancouver, nothing justified her husband's attack. Tanzim had to work hard to change the minds of teachers leery about getting involved in light of the husband's well-connected relatives. He prodded them in the same way he did his students. Tanzim reminded them that every important social movement had its roots in Dhaka University. He argued that had Rumana been from any other university, the attack would not even have come to light. He said that taking up her fight for justice could launch a movement against domestic violence.

Alena Khan told Rashed to expect, in the early stages of the case and because of the intense media interest, to devote every waking hour to their effort to bring Sumon to justice. The Kabirs would most certainly assemble a team of fifteen to twenty lawyers; the Monzurs had the two of them and her junior. Most importantly, Rumana was safe only as long as Sumon remained behind bars. Anusheh was never completely out of danger; those seeking to influence the child as a witness at trial could try to kidnap her.

Aside from the courts, Alena would concentrate on the police, recognizing that under political pressure to protect Sumon, they could ignore evidence or even contrive evidence if not held accountable. She had challenged police conduct in two notorious cases. In 1997, she'd filed a case against police of hiding evidence after the acquittal of four policeman for the gang rape of Seema Chowdhury. They had detained the teenage garment worker when she and her fiancé were out for a walk. After a public outcry, the policemen were arrested. But Seema had also been jailed "for her own safety." Four months later, she was dead. A post-mortem revealed she'd been tortured in custody. More recently, in 2006, Alena helped mobilize women's organizations to probe the death of a popular rights activist, Nasreen Huq, as a possible murder. Nasreen had been leading a campaign against a British company's controversial plan to develop an open pit mine in Bangladesh's poorest province, when her own driver rammed her against the wall of her garage.

Alena told Rashed that public perception of Sumon's crime could dictate how far the case against him progressed. She assigned Rashed the role of mobilizing human rights groups and the media to Rumana's side, as a way of reaching lawmakers. Rashed enlisted a young cousin, a recent MBA graduate who worked for a British-owned chain of supershops (a combined department and grocery store) to monitor leading media and to post on the Justice for Rumana platform. Rashed also set up a daily call with his uncle Moynul at ten every evening—to accommodate the time difference between Bangladesh and the Netherlands—to strategize.

A distraught and angry Kabir dominated television coverage while Rumana was in India. He claimed that his daughter-in-law was faking blindness, that she was using makeup to discolour her eyelids. He said she had attacked his son first, that his son was forced to defend himself. He denied reports that his son was angry that she planned to continue her studies abroad; in fact, his son had a business and had sold it to support her education. As for trouble in the marriage? "Every husband and wife bicker and argue." Kabir was angriest when he called Rumana immoral and shameful. His choice of words, *onotitik* and *lojjaskor*, could not be more condemning. He offered "evidence" to reporters: copies of photographs of Rumana in mixed company, and of her posed alone with the student Sumon had named, as well as a lewd email she had written to him.

Rashed's young cousin examined Kabir's photographs and traced most of them to Facebook posts. Rashed readily concluded the photos were but a record of social events at Rumana's college. As for the purported email, Rashed dismissed it as amateurish fakery. Never mind that the ungrammatical and unpunctuated English was unlike anything Rumana would ever write, the author's rush to produce evidence to incriminate was apparent from the email's opening words—"good morning, navid. i really don't want u to think of me as 'cheap' or 'bad' who is cheating on her husband. . . ".

Though confident that leading newspapers would ignore Kabir's supposed evidence, Rashed called several editors as a precaution. All assured him they had no plans to publish Kabir's material. Rashed was caught off guard, however, when a junior reporter at the country's major tabloid, the credible *Manab Jamin*, tipped him off that the paper would publish the photographs in the next day's edition. Rashed phoned the editor—"Let me tell you the true story"—and persuaded him to pull the piece.

It did not surprise Alena to get a call from Anisul Huq, a member of one of the country's most respected legal families. His father, one of the founders of the Awami League, had prosecuted war crimes from the War of Independence. At the time of his death in 2002, he had been prosecuting the former army officers accused of assassinating President Mujib in 1975. His son Anisul took on that role in 2007 and saw the trial through to its conclusion with the upholding of the death sentences. (The upward trajectory of Anisul's career would continue; on his election to parliament in 2014, he would be appointed minister of justice, law and parliamentary affairs—and reappointed in 2019.)

Anisul said his was a courtesy call, to tell Alena that the Kabir family had asked him to join Sumon's defence team, but that he had not yet responded. Alena hurried Rashed into a car so that they could go see Anisul in person. "We can't risk the opposition taking a lawyer the calibre of Anisul Haq."

Admitting that he knew nothing of the case beyond what he'd heard in the news, Anisul asked his two visitors: "Is it true that his wife has lost the sight of both eyes?" Told it was so, he said he would not take the case. However, he had a question of law for Alena: Why had she filed a complaint of attempted murder under the penal code and not under the Women and Children Repression Prevention Act? Was it because she intended to ask for the death penalty? If so, both laws provided for such.

"I'd lose under the women and children law," she replied.

The rate of conviction under that law, enacted in 2000, was only three percent. But she said no more about it. To explain her reasoning would have pointed out the senior lawyer's incorrect assumption that Sumon's offence met one of that law's provisions, that his intent had been to force payment of dowry from Rumana's family or push her into begging or prostitution.

Alena was reminded of what women's rights advocates were up against: a common perception that a husband had the right to beat his wife, and that she ought to have the mental strength to endure it.

After Rumana's second day at the Sankara Nethralaya eye hospital, Monzur took her back to the hotel but returned later, on his own, to meet with a senior consultant to review the findings, contained in the case summary.

The page-and-a-half document, written in technical medical language, described how Rumana presented at her first appointment. It went on to state that tests by the Sankara hospital revealed in the left eye, "total hyphema with subconjunctival dehiscence"; and in the right eye, "vitreous hemorrhage and retinal detachment." It concluded that the absence of perception of light and "disorganized" globes in both eyes indicated a poor visual prognosis, and that "nil further intervention is needed at present."

Monzur trudged back to the hotel. A last thought the consultant had shared haunted him. He'd speculated that the assailant must have preplanned the attack, because it had destroyed all options to restore sight. If true, if Sumon had put that much thought into the attack, the sheer cruelty of it crushed Monzur.

At the hotel, he reported to his wife and daughter the hospital's findings in the fewest words possible. "Nothing can be done."

Rumana asked her father to take her from the bed to where her daughter was watching television, so they could snuggle as they did in days before.

Late that evening, Monzur's cell phone rang. The caller asked—in English—if he was the father of Rumana Monzur.

It was Peter Dauvergne. He told Monzur that when UBC's president, Stephen Toope, learned that Rumana's family had taken her to India to seek treatment, he thought of an alumnus who ran the Aravind Eye Hospital in Pondicherry. Peter said that UBC had arranged for doctors there to examine Rumana.

Monzur put Rumana on the phone.

"Peter, I can't see anymore." Rumana convulsed in tears. "I won't be able to see anyone anymore."

"Rumana, Rumana." Then, "Rumana, do you want to come back to Canada?"

"Yes, I do! I do want to. Canada was where I achieved everything. I came back, and I lost everything."

"Okay, Rumana. We'll make sure you come back here."

The next day, Monzur hired a driver and a minibus for the three-and-a-half-hour drive south to Pondicherry. The family's mood lightened. Anusheh narrated to her mother the passing scenery of boats and canals, adding how amazed she was at all the greenery.

That afternoon, at the Aravind hospital, Rumana saw specialists and underwent several tests. The next day, Monzur met to discuss the doctors' findings.

On his return, Rumana asked, "What did they say?"

"They said the same thing."

Two days before the Monzurs were due back from India, Rashed heard a rumour that the Kabirs were planning to hold a press conference to reveal a pattern of infidelity by Rumana. Worried they might recruit stand-ins to say they'd had affairs with her, Alena had Rashed ask Rumana's friends at UBC to urgently send testimonials attesting to her character. On Sunday night, the residents at St. John's faxed Rashed twenty-two statements about their friend.

Mohsen contributed one. Frustrated that Rumana should have to endure another onslaught of false accusations, he also revived the idea of a rally. This time the other residents warmed to it. He set the date for the following Sunday, June 26, on the plaza of Vancouver's art gallery, the city's former courthouse and a popular spot for protest.

Rashed shared the testimonials with media outlets whose political or religious leanings he expected to tilt in Rumana's favour. On Monday morning, a handful of daily newspapers in Dhaka quoted from them:

"Rumana had a flawless reputation."

"Not only did [she] cover her head as a symbol of the Islamic values which she practised all the time, but she was surrounded by her female friends all the time."

"She regularly dined with two girlfriends."

"She would stand out in the cold rain to talk long distance to her daughter."

"Whenever I went by her room she was praying, phoning her family or studying."

"She was like an elder sister."

In addition, some quoted an open letter sent on behalf of the Bangladeshi community in Vancouver: "[I]n a community so small it is simply impossible to have an extramarital affair without being noticed by the community members."

Prominent women's rights activists, in columns and blogs, condemned what the character testimonials insinuated, that blame lay with the victim. With undisguised sarcasm, they asked if the portrayal of Rumana—as devout, studious and family oriented—implied that, otherwise, a woman who cheated on her husband, who was corrupted by Western morals, deserved what she got?

The rumoured press conference in Dhaka didn't materialize.

However, verbal jousting about the attack on Rumana found fertile ground on the internet. The extreme savagery of the assault made it a leading topic on Facebook and on Choturmatrik, a popular new Bangla-language community blogging platform:

> "It took a monster to bite the nose off his wife to wake us up to the reality that we have a very serious problem in our society, but in all likelihood this culture of silence and mana chola [societal shame] will continue."
>
> "Whose face are we saving?"
>
> "Shame! Shame! Shame!"
>
> "If [women] did not maintain their modesty, they could not blame men for the rampage of harassment, acid attack, rape and domestic violence."
>
> "You can't make a sound of clapping with one hand."

Competing narratives, whether sown in the media or on social media, had already begun to take root on the street. In a country mired in poverty and plagued with low literacy rates, gossip prevails. The idea of Rumana the sympathetic victim could be brushed aside if the public bought the narrative of Sumon as a husband wronged, goaded by his wife's infidelity. Were that to happen, it would give credence to a subsequent conclusion by the police that Monzur's complaint was a private matter, an issue of honour between two families, where retribution for a wife's betrayal was not considered domestic violence.

Rumana and her family landed in Dhaka unaware of the media coverage or the upcoming rallies in Dhaka and Vancouver. A mob of reporters surrounded her as she emerged from the airport exit, seated in a wheelchair that her father pushed. Her head shrouded in a scarf, and her eyes obscured by dark glasses, she had little to say: "He has made my world dark. I can't see my daughter. My daughter is so young. My mother is sick and now he has done this to me. . . Please press for his trial."

Alena Khan hopped into Rashed's car beside Rumana. She had news to share before anyone else could, and she needed to see Rumana's reaction to it. Students at BUET, the lawyer explained, had issued a statement that reports that Sumon was a graduate of the school were untrue, that there was no record of Sumon completing his degree.

"What?! He didn't graduate?"

Alena was satisfied that this came as news to her client, yet more confirmation that her husband was a serial liar. Rumana realized that without a degree Sumon couldn't even have applied to the MBA program.

On the ride back into town, Rashed disclosed to Rumana what Sumon had told reporters upon his capture: that she'd had an affair when in Canada.

Rumana suppressed a laugh. "I knew that would be his defence, that that would be the first thing he'd say." When Rashed told her about the photographs and purported email exchange that her father-in-law was handing out, she said immediately that they had to be Sumon's work: he had the passwords to her Facebook and Yahoo accounts, and he'd stolen her camera.

No media had published the photos, but Rashed said he was still concerned. The amount of ink and airtime the media had devoted to Sumon's accusations were allowing the Kabirs' side of the story to gain traction: "The media say to me, 'The husband has said nasty things about Rumana. If what he's saying isn't true, why isn't she saying anything?' Hema, if you stay quiet, people are going to think there must be some truth to it all." Rumana accepted Rashed's proposal, that after a night's rest at Labaid, she would hold a press conference at the hospital.

Shehneela was setting the table for dinner when her mother telephoned her: "Turn on the television. Is that person Hema?"

Shehneela's mother-in-law was already watching the news. Were it not for the caption identifying the beating victim as "DU teacher Rumana Monzur," Shehneela would not have believed that the person on the screen was her childhood friend. Her mother-in-law said the attack had been on the news for days. Shehneela had caught snippets but scrupulously avoided the story, regarding it as "morbid."

She went straight to a photo album from her Agrani days. On seeing her friend's beautiful smile and bright eyes, she wept.

It had been four years since Shehneela had seen Rumana, when they both attended the goodbye lunch for Farzana Morshed. Rumana had left the lunch early. In her wake, others gossiped. "Do you know, her husband doesn't do anything. He's got some business of CNGs, but he relies on her." Shehneela had kept to herself that she didn't like Sumon and avoided him.

On Shehneela's brief visits home from India during her first year of university, she'd head to the Monzurs', keen to make up for lost time with Rumana. If she saw that Sumon was visiting, she didn't go farther than the front door. She'd tell Rumana she'd come back later: "I just came to say hello."

In the morning, Shehneela called the principal where she taught and asked for the day off. She went to Labaid hospital. Even as she approached Rumana's bed, her friend said her nickname, Tupah: "I know you by your smell." Shehneela could not stay long; Rumana's father and some teachers from Dhaka University were standing by to accompany her to a press conference.

Rumana sat flanked by her father and lawyer. Her eyes remained closed and her head flopped slightly back, her strained neck muscles still unable to fully support her head. Normally, only reporters attended a press conference. This time, as well as Rumana's colleagues from Dhaka University, high-profile activists and advocates from various women's and human rights organizations and NGOs came out in force. Many were from revered families linked to the birth of Bangladesh and had storied careers. Now the head of a non-profit that supported research on poverty, Mugha Guhathakurta had watched on the night of Operation Searchlight Pakistani soldiers drag away her father, an English professor at Dhaka University. He was later found shot dead. The lawyer, Sara Hossain, daughter of Kamal Hossain, known as "the father of the Bangladeshi constitution," headed Bangladesh Legal Aid and was the impetus behind the year-old Domestic Violence Protection and Prevention Act. Khushi Kabir, a renowned activist who headed Nijera Kori, an organization to empower landless peasants, was one of the women the world over collectively nominated for the Nobel Peace Prize in 2005.

The conference was conducted in Bangla, but back in Bangladesh less than a month after almost a year abroad, Rumana occasionally inadvertently slipped in words in English. In a tremulous voice, she began by describing what happened on the afternoon of June 5, 2011. Monzur repeatedly removed his glasses and methodically dabbed a handkerchief at one eye, then the other. Rumana went on to call for the case to be shifted from the regular courts to a "speedy trial tribunal" (in 2002, in response to a surge of violent and gruesome killings, gang rapes and terrorizing of minorities, the government enacted a law allowing it to designate cases to be tried before a special tribunal and resolved within sixty days). In the country's overburdened justice system, five years had become the average elapsed time from the initiation of a case to a pending verdict.

A reporter interjected. "Was June 5 the first time you were assaulted?"

"No, it wasn't. He tortured me since the day we got married. Later, every time, he would beg for forgiveness. He'd say, 'Please forgive me this time. I made a serious mistake. It was wrong of me, it won't happen again.' In every instance I believed him. I loved him—" Rumana whimpered. "He said he wouldn't let me live. He threatened that he would find me and kill me. I'm afraid for myself, for my daughter, for my family. Please put him away. . . Please help me live. Please help my daughter to live."

Another male reporter called out. "Your husband says you were unfaithful to him, that you had an extramarital affair with an Iranian man while studying abroad. Is it true?"

Cries broke out: "Shame! Shame!" Chairs scraped on the floor as Rumana's supporters leapt to their feet:

"The violence done to Rumana is the crime. She is not on trial. He is!"

"Accusations of immorality are an old trick, to distract attention, to justify domestic violence!"

"An allegation like that shakes the confidence of women in this male-dominated society!"

Delwar Hossain added a male voice to the rebuttals: "My wife is my property and I am going to kill her because she did something I don't like? Does impropriety—even if true—mean a husband has the right to kill his wife? Nobody gave this man the right to take justice in his hand!"

The criticism raining down on the reporter brought the conference to an abrupt end. As the reporters walked away, a television journalist muttered, loud enough to make sure he was heard, "These kinds of incidents don't happen out of the blue. There has to be more to this."

Within two hours, Gitiara, from Dhaka University, and the anthropologist and columnist Rahnuma Ahmed released a statement condemning attempts to justify the attack and character assassination by "a section of the media and some individuals on social media." The statement appended forty names of mostly women lawyers. After a flurry of emails among several women activists calling for a stronger statement, they released a second one, appending seventy additional names, female and male, across a breadth of civil society: "A woman's fidelity or character is immaterial to the prosecution of a case of criminal violence. Allegations of infidelity are an attempt to deviate attention from the attacker and shift blame to the person attacked."

Television coverage of the press conference ran at length the reporter's offending question and Rumana's supporters rounding on him. In one glaring omission, none reported the rebuttal from Amena Mohsin: "Why don't you ask instead where Sumon was for ten days? Why don't you want to know who offered him protection?"

Late that evening, Rumana's uncle Moynul called her. For the first time since the attack, Rumana heard someone declare to her, directly and forcefully, that reporters asking her about Sumon's allegations of infidelity was wrong and unacceptable.

He was emphatic. "You are not the one with any guilt. No matter what anyone says, no one has the right to do what Sumon did to you. Even if you liked someone, no one has the right to do what he did to you."

Some days later, Rumana learned that Alena had asked her friends in Vancouver for character testimonials. Upset, she told the lawyer she felt ashamed on her friends' behalf.

"You and I know what Sumon said about an affair isn't true," Alena replied, "but people in Bangladesh might not believe you."

Hardly were the next morning's papers on the street, with accounts of the press conference, when, in an unprecedented move, women parliamentarians across all parties joined in a motion of censure (normally members of the ruling party do not participate in censures) against the oppression of women.

Thirty women parliamentarians then proceeded to Labaid and formed a human chain on the road in front of the hospital. One pledged on behalf of the prime minister, Sheikh Hasina, that the government would stand by oppressed women "regardless of which party they belong to."

Television cameras followed the agriculture minister into the hospital to Rumana's bedside. The seventy-year-old woman caressed Rumana's forehead. She bent close to her ear: "I don't know why women like you tolerate torture like this." Rumana wept. She hadn't known any better than to keep her silence. In doing so, she felt she hadn't lived up to either her education or her esteemed position as a teacher at Dhaka University.

Over the next day, various groups formed human chains, held candlelight vigils and demonstrated in support of Rumana. Prominent citizens made pilgrimages to her bedside. Among them, Arefin Siddique, the vice-chancellor of Dhaka University— making a pointed public appearance—Dhaka's mayor, Sadeque Khokha, and Bhasha Matin, aged eighty-six, one of the last surviving student leaders of the language movement. By the *tap tap* of a cane as he entered her room, and the wrinkled hand holding hers, Rumana knew the visitor was elderly. But in a reversal of an act of respect by the young for an elder, he touched her feet. "Please forgive me," he said to Rumana. She felt as if he was apologizing for being a man.

Amid growing public support, Tanzim secured several large newspaper advertisements, free of charge, for the rally at the Shaheed Minar. DESH TV, a Bangla-language satellite and cable television channel, agreed to broadcast it live. Much more difficult for Tanzim was to convince Monzur to join the roster of speakers. He repeatedly refused, citing the political sensitivity of the case.

Shehneela and her mother went together to Dhanmondi to call on Rahima.

Talk among the women relatives gathered there was angry, sorrowful.

"The fathers were friends."

"How could their son do such a thing to a friend's daughter? He spoiled a girl's future."

"Do you know he didn't pass his studies at BUET?"

"How could he attack her in front of his own daughter?"

"He tortured her mentally and physically for the whole marriage. How could she not let anyone know the truth?"

The women relatives who were taking turns staying with Rumana overnight spoke of her bouts of crying that left them struggling for words. Compelled to say something, they could only think to ask, "Hema, why didn't you tell us?" Her answer was bewildering: "I thought I could fix him. I was hoping that my love could make him okay."

In the years to come, plagued by the question of why Rumana had kept silent during her marriage, the family would return to their own conjecture: that in falling for Sumon, Rumana, who had excelled at all she did, could not admit she had made a bad decision.

Puzzled at why Rumana wouldn't have confided in her own mother about the abuse, Shehneela felt a rush of anger. What was the use of her education if she didn't speak up at the time?

After attending a bail hearing at the Dhaka courthouse, Monzur came directly to Rumana's bedside. As he held her hand in his, he could not control the trembling of his own. "Hema, maybe we should withdraw the complaint. You'd have to testify at the

trial. The other side will say all kinds of ugly things about you."
Rumana pushed aside her father's qualms: "They've already
done the worse they could to me."

Since her return from India, she'd been interviewed three
times at her bedside by the Detective Branch. She felt confident
that they believed her. Several times after her answers, she'd heard
the senior officer turn to talk to someone—presumably the junior
who'd accompanied him—and say, "I told you he's lying."

On the day of the rally at the Shaheed Minar, as Tanzim set up
a sound system on the platform of the monument, a man accosted
him. He said he was from the university and with the ruling party.
He told Tanzim that individual teachers could not hold a rally in
the name of Dhaka University. Omar intervened and pushed him
off, but not before the two had exchanged harsh words.

Several thousand turned out for the rally. Some sixty faculty
and administrators, including the vice chancellor, sat barefoot and
cross-legged on the platform. Some held placards, in Bangla and
English: "JUSTICE DELAYED IS JUSTICE DENIED" and "WE WANT
PUNISHMENT OF MONSTER SYEED." Tanzim read a statement
declaring that the fight for justice was not restricted to Rumana,
that it was on behalf of all victims of domestic abuse, and that the
greater cause was women's rights. Several speakers demanded that
police press charges against Sumon, and that the case be tried by
a speedy trial tribunal. DU's vice chancellor was blunt: "In fact,
Rumana has been practically murdered as nothing is left when the
eyesight of a teacher is taken away."

Silence fell over the crowd when Monzur stepped to the
microphone. To secure his participation, Tanzim had had to plead

with him, finally persuading him that it was vital that the victim's father express his solidarity with the rally.

Clasping his arms and hands tight to his body, as if necessary to hold himself together, Monzur described the family's futile search for treatment in India. He continued, his tears coming in a torrent:

> "As a father I am in deep pain, but what I saw in the last few days made me believe that all of [you] are feeling the same pain. . .
>
> "I don't know what will happen now. My request to all of you is to keep praying for Rumana. Maybe Allah will not be able to ignore your prayers. . . My request to you is to make sure that my daughter gets justice, to make sure the person who tortured her like this receives such a punishment that becomes an example."

As a grieving father, Monzur seemed to fold within himself and shrink. His wiry, still athletic, frame seemed fragile.

On the plane ride home from Dhaka to New Jersey, Farrukh Mohsen could think of little else but the image on television of his lifelong friend, Monzur, looking utterly broken, pleading for justice for his daughter.

Farrukh had been in Bangladesh to visit relatives in his ancestral village. With some time to spare before he had to leave for the airport, he had turned on the television and caught a live broadcast of the rally at the Shaheed Minar. He was shattered by what he saw; he could not fathom how the marriage between the son and daughter of two of his closest friends could come to such violence. He recalled that neither set of parents was excited about Sumon and Rumana marrying, but that the son was insistent and Rumana wanted the wedding. Farrukh remembered thinking it odd, during a visit to the Monzurs', to see the young couple living with them rather than with the in-laws. But nobody had said anything about it.

Once home, Farrukh called Kabir and Monzur, in turn.

The trouble, Kabir told him, began with Rumana getting "friendly" with an Iranian student in Canada. He said he'd have his daughter mail copies of photographs of Rumana with the man and an email she wrote to him that was evidence of her immorality. Farrukh decided he'd wait and see before passing judgment. He found unthinkable another accusation on the call, that Rumana was in on the deception that Sumon had graduated from BUET, that she and Sumon had shown Ruby and Kabir a diploma. But what seemed truly fantastical to Farrukh was the story that the two had planned a joint suicide and that Rumana had given an overdose of pills to Sumon but had not taken any herself.

When the package arrived, Farrukh had no clue what to make of the intimate content and language of the email. However, he saw how the photographs would inflame Kabir with his conservative outlook: Rumana, a married woman with a young daughter, gone abroad without her husband, standing with unmarried males in a group or in close contact with one. Kabir would consider such behaviour haram. As a consequence, what respect and regard he had for Rumana would have died.

Farrukh put himself in Monzur's shoes.

Monzur would have had no concern about his daughter going abroad to study, and would have wanted her to go. He'd see the photos as harmless: friends, females and males alike, arms around each other's shoulders, laughing and smiling for the camera. Farrukh saw them the same way. His children posed for the camera like that all the time, but they were born in the US. Monzur's family was liberated and had a broad outlook. In contrast, Kabir's son had hardly left Bangladesh.

Unlike his call with Kabir and Ruby, Farrukh's call with Monzur was brief. Monzur was willing only to accept words of comfort, refusing to speak of the attack or hear mention of the Kabir family. Farrukh sympathized: a protective father like Monzur would have taken the defaming of his daughter and the assailing of her character very hard. Sadness flooded Farrukh at the thought of his two friends, each diminished, each broken by what had happened, on opposite sides of a chasm of blame and hurt.

Two days after the rally at the Shaheed Minar in Dhaka, the scene repeated itself half a world away. Several hundred came out to the rally in downtown Vancouver.

In the days leading up to the Vancouver rally, the story had garnered national headlines across Canada of the UBC graduate student who'd gone home to Bangladesh in a break from her studies and been attacked and blinded by her husband.

The award-winning roving foreign correspondent from the *Globe and Mail*, Stephanie Nolen, based in New Delhi, called Rashed and asked for a telephone interview with Rumana. Rumana declared she felt no safer with her husband in custody. "He's in jail now but he has friends and he can do anything because he has money." Asked about the focus of Bangladeshi media on the charge of infidelity, she said: "I don't care what Sumon is saying, it doesn't give him the right to do this to me." She said she wanted to make clear why she, an educated person, had tolerated him so long. "Because I really loved him. Every time, he convinced me, asked for forgiveness, that's why. I had a daughter and my daughter needed a father. I didn't want her to be deprived of her father's love because of me."

At the Vancouver rally, Mohsen was cheered to see a strong press contingent. His fear that it would turn into a showdown with supporters of the husband was for naught, though he'd guarded against it by lining up speakers from the administration of UBC and representatives of women's and human rights and civil society organizations. The placards for the rally—in Bangla and English—addressed the bigger issue of violence against women: "Support Rumana," "Respect Women's Rights to Education," and "End Violence Against Women."

In his own remarks, Mohsen emphasized the global problem of women subjected to violence "for no good reason other than the fact that they are women." Several women came forward to the microphone to share their own stories of abuse by an intimate partner, or the stories of others, among them a woman blinded after being shot twice in the head by her estranged husband; a wife whose husband had chopped off her fingers.

How, Tulip wondered, could Hema have kept secret the abuse in her marriage? How was it that she had not confided in her parents or her friends? But then, had Tulip really given her friend an opportunity to share? In the first months after Rumana married, Tulip had tried to make plans to meet with her, but it seemed difficult for Rumana to commit, so she gave up. Tulip had only recently moved back to Dhaka from London, where she'd worked as a UK diplomat.

Tulip had vowed that once Rumana was back from India she'd pay her daily visits. Shehneela had also become a regular visitor. Rumana began to confide in them both. When she told them about the slap on the first night of her marriage, Tulip said only, "Hema, forget it. Just forget about it." Shehneela, who had been holding Rumana's hand in hers, replied by pressing her hand more tightly.

Each time Tulip visited Rumana, she ruminated on the poor quality of life her friend would experience if she remained in Bangladesh. Not only did Dhaka lack social services, the city was inaccessible for the physically disabled. Even able-bodied persons could find the city hard to negotiate, its few sidewalks mostly broken or fallen in and trash or hawkers occupying the limited available space. Rumana's family seemed uneasy dealing with her blindness, seeing her as a diminished human being, her former life gone. As far as Tulip could tell, only Anusheh, who sat happily on the hospital bed colouring or doing puzzles, was helping her mother adjust. When an auntie arrived with a new dress, she guided her mother's hand to it: "Mamma, touch this. See how it feels. It has ruffles."

And what of the young girl? Surely she would need counselling. Tulip had also taken to visiting the family at Dhanmondi daily. She had overheard the aunts speak of how the child, chancing on a newspaper with a photograph of her mother and father, had ripped his image from it. How, when she came across some item belonging to her father, she pointed to it and said, "Daddy did naughty things." How she'd lost a baby tooth and at seeing barely a trickle of blood, screamed.

Tulip cornered Monzur. She asked again what was he thinking about Rumana's future. As before, he didn't answer. Tulip sought out Rashed: What was the point of Hema languishing in bed, why not seek other medical opinions abroad? Rashed put her in touch with Moynul. Between them, they contacted leading eye care hospitals around the world. One after another said that no treatment could restore vision in eyes that do not respond to light. Tulip went to Rumana. She urged her to consider her and Anusheh's future, and to think about moving to Canada. "You have a natural home in Canada. If you have a good relationship with your university, I'm sure they would help. There's no harm in contacting UBC."

Catherine Dauvergne was in the stands cheering her daughter on at an out-of-town swim meet when an email came from a Sayeeda Salim—Tulip—raising the idea of Rumana Monzur relocating to Canada.

Catherine had an idea. She reached UBC's dean of medicine. "Is there something we could do for her if she were here, in Vancouver?" Soon, she was talking with Dr. David Maberley, a surgical retina specialist and head of ophthalmology and visual sciences in the faculty of medicine, and affiliated with the Vancouver

General Hospital. Had he treated any similar cases? He had—a victim of an attempted murder, whose assailant, the parent, had stabbed her in her eye. Such details were not important to him: "My job is to fix the eye."

He said he couldn't comment on whether restoration of some sight was possible for Rumana without seeing her medical reports, "but I would never tell a young person who's suffered severe eye trauma that there's no hope of recovering some useful vision." Normally, however, the best chance of saving the eye was to operate within four to six hours of an injury. Rumana needed to get to Vancouver as quickly as possible.

Catherine shared the urgency with Tulip. It had been more than three weeks since the attack. Upon hearing Catherine's news, Rumana was insistent that she would go to Canada only together with her daughter, that she'd worry about the girl's safety if she left her behind. To take Anusheh out of the country, Rumana had to arrange a court order granting her temporary custody. On Catherine's news, residents of St. John's began a city-wide fund-raising campaign to help cover Rumana's expenses.

Tulip observed Monzur's response to the Vancouver offer. She was disappointed to see that he was regarding the trip as he had the trip to Chennai—only to seek medical care. She called Catherine to share her worry about what life held for Rumana and her daughter if they remained in Bangladesh. "The blind are regarded as a social burden. Nor would this be a good environment for Anusheh to grow up in. In this country, people gossip a lot. You have to have a thick skin. The attack was big news here. People can be nasty and malicious. No matter what school Anusheh went to, she'd be targeted."

"Tell Rumana's father exactly what you've just told me," Catherine told her.

Tulip found Monzur sitting on the floor of the lounge. His wife was trying to console him. Tulip said nothing.

The Canadian High Commission had visas ready in days, on July 4. The family decided that Monzur and Rumana would travel ahead to Vancouver. Rahima and Anusheh would follow when the temporary court order came through.

At Rumana's direction, Monzur went to withdraw money from her bank account for the trip. He found a zero balance; Rumana had told him it would contain the equivalent of eight thousand Canadian dollars. The teller apologized. He said that the attack had not yet been in the news when Sumon had presented what in hindsight was a forged cheque.

When Rumana asked Tulip to include her published articles in her packing for Canada, she learned what Rahima had been unable to bring herself to tell her daughter. On the day of the attack the building's guard, having heard Sumon yelling on the terrace, later found remnants of a fire. Sumon had burned not only Rumana's scholarly articles, but also every one of her paintings.

ten

DR. MABERLEY SAT WAITING FOR RUMANA. HER FLIGHT HAD just landed, and he expected Catherine Dauvergne to deliver her soon to the Eye Care Centre of the Vancouver General Hospital. The operating theatre was booked; after his initial examination, he'd do the first of four surgeries.

The doctor envisaged two surgeries on each of Rumana's eyes. The first was exploratory, to assess the damage. He'd then close up the eye and give it a few days to heal and, in the meantime, conduct an exploratory surgery on the other eye. He'd go into each eye a second time to look for salvageable retinal tissue with which he could then repair and reconstruct the eye. Each of the surgeries was a delicate procedure of several hours; care had to be taken to guard against the escape of the gel-like fluid that helps inflate the eyeball and gives it its round shape.

Upon Rumana's arrival, Dr. Maberley's immediate decision was which eye to operate on first, the left or the right. He compared their outward appearance, avoiding retracting her eyelids so as to put no pressure on the eye globe. The right eye looked less bloodstained than the left, which suggested it was less likely to be ruptured and therefore had better odds of recovering some sight. He elected to start with it.

In the operating theatre, Dr. Maberley replaced the bloodstained cornea of the right eye with a prosthesis that he could operate through on the second surgery. Then he loosened the muscle off the eye. Contrary to what he had anticipated, the globe was ruptured. It resembled a crushed grape. Fortunately, the injury had not gone all the way through to the back wall of the eyeball. Hopefully, on the second operation, he'd find viable retinal tissue to work with.

Two days later, Dr. Maberley undertook an exploratory surgery on Rumana's left eye. It, too, had been ruptured. He saw why the stain of blood was so massive: the gouging had penetrated to the last layer before the back eye wall, to the choroid, the layer made up of a network of blood vessels that nourish the retinal tissue. The blood from the hemorrhaging would have been trapped in the eyeball; any pressure on the eye would have caused severe pain.

When Dr. Maberley went back into the right eye, he found the back eye wall to be no longer intact. Only a portion of it remained. Spattered against it, only a small remnant of retinal tissue, not enough to salvage.

Hope for any restoration of sight rested with Rumana's left eye.

On Rumana's tenth day in hospital, Dr. Maberley undertook the second surgery on the left eye. What he saw shocked him. The

damage was the worst he'd seen in his decade and a half as a retinal surgeon. The eye was laid waste. Even the one-cell-deep layer
of pigment between the retina and the eyeball was gone, leaving
exposed the stark white back wall of the globe. All that remained
of the retina was a shrivelled ball.

His job reduced to ocular taxidermy, Dr. Maberley added sili-
cone to replace the lost fluid and closed the globe.

Though the last operation on Rumana's eyes had ended long
after midnight, a few hours later, Dr. Maberley made his way to
Rumana's room when he knew she would be awake. He wanted
a good hour to speak with her alone before her father arrived for
his daily vigil. When the doctor arrived he found she already had
visitors, two of a daily rotation arranged by Sarah Meli. The countries they heralded from—Belgium, Germany, Malta, Iran, India,
Pakistan, Norway, Canada—could turn Rumana's bedside into a
general assembly of the United Nations.

Dr. Maberley returned when Rumana was alone. He settled in
the chair by the bed. He was frank: the surgeries on both eyes were
unsuccessful; nothing could be done.

Rumana felt herself falling into a bottomless abyss.

She had fully believed that she would regain some sight, that
the darkness would lift from her world. She had counted on seeing
her young daughter's face again and on starting the life that she'd
planned for the two of them.

Dr. Maberley knew the news he brought could only be devastating. This was a young patient with a lifetime ahead of her.
Knowing Rumana needed time to take it in, he kept talking.

"It will be awful for a while. You'll probably wake up every morning wishing you could see again."

Rumana focused on the doctor's voice.

"You know, Rumana, you will be able to do everything, but in a different way. You won't be given a driver's licence, so you won't drive a bus or a car. You'll have to give up photography, and art exhibitions won't be your top priority. . . "

She knew that the doctor was trying to bolster her spirits.

He said he had a story for her: a blind lawyer was arguing a case in court when a power failure threw the courtroom into darkness. The judge called a recess until power was restored. The blind lawyer raised an objection: "Respectfully, Your Honour, I have a disability. Now, everybody else has a disability, and I am the only abled person. I am prepared to keep going."

Dr. Maberley finally got not only a smile out of his patient, but a laugh.

Blindness, he told her, did not hinder achievement or end ambition. He shared with her example after example of people who lived with blindness and yet were exceptional in their lives, who'd contributed to their community and the country. "I have full confidence that you will be able to overcome your blindness. In this country, you can do anything. You have no idea how well you are going to do."

Dr. Maberley told Rumana he would arrange for an introduction to someone from the Canadian National Institute for the Blind, a non-profit organization that helped the blind lead independent lives. Finally, he asked, did she want to talk to the press or should he? Rumana said he should. She did not want to hear—ever—the details of the permanent damage Sumon had done to her eyes.

That evening, back in his hotel room, Monzur wept freely. Waves of guilt crashed over him. He chided himself for assuming that as long as his daughter had the right education and outlook, nothing catastrophic could befall her. Now he saw that for all the preparations he and Rahima had taken in raising her, and for their belief that she had ably made the transition to adulthood, she had lacked maturity in one important way: in judging the character of a boy. With any other marriage proposal, he and his wife would have investigated the family, along with the boy's character, education and outlook. Instead, they had trusted the Kabirs to care for Rumana's happiness and protect her from adversity.

Still, how was it, even when the young couple were living under their own roof, that he and Rahima had not picked up earlier on whatever misunderstandings or disagreements the two were having? In agreeing to the Kabirs' request to wait until their return home to Bangladesh, he'd put his faith in the two families reaching an amicable arrangement. That, too, was a mistake.

Perhaps the pivotal moments when a life could go one way or the other are many. Until, one by one, like the last flashes of a warning light, they are gone.

Alone, finally, Rumana succumbed to a crippling sadness. She didn't know how to live as a blind person. She had only ever met one person who was blind: a student enrolled in one of her undergraduate classes; she'd had to enlist his fellow students to read the exam questions and write his answers. Otherwise, she had encountered the blind only at a distance in Bangladesh. Riding in a car or rickshaw, she might pass a blind person at the side of a road, or when stopped at a traffic light, see one among the beggars and hawkers. Or one among the poor lined up outside a mosque after Friday prayers, hoping to feel a few taka dropped into their outstretched palm.

Rumana asked herself, was it even possible for her to continue living?

The questions that had possessed her in the immediate aftermath of the attack kept cycling in her mind: Why couldn't she have stopped the abuse? How could she have avoided the attack? Why didn't she run? Why didn't she turn her face away, to protect her eyes? Feeling an approaching panic attack, Rumana braced herself against it, stopping the memory from playing out.

She calmed herself, restored her normal breathing. She tried to take inspiration from Dr. Maberley's encouragement. Was there anything she could do to make her situation better?

She had no answer.

The permanence of darkness had collapsed her world. It was as if the hospital room itself was suddenly smaller, the ceiling lowered and the walls squeezed inward.

This is the end of everything I have achieved and everything I could have achieved. I have to bury my ambitions.

In times of duress during her marriage, Rumana had found solace in reading the Qur'an. She reached for the iPad along with the click wheel that a cousin had given her. They'd installed an app that alerted the faithful to daily prayers, five times from dawn through to the evening. She had used it to delineate her darkness, so she had an idea when she should be awake and when she should be sleeping.

This time, she opened it to listen to recitations of the suras from the Qur'an.

A peace drifted over her. As the lilting voice recited the verses, she felt as if Allah was speaking to her, telling her that he would not give her a burden that she was not able to carry. It came to Rumana that in the hardship that had befallen her, Allah was testing her.

Rumana acknowledged the hard truth: I am not going to see again.

She saw a choice: spend her life confined to bed or rise from it.

Helpless hardly described how she had been feeling. She had relied on others for everything and anything. To feed her, to tell her when to open her mouth. To reach for a tissue. To take her to the bathroom, wait for her there, take her back to her bed.

What good are my hands and feet if I don't use them?

She eased herself off the left side of the bed, waited for her dizziness to subside. Keeping one hand on the bed and careful not to let her feet lose contact with the floor, she reached forward until she felt what had to be the bedside table. Atop it, her fingers grazed the cold ribbed plastic side of the jug that held water. Good. The jug is filled. I won't have to call a nurse. Beside the jug, she found a plastic cup.

On the far side of the bed, she ran her hand along a rounded slender edge: the adjustable tabletop. She made a slow sweep of its surface and found the Vaseline she used to soften the scar tissue on her lips. Next to the Vaseline, the box of tissues. What does it matter that I can't see the jar or the box? I know what they are and where they are.

She extended one foot to explore the floor beyond the table. She bumped up against the overnight bag Tulip had packed for her.

Believing the entrance to the bathroom to be on the far side of the bedside table, she ran her palm along the wall until she came upon a door frame. Continuing past the doorway to the bathroom, she searched with her foot and found the leg of a chair; she had heard Dr. Maberley and visitors speak from there. She made her way past the chair and located the door to her room.

Worried she might lose her bearings, she retraced her steps, keeping one arm reaching high in hopes she'd come upon the television. Sure enough, it sat atop a cold metal shelf. Once back in bed, a strange feeling overcame Rumana. The room was no longer dark. It was bright, glowing and colourful.

Rumana stayed seventeen days in hospital. During that time, a plastic surgeon, Dr. Douglas Courtemanche, reconstructed her nose. He first chatted with her at length to better envisage her facial expressions and the movement and wrinkle of her original nose to help him refine his drawings of its replacement. In the operating theatre, he fashioned a wedge from cartilage scavenged from the nasal cavity and covered it with skin harvested from the back of one of Rumana's ears, the shiny and smooth surface there a good match with what remained from before.

On the day of Rumana's discharge, Rahima and Anusheh arrived from Dhaka. Catherine and a team she'd assembled had arranged a three-bedroom, two-storey townhouse at the Acadia

Park residences on campus. The residences were unfurnished, but her team had scoured the university's warehouses for furniture so that it was move-in ready. The pedestrian-only area of the park was reserved for families with at least one member who was a student at UBC. Instead of the screech of circling gulls Rumana had been accustomed to hearing at St. John's College, her new neighbourhood greeted her with the sounds of children on the playground and basketball court outside the Acadia Park commons.

Rumana was upbeat. On one of her final days before discharge, a woman assigned by the CNIB to be her independent living coach paid a visit. Lynn Jensen (herself blind in adulthood, after an illness) got Rumana out of bed to demonstrate how she was most helpfully guided: as the blind person, she grasped the arm of the sighted guide—Lynn played that role—just above the elbow, and they walked together at a normal pace. To be properly guided gave Rumana a sense of liberation.

Lynn's next few visits were to the Monzur family's townhouse. At first, it was pandemonium. Anusheh screamed at the sight of Lynn's guide dog and took refuge on the couch. Howie, a six-year-old black Labrador retriever, terrified the child; in Bangladesh dogs were seen as dirty, impure, even evil. The family had much to learn from Lynn's lessons. The first rule for living as, and with, a blind person: organize the living space and avoid clutter on the floor. Rumana required an entirely new level of focus for every activity now, even eating and drinking. When reaching for a glass, Lynn instructed, keep one hand on the table to help stay oriented. When eating from a plate, start at twelve o'clock and move in a rotating pattern toward the centre. To avoid "empty fork syndrome," pay attention to the weight on the cutlery—that required additional explanation, as Bengalis eat with their fingers. The lessons in the kitchen abounded: when using a knife and cutting board, keep the blade in constant contact with the board's surface; centre a pot on the burner before turning it on, and check that no dishcloth is close enough to catch fire.

"Assistive devices" became essential to everyday life. Rumana was excited to have a talking watch and a PenFriend, a digital recording device to affix audio bar-coded labels on items. She started with clothes in her closet, so she could coordinate what she wore, and cans and jars of food, so she could help prepare meals for Anusheh.

Rumana's initial optimism soon slipped away.

Navigating the minutiae of daily life was overwhelming. Even brushing her teeth—getting the toothpaste on the brush, the toothbrush into the mouth—could frustrate her. (This challenge was solved by putting toothpaste in the mouth instead.) As part of Lynn's lessons for the family, she'd had Monzur and Rahima blindfold themselves to better understand their daughter's disability. However, try as they might to be helpful, they sometimes only hindered Rumana's progress. The first instinct of Rahima—who had her own problems with balance—was to say "Sit, sit" and do for Rumana what she needed to try for herself. As Rumana kept bumping into furniture and bruising herself, her parents couldn't stop themselves from calling out, "Hema, be careful." The engineer in her father would spell out precise measurements—the extent of a reach, the size of a table, the distance from Rumana— to what she needed or where she wanted to go. Only Anusheh intuited what was most helpful: "Mamma, it's on your right"; "Go straight. . . now put your hand out." She told any new visitor to the house: "My mom sees with her feet."

After four weeks, when Rumana's eyes were fully healed from the surgeries, Dr. Maberley measured her for custom eye shells. An ocularist then hand-painted the iris—Rumana chose amber green, thinking a translucent colour preferable to her natural colour of dark brown. A black dot was added for the pupil, and to give the white of the eye a natural look, red nylon fibres were inlaid to replicate blood vessels. Apart from the aesthetics, an eye shell protected against infection.

Beyond medical appointments, including weekly appointments for both her and Anusheh with separate psychologists, Rumana shut herself inside the townhouse. She relied on her father to be her sighted guide. Going anywhere with him was agonizingly slow; he wanted to guard against falling. St. John's residents visited almost daily. They offered to take her on an outing to the college, a twenty-five-minute walk across campus, but she didn't yet want to be seen in public. She didn't feel herself; she still couldn't fully open her eyelids—the force of the attack had temporarily damaged their elasticity—and her new nose took getting used to.

In August, only Monzur went to Pennsylvania to attend Mashrur's wedding. He continued to Dhaka, to tie up loose ends and empty the Dhanmondi apartment. To help Rahima and Rumana in his stead, two of his brothers stepped in: Moynul came to Vancouver from the Netherlands and Mahmood from New Jersey.

Family in Dhaka tried to cheer Rumana with their phone

calls, but the conversations died almost from the start. It rang hollow to ask Rumana "How are you?" As callers stumbled to fill the awkward silence, they'd ask how the weather was that day in Vancouver, or what time it was. Then, thinking that what they'd asked required sight to answer, they'd mumble apologies. Only Jolly's husband, Maqsood, his deep baritone resonating down the line, always found encouraging words. He reminded Rumana of her mastery in her studies and of her achievement in being hired by Dhaka University, encouraging her to tell herself that she'd proven her worth before and would again.

Of all that the attack had taken from Rumana, the most gut-wrenching was that she would never again see her daughter's face. Would she remember how Anusheh looked when she was happy and laughing? Or sad, or scared? It pained Rumana that she would not see her five-year-old daughter transform from a girl into a teenager, from a teenager into a young woman.

Grief devoured her.

Unsettled after his calls with Kabir and Monzur, Farrukh vowed that he'd visit the Monzurs at the earliest opportunity. He came to Vancouver late that summer to encourage Rumana, whom he had known since birth—he hardly knew Sumon—in her blindness and to tell her to look forward to the day when she would resume her studies.

During his visit with Monzur, Farrukh abided by his prohibition against mention of the Kabirs. However, he found Rumana herself open to his inquiry about her marriage. Her divorce certificate had been issued; Sumon was now her ex-husband. Farrukh was perturbed to learn that her marriage with Kabir's son had been troubled from the start. He sympathized with Rumana trying to make her marriage work, and with the inclination of both families to preserve the marriage between their children. Divorce was a fearful measure. Though the changing times had made it less of a taboo, divorce was still frowned upon, still carried a stigma.

Farrukh came away seeing an unbridgeable divide between the Monzurs and Kabirs. On one side, the more progressive-minded Monzurs; on the other, a conservative family with a traditional Bangladeshi mother-in-law. What one family would have seen as abuse, the other had taken to be the natural order of marriage.

As summer turned to fall, a growing tension strangled the air in the Monzur townhouse. Before Monzur and Rumana had left Dhaka, Alena Khan had said to expect progress on the case once the outcome of Rumana's medical treatment became clear, and to expect the government to send the case, if it came to charges, to a speedy trial tribunal.

The prospect of returning to Bangladesh for a trial, quite apart from the trepidation around both her and her daughter having to testify, filled Rumana with dread. She feared that the moment their plane touched down, the family's security would be at risk. When her father had gone back to Dhaka to empty the apartment, he hadn't been back in the city a full day when he'd narrowly missed an encounter with Ruby. On his return from an errand, the maid told him that Ruby and two of her sisters had knocked at the door. Getting no answer, Ruby had yelled out, "I am Sumon's mother. We've come to see Monzur." The maid yelled back that he was not home. At that, Ruby and her sisters had left. Rumana anticipated that, once in Dhaka for the trial, her family would face intense pressure—even blackmail—to withdraw the complaint.

In October, the High Court in Bangladesh instructed the Detective Branch to update the court on the case by the end of the November. For such a high-profile case as Sumon's, his remand into investigative custody, going on five months, was unusually long. In a justice system often criticized as corrupt, long remands could work both for and against a detainee. The longer the remand, the more time and opportunity family and supporters have to bribe police, prison authorities, court employees, clerks, lawyers and brokers. On the other hand, long remands also leave the detainee vulnerable to harassment and abuse by police or guards seeking to extort money to grease the wheels toward bail.

That month, Rumana granted an interview to the *Vancouver Sun*. The article described her as looking thin and speaking in a voice barely above a whisper. It said that the only time she became animated was when she spoke of completing her studies, and that her CNIB coach had cautioned her to be patient about returning to school, that she needed more time to adjust to her blindness. She spoke of difficulty coping with her blindness and said her greatest challenge was being a mother to her daughter. She was in counselling: "I am not okay. Sometimes I feel someone snatched myself from me and I am living someone else's life." Asked about the case against her husband, she was dismissive: "I'm focused on my recovery, not on him. How can he be punished properly. His life hasn't changed. I have lost my sight."

In Dhaka, Alena and Rashed awaited the report from the Detective Branch to the High Court. The DB could say it had not concluded its investigation. Or if it had, it could submit a charge sheet. On the charge sheet, it could agree with the attempted murder charge Alena had asked for, or it could conclude a lesser offence had been committed, which would open the door to bail. Or it could conclude no offence had been committed, which would allow Sumon to walk free. Alena said that if released on bail, Sumon could flee the country to avoid trial. Either way, if out on bail or a free man, Sumon would put Rumana and Anusheh in danger no matter where they lived.

In late October, prison authorities transferred Sumon from Dhaka Central Jail to Bangabandu Sheikh Mujib Medical University. A transfer to the country's first-ever medical university spoke of the prisoner's importance. At Dhaka Central, a two-century-old jail house populated with eleven thousand inmates, four times its capacity, food was bland—the breakfast of dry bread and molasses had not changed since British colonial times—water was not potable, and prisoners ate outside sitting on the ground. Disease, particularly tuberculosis, was rampant. The poorly ventilated buildings baked in summer and dripped with dampness in winter. In contrast, prisoners incarcerated at BSMMU received expert medical care and proper food. Of particular advantage, they had liberal access to their lawyers and family. Alena worked her prison contacts and learned that Sumon had been doing poorly in jail—other prisoners apparently bullied him.

On Tuesday, December 6, Rumana woke to hear her father in the living room on the main floor below, talking to someone whose voice she recognized. It was the media relations officer from UBC. She went downstairs and Randy Schmidt broke the news to her—Sumon had been found dead. He'd died in a prison hospital. Monzur had already known; Rashed had called.

Randy asked Rumana if she could provide a statement; was now a good time? She told him to say that the news was shocking, that the last six months had been very difficult, and his death didn't make her situation any easier.

There would be no trial.

Later that day, over lunch, Rumana said to Anusheh, "I need to tell you something. The bad guy was found dead in the hospital."

Anusheh was quick to answer. "He can't hurt me the way he hurt you, then."

Prison officials at the hospital in Dhaka held a press conference, at which the Kabir family was present, to address the circumstances of the high-profile prisoner's death. At quarter to five that morning, Sumon's prison roommate, thinking that Sumon had been rather long in their bathroom, called out to him. Getting no response, he summoned a guard. The guard found Sumon lying unresponsive on a blanket on the washroom floor. He had died of cardiac failure, officials said, with no further elaboration. They addressed why Sumon had been transferred from Dhaka Central Jail to the hospital, citing issues with his eyesight and that he'd shown "signs of mental instability."

Furious at the insinuation that his brother had taken his life, Shawon told reporters that he and his mother had visited Sumon only a week ago and that they had conversed as usual: his brother asked about the latest efforts to secure bail. An embittered Kabir lashed out at the media. "We tried hard, but we failed because of pressure from you." He gave an anguished cry. "Rumana is not innocent! That side has killed my son."

In New Jersey, Farrukh was deeply shaken to learn the news. First the maiming of Hema, now the death of Sumon. It grieved him to think of his friends, Monzur and Kabir, two of the four who'd bonded in their youths and shaped each other at a formative time of their lives, each having suffered unfathomable loss. Now the two were forever locked in enmity.

Farrukh believed neither could be faulted. He loved them no less. They were each a good human being. So many hearts broken over this, never to be repaired.

Shawon went to reporters with his family's suspicions that his brother had been murdered. He explained bitterly that he had attempted to file a complaint of murder at the police station in whose jurisdiction the BSMMU was located, but the police had refused to accept it. He cited the report of the doctor who'd certified death, which noted marks on the wrists (explained by prison officials as handcuff marks) and discolouring on the neck. He asked why the hospital superintendent and what Shawon referred to as "other unidentified persons" visited his brother's room in the middle of the night, all the more curious since reports were that his brother, when found on the bathroom floor, had a plastic bag over his head.

Finding no interest from traditional media, the Kabir family turned to fringe news outlets online. Stories quoted Ruby accusing Rumana of having tried to kill her son days before their altercation that led to his being taken into custody. She said that

Rumana fed him wood apple juice laced with sleeping pills and it had landed him in hospital. The Kabirs intimated that Monzur was culpable, that as a retired major he had connections to help pull off a murder. An anti-Islamist online weekly tabloid went so far as to suggest the involvement of the Iranian graduate student in Canada or Iranian medical students in Bangladesh.

Anonymous bloggers, writing in Bangla and English, populated the internet with abuse and unfounded theories. The website—using Sumon's formal name—"Hasan Syeed Hottar biochar Chai (We want Justice for Hasan Syeed's murder)" and the Bangla community blog "somewhereinblog.net" recycled accusations that Rumana had an extramarital affair in Canada with the Iranian student and posted what it claimed to be incriminating photographs. Comments heaped vile and vulgar names on Rumana. The website even cast doubt on her accusations of torture with an album of photographs titled "Happy family time together"—the couple seated on a tourist bus, riding bumper cars at a leisure park, at a party for their daughter's birthday.

The gossip on the street alternately condemned Rumana— Rumana faked her blindness as a ruse to leave the country; Rumana resumed her affair—or was elated for her—Rumana can see again; Rumana remarried.

"I don't want a single taka of the Kabirs' money, not for me, not for Anusheh."

"But Hema, the Kabirs stole your money."

It took a bank manager in Dhaka who knew and alerted Monzur for Rumana to find out that what Rashed said was true in the sense of Anusheh's share of Sumon's estate as the sole surviving child. According to the manager, Kabir had come to the bank to cash out assets held in his son's name. He presented a succession certificate—which gives access to a deceased's assets—issued by a family court judge. He portrayed himself as a grieving father who'd lost his son while the son's ex-wife was still carrying on an affair in Canada. The manager refused to make Kabir's transactions. Rashed had Alena investigate, and she learned that the Kabirs had convinced a judge that the young child of their deceased son was living with them and that they needed access to her share of his assets to provide for her care.

To Rashed's consternation, Rumana insisted that she would also forfeit the denmohar negotiated between the two families and specified in the Nikahnama of the cash and assets owed upon divorce.

Rumana told Rashed her sole concern was that the Kabirs not try to wrest custody of Anusheh from her. To safeguard against that, for as long as her daughter was a minor, she would not take her back to Bangladesh. Rashed finally persuaded her that Anusheh should not be prevented from returning because of a fraudulently obtained succession certificate, and that one important reason to press for payment was to preserve some negotiating room if Rumana had no choice but to go to family court in Dhaka to settle custody. Rumana finally conceded.

Alena filed a petition with the family court to say that Anusheh was living with Rumana in Canada and to hold the Kabirs to their legal obligations. What Monzur found particularly grievous was what the Kabirs argued in opposing the petition, that because Monzur's complaint against their son had not progressed past the stage of a police investigation, his assault on Rumana was unproven.

Monzur and Rahima worried that their daughter had slipped into depression. Rumana doesn't talk, they told each other. She stays in her sweatpants all day. Doesn't seem interested even in eating, doesn't go out. They never saw her cry, but they were certain she did in her bedroom.

At the one-year follow-up appointment with Rumana, her plastic surgeon, Dr. Courtemanche, noted in his files that her mood was "very flat." It raised no concern for him. He detected, beneath her subdued manner, evidence of a bubbly personality. Their conversations often turned to cricket; more than once she teased that he had no idea just how good a batsman she was. And he knew that patients who have suffered trauma to the face and undergo reconstruction need time to live with the change in their appearance.

If Monzur and Rahima felt helpless to reverse their daughter's sadness, they took heart in the dedication of her friends who kept up their visits. Among the most faithful were Mohsen, Sotonye and Sarah Meli, who, on first word of the attack, had been the mainstay of keeping the community of the college apprised. With each visit, Rumana talked—vented—about the tribulations of her marriage. Anger at the Kabirs' late son still smouldered in her, but by speaking aloud of the abuse, she began to heal from her trauma.

It was Anusheh who helped her mother realize that her greatest loss was not so. "You can still see me, Mamma—with your hands."

It struck Rumana that Anusheh was right. She *could* still see her. Not by sight, but by touch, by breathing in her scent, by hearing and interpreting the sound of her voice, her laugh, her tears. In fact, the brain reroutes sensory pathways; information and signals from Rumana's intact senses of touch, hearing and smell were gradually expanding from their usual locations into the visual cortex.

Rumana recognized that she had allowed her profound grief at her loss of sight to defeat her. She lectured herself: "Hema, you can't just sit in a corner and grieve. You're a mother with responsibility to protect and raise your young daughter. Let learning the skills to live with blindness take care of itself. Put your energy into finding meaning in your life, beginning with your daughter—and the other passion that brought you happiness."

In September 2012, fifteen months after the attack, Rumana was ready to resume her studies. She contacted UBC's Centre for Accessibility for help. It connected her with a second-year law student, Graham Hardy, blind since birth, to help explain assistive technology and to introduce her to the university library's equipment and services for the visually impaired.

Graham's enthusiasm for his field of study turned Rumana's mind toward law as an option for her. Her father, despite reservations about a legal career in a new country, allowed that practising law could be more practical than her previous academic career: "Law requires logical deduction; your work is with your brain. With political science, you have to make field trips." Rumana worried that she couldn't match up to someone like Graham, who was fluent in Braille and lived independently with his guide dog.

The centre encouraged her. Her doubts eased, and the characteristic Rumana bloomed forth.

Rumana set herself a goal: start law school next year, beginning in the 2013/14 academic year.

She set a schedule: write the Law School Admission Test this coming December; then complete her master's thesis.

"This is Hema's normal behaviour," Monzur told Rahima. Cheered, they felt their own grief begin to recede.

Sotonye and Sarah were skeptical that in the two and a half months left before the LSAT date their friend could be ready to write it. "Rumana, you don't know Braille, and there isn't enough time for you to learn it." She refused to entertain their doubts. "What do I have to lose?" Seeing Rumana's determination, her two friends came daily to the townhouse to read aloud study materials and help her work through practice exams.

At the test, the invigilator gave Rumana a separate room and allowed her seven hours, twice the time allowed a sighted person. She was provided with a reader to read aloud the questions and multiple-choice answers, and a scribe to circle her choice. For the logical reasoning section requiring her to draw Venn diagrams and graphs, she was supplied with magnetic strips, discs and a board—at home, she had practised using Anusheh's bangles and pipe cleaners. At times during the test, Rumana's concentration flagged. She worried she might have to give up, but she persisted.

The LSAT behind her, Rumana next revamped her thesis to use secondary instead of primary data.

Tulip's foresight that Rumana would benefit from advanced accessibility services in the West proved right. In Bangladesh, universities only began opening their doors to the physically disabled in the late 1990s, and only after students at Chittagong University went on a hunger strike. The blind student Rumana once had in her classes had none of the services available to her. In contrast, the UBC library assigned her a research assistant who, at her instruction, collected articles to send to the university's Crane Library (named for a deaf-blind student who'd attended UBC in the 1930s). Volunteer readers recorded the articles on CDs, which Rumana listened to, then dictated notes on a voice recorder for an assistant to type out. The process was repeated numerous times until Rumana had digested the content sufficiently to start structuring and drafting a thesis. Each draft she dictated was typed and read back to her by volunteers, until she was satisfied she had a final version to submit.

Rumana's new life began to fall into place. In March, she was offered admission to UBC's law school for the fall. In April, she submitted her thesis: "Securitization of Climate Change in Bangladesh: The Repercussions of Rising Sea Levels for Human Security." The political science department scheduled her oral defence for June 28. To help her prepare, assemble, edit and format a PowerPoint presentation and an accompanying script and commit everything to memory, Sarah dropped her summer classes and Sotonye set aside work on her own master's thesis.

On the day of Rumana's defence, the entire family readied themselves to attend. For the first time in more than two years, Rumana, with Anusheh's guidance, put on makeup. Rumana directed her daughter to mix a shade of foundation that could disguise the slight change in skin tone between the tip and the bridge of her nose, and mix a shade of nail polish to go with her outfit. To balance a studious look with style, Rumana paired a sensible black skirt with a royal blue and black top, with a modest split crew neckline outlined in a ribbon of sequins, and a thin black sweater. She chose a dark blue head scarf in cut velvet and chiffon that was run through with delicate silver threads. For shoes, black pumps.

Some sixty faculty, students and friends were in the audience in the large conference room at the Liu Institute for Global Issues. For the better part of two hours, with Sarah at the computer to advance her PowerPoint slides, Rumana presented her thesis and fielded questions. Except perhaps when Rumana was answering a question and her gaze didn't quite meet the questioner's eyes, one could forget that she was blind.

When Rumana concluded, the room erupted in cheers.

Finally, Monzur felt the shock of the attack subside. "Hema will go on," he told Rahima. "All the systems and help are here for her. She will get assistance from her daughter. Allah has tested us and finally helped us."

As she had planned, in the autumn of 2013, Rumana enrolled in UBC's faculty of law.

It had taken one of Rumana's Agrani friends, Zana Shammi, months to work up the courage to call her. Zana had first learned of the attack after she received no response to a birthday greeting she had sent Rumana on Facebook. Curious, she saw messages praying for her friend's recovery. She followed links and saw television news clips. She couldn't believe what had happened to the sweetest girl at Agrani, the one whom she used to tease, "How come you're so-oh nice?"

In the spring of 2012, she came from Toronto to visit Rumana in Vancouver. A videographer, she had conceived a documentary project, taking Rumana's marital relationship as one example to spark conversations to empower women in Bangladesh trapped in abusive marriages.

Two years later, Zana, on a visit from Toronto to Dhaka, tracked down a telephone number for the Kabirs. Ruby answered. Zana identified herself as a journalist, who before moving to Canada had been a reporter for Dhaka's first private television channel. She asked if she could visit.

Ruby said yes.

Zana dressed modestly to visit the Kabirs. She had her seventeen-year-old brother accompany her, thinking that seeing her accompanied by a male would also improve the odds of them warming to the purpose of her visit—securing their participation in her documentary.

Quick to offer food and drink, Ruby bonded with Zana over their shared ancestral origins in the Noakhali district of the Chittagong Division. Ruby was gracious and talkative, and Kabir emerged to join them. When Ruby effused over the good looks of Zana's brother and offered to make a match for him, Zana saw an opening. "It must be hard for you both. You lost your son."

Ruby broke down. She said that the entire media had been against the family, that no one had thought to say "You've lost your son" or to ask how she and Kabir were coping. Bitterness spilled from her husband. Kabir said he'd been so furious at his son's death that he'd wanted to file a suit against Rumana's father for the loss of the young man. He hastened to add that he wasn't saying what his son did was right—it was wrong, of course—and he was sorry about what had happened to Rumana and wished it hadn't.

Zana asked Kabir and Ruby outright whether they would consider speaking on camera about it.

Ruby began to pour her heart out. She said her son and daughter-in-law had been a happy couple, that he'd been crazy about her, that he was so in love, so obsessed with her that he couldn't do enough for her. Kabir turned quiet. He said the family had pending court cases against the Monzurs; they'd have to take the advice of their lawyers.

When Zana called back, the answer was no.

Back in Toronto, she contacted the Kabirs' daughter in Texas, hoping to enlist her to help change her parents' minds. The answer was again no. However, unprompted, Sabira spoke warmly of Rumana, said she was so nice, a real sweetheart. She echoed what her mother had said, that Rumana and Sumon had been madly in love. He had supported her going abroad for schooling, he'd paid her tuition. She allowed that what her brother did was very wrong, but Rumana had provoked it. Sabira said her own everyday wardrobe in the US included jeans and T-shirts, but when she returned to Bangladesh, she wore a sari or a shalwar kameez and her head was covered. Rumana, she pointed out, had not shown that same respect; when she returned from Vancouver and landed at Dhaka airport, she was dressed in Western clothes.

In the summer of 2015, between her first and second years of law school, Rumana made her first foray into speaking out as a survivor of abuse. She gave a TEDx talk in Vancouver about ending violence against women. She stood alone on stage and, clasping her hands around the top of her white cane, began by giving statistics, continent by continent, of the percentages of women who face violence. Then she made it personal. "I never thought it could happen to me, who was teaching at the most renowned university in Bangladesh. Until it did." Preparing for and giving the talk gave Rumana the confidence to turn her mind toward activism.

The next summer, before her final year of law school, at the whirlwind daylong job fair hosted by law firms looking to recruit summer students, Rumana wondered how the work world she would soon rejoin would treat her. She singled out the firm that ultimately hired her as her own first choice. Unlike other recruiters, Kerry Sheppard, a senior partner in the Vancouver office of the international law firm DLA Piper, did not tell her where she could put her white cane and did not ask about her blindness. He did ask why she'd taken two years to complete the first year of the program. She answered that she'd gone abruptly from sight to blindness and that, if he wished to know more, her resume had a link to her TEDx talk on reducing violence against women. What she did not say was that she had to first master JAWS (Job Access With Speech, a screen-reader program that converts digital text into spoken words) and adapt her method of learning and recall (those who are visually impaired or completely blind rely intensely on working memory, which some liken to a temporary storage bin of information, incorporating both short-term and long-term memory).

As Rumana rebuilt her life, she had little time to concern herself with the long-running dispute over the settlement of Sumon's estate. She left it to Rashed and Molly, to whom she had given power of attorney, to deal with lawyers and attend hearings at family court in Dhaka. Often proceedings had to be postponed because of the Kabirs' frequent travels out of the country.

In 2016, the families agreed to pursue an out-of-court settlement. Rashed and Farrukh acted as mediators; Rashed for Rumana, Farrukh for the Kabirs. When the accounting of the estate revealed the Paribagh apartment to be in the names of Sumon and his brother, Rumana wondered if that explained the Kabirs' initial haste to cash out accounts—that they feared if she pursued compensation for her injuries, it could bankrupt them. Rumana said yes to every deduction from the denmohar that the Kabirs asked for—including the gold jewellery they had given her for her wedding—leaving a final sum of about five thousand Canadian dollars. When Rashed presented the amount the Kabirs proposed to pay Anusheh, Rumana told Rashed she would accept it on one condition: the Kabirs would have no visiting rights with Anusheh. They accepted her condition.

To Rashed's exasperation, Rumana subsequently told him said she would take no payment from the Kabirs for either her or Anusheh. "Allah would not put me in a situation where I'd have to use their money." Rashed tried for weeks, but could not change his cousin's mind. He finally convinced her when he said the money may one day be needed for Anusheh's education.

All said and done between the families, Kabir lamented to Farrukh that communication with his granddaughter would not be restored. Farrukh listened to his old friend speak of his rapidly worsening heart and of his limited time. To think of the once-handsome man now so evidently in decline weighed heavily on him.

—

When Rumana and Anusheh arrived home from the girl's Saturday morning swim lesson, Monzur told his daughter that she had missed a phone call. He had spoken to Kabir, but only long enough to tell him where Rumana was and that he'd tell her he had called.

Rumana was annoyed. It had to be about money.

The next Saturday, Kabir called again. Monzur and he had the same short exchange.

On Kabir's third try, this time on a weekday, Rumana answered.

Kabir launched into an apology. He said what their son had done was wrong, that the family was ashamed for having spoken out against her. "I don't know how I could have said about you what I did."

Rumana was willing to listen to Kabir, but not to appease his guilt. She believed that had either parent known what their son was planning, they would have stopped him, but she could not forgive them for their actions afterwards. They knew her well enough to know what their son said was untrue, yet they had gone ahead and smeared her and levelled false accusations about her to the press.

Shawon came on the line. Rumana had no issue with Sumon's younger brother. She told him that she was in law school. He shared with her that something good was happening in the lives of their family—their immigration to the US had been finalized. Then, clearly nervous, he apologized for the nasty remarks made about her online. He did not say who authored them, only that they were fake profiles. "Please forgive us."

Shawon's parents came back on. Ruby cried. She, too, said she wanted to apologize, and she asked forgiveness. Kabir asked if they could speak to Anusheh. He said he did not know how much time he had left to live—his heart was giving out. Feeling manipulated but without a choice, Rumana agreed, with one condition: they could speak of themselves only as friends of her father. In Rumana's mind, what their son had done to the mother of his child, in front of his child, was a forfeiture of the moral right of any of the Kabirs to have a familial relationship with Anusheh—at least for as long as Anusheh was a minor.

Rumana took her daughter on her lap. She explained that friends of her father wanted to talk to her, that they used to be her Dada and Dida.

"What do they want to say?"

"They just want to ask how you are doing, nothing else. Just say salam to them."

Rumana put the phone on speaker.

Anusheh said hello but quickly had difficulty with the vernacular of the Kabirs, which was more colloquial than the Bangla spoken by the Monzurs. As the call grew awkward, Rumana had to keep interpreting, to tell Anusheh what the Kabirs were asking—how was her school, did she have friends, what was her favourite food.

Some weeks later, a present arrived in the mail for Anusheh's eleventh birthday. The large box of crayons and art supplies was suited to a much younger child.

—

The fourth of the engineering students who'd bonded as roommates more than fifty years ago, the poet and idealist among them in the day, Mustafizer, received a diagnosis of terminal cancer. Regretting unfinished business in his life, he told Farrukh that he hoped to see a reconciliation between Monzur and Kabir before it was too late.

Farrukh told Mustafizer, who was retired from his teaching job at a college in California, that he not been able to even broach the subject with Monzur. Mustafizer beseeched him: "Do not give up. Keep trying to move the two of them closer together."

Farrukh called Monzur. "Kabir is not well. His condition is poor. I think you should visit. When are you going to Dhaka?"

Monzur took his friend Farrukh to be a true gentleman; he would not say one thing and mean another. By coincidence, he and Rahima were going to Dhaka in a matter of weeks.

Monzur asked Rumana if she had strong views either way about him calling on Kabir. "I know him only as your friend," she said. "You are free to decide."

In Dhaka, Monzur waited until one afternoon when he had a brief window of free time and mid-afternoon traffic would allow him a quick trip across town to Paribagh. He dialed the Kabirs' home number. Kabir answered.

"You are at home. Can I visit?"

"Please."

At the door, Ruby greeted Monzur and showed him to the bedroom. With enormous effort and obviously fighting pain, Kabir struggled to a sitting position. Monzur's eyes watered. When he first saw Ruby, he thought she had aged beyond her years, but Kabir was a shadow of how Monzur had last seen him.

The men embraced.

Tears ran down Kabir's cheeks. "Forgive me for all that has happened. I can't change anything back to what it was before."

"Please forgive us for what happened," Ruby added. "Forgive my son also."

Monzur waved his hand across the air between them. "Forget everything that has occurred."

Ruby served drinks and snacks as the two friends, one propped against his pillows, the other sitting on the edge of the bed, chatted. The frail older man spoke of his two heart bypass surgeries and how he needed a third, but his cardiologist in the United States said he would not survive the operation. They asked after each other's sons. Kabir said Shawon had moved to Austin to live with Sabira and her husband. Monzur said Mashrur lived with his wife in the Netherlands, where he had a business in technology training. Neither mentioned Sumon or Rumana.

After thirty-five minutes, Monzur rose to leave.

"You may not see me again," Kabir said. "There may not be a next time." They embraced once more.

Some months later, in early December 2017, Kabir would succumb.

In May of that year, Rumana and Anusheh, along with Tara, who had come with Mashrur from the Netherlands to attend Rumana's graduation from law school, went on a shopping mission. They were looking for two dresses for Rumana: one to wear to the convocation ceremony and one for the dinner afterwards. Tara drove Monzur's car. Unfamiliar with Vancouver, she relied on Rumana for directions; Rumana would tell her what buildings to watch for in advance of any turn to direct them to the Pacific Centre mall. Once there, it was Rumana who explained the location of the mall's escalators.

Tara and Anusheh browsed the racks of dresses at a couple of stores looking for the colour and styles Rumana favoured. Anusheh explained to Tara that using examples from nature in descriptions of colour or texture was most helpful to her mother. Rumana took home a sleeveless dress in the grey of a cloudy day, puckered like sand marked by waves, with a cluster of pink-flecked black and silver beads along a V-neckline; and a second V-neck dress, in teal, intricately beaded and sequined, with cap sleeves, and scalloped lace bordering the neckline.

Dressing for the ceremony, Rumana asked Anusheh to choose the dress in which she looked most cheerful. Anusheh chose the teal dress. Rumana applied her own makeup. As always before leaving the house, she had someone check her clothing in case she had leaned against the kitchen counter, where there might be a spill of flour or spice—the worst was turmeric.

Rumana sat with the dignitaries on stage. She'd been given the honour of offering brief remarks. When it was her turn, a sighted guide offered her his arm and, head held high, she walked with him confidently to the podium, her heels clicking across the stage. Rumana spoke of choosing UBC for her master's, went on to describe the attack that took her sight, then expressed her gratitude to the university and her "UBC family" who, when she was "lost," gave her direction. She made sure her remarks ended with humour: "I will never forget your warmth, love, support and tolerance, especially when I hit some of you with my stick." The audience rose to their feet.

Sometimes Rumana forgot she was blind. Her creativity illuminated her world. She could rely on her trove of memory from her sighted life, so her mind's eye saw vivid colour and detail. She saw the posture of the person she was speaking with, saw their gestures as they spoke, saw them lift their coffee mug to their lips. To establish and keep eye contact, she homed in on a speaker's voice. Taken in by her warmth and her smile, they also could forget—or not notice—that she was blind.

This is not to say that aspects of Rumana's life from before didn't elicit occasional longing in her. Her sighted self had never been clumsy or careless. She'd had to recalibrate to a slower pace. But she was now more patient, better organized, her concentration intense, her recall and memory precise. She enjoyed fashion as much as ever and was meticulous about her appearance in public.

After Rumana's graduation, the Monzurs had to move out of student housing. So that Anusheh, now entering grade six, would not have to change schools, they decided to remain on the UBC lands. The family applied to rent an apartment in a building under construction and slated for completion in 2017, just inside the main gate to the UBC campus. The six-floor building had easy curbside access, which was convenient for Rumana when she used Vancouver's HandyDART, public paratransit that provided door-to-door service for the disabled.

Rumana and her father made three visits to the apartment before their move-in date. She studied the fob and intercom system at the front entrance, the layout of the lobby, stairs, elevators and hallway. Inside their apartment, she found her way through each room, taking note of which side of the doors the handles were on and which way they opened. She memorized, by touch, the window ledges and the layout of counters in the two bathrooms and kitchen. Monzur measured and gave her exact dimensions of each window and its height from the floor, the direction it faced and the view it showed. Rumana began to make a mental map of the apartment and to plan the furniture arrangement.

Once the family moved in, Rumana planned the hanging of pictures on the walls. Just inside the entranceway, she had her father hang three acrylic paintings by Anusheh: a waterfall inspired by a visit Rumana and Farzana Morshed made with their daughters to Niagara Falls, a forest landscape that camouflaged a deer, and a close-up of wildflowers. Another wall displayed three framed family photographs, including one of Rumana at her convocation. For her own bedroom, on the wall with the largest expanse, she purchased an oversize print of a flower, the petals of which were streaked with maroon and burgundy, two of her favourite hues of deep, rich red.

author's note

MANY IN DHAKA HAD HOPED THAT THE MASSIVE OUTCRY at the assault on Rumana Monzur would spark a movement against domestic violence. As it happened, her husband's death, six months on when he was still on remand, nullified the complaint. Some activists lamented that because it "didn't go anywhere," other women suffering abuse might not come forward. If such a high-profile victim—a member of the faculty of Dhaka University, an institution synonymous with the identity of Bengalis and the development of Bangladesh—couldn't get justice, how could they?

"Torture" was the word most commonly used to describe the abuse as the drama of Rumana as victim and her husband, Syeed Sumon, as perpetrator played out in the media. "He tortured me since the day we got married," she told reporters. "I didn't torture her," Sumon said on his arrest, "she tortured me." A government minister visited Rumana in hospital and whispered to her, "I don't know why women like you tolerate torture like this." Indeed, even when the violence causes a woman grievous harm, it is unlikely to be reported to police. Perhaps only by elevating the language of abuse can society chip away at cultural norms that see a husband's violence against his wife as necessary to maintain his authority. The characterization of domestic abuse as torture may also help compel society to face up to its tolerance for violence and complacency about living with it.

I asked Sara Hossain, a leading women's rights advocate and lawyer practicing public interest and family law, to reflect on the case of the assault on Rumana. She spoke of the shortcomings in the country's legal system. Despite the enactment of laws to protect women from domestic violence, enforcement was lacking. She added that "reliance on the rule of law is not enough because of the nexus of justice, power, political influence and corruption." Public support for Rumana swelled at rumour that her husband had influential persons on his side, leaving her up against the weight of the state.

I am reminded of the essay by Ursula Le Guin, "It was a Dark and Stormy Night: Or, Why Are We Huddling about the Campfire." The American author describes our penchant for remembering stories and inviting their retelling as owing to our living life "in the middle." The virtue of remembering and sharing a story is to "come to the end together, even to the beginning." To allow for different beginnings and endings in stories such as Rumana's, can we imagine societal structures where women can live safely? Where progress or setbacks in women's rights rely on more than—if at all—the actions of the police, prosecutors and the courts? More broadly, what systems, values and institutions enable and perpetuate violence that in effect give license to mete out harm, and that depend on retribution and punishment by the law to address the problem? Justice would be better served if girls and women were not harmed or abused in the first instance.

In the Bangladesh government's first-ever survey of domestic violence in 2011, eighty-seven percent of married women reported having experienced some form of abuse from their partner. Asked if it had happened within the last twelve months, nine out of ten answered yes. In some ways, the relationship of Sumon and Rumana in its culmination of a near deadly assault is a textbook case. Theirs was a relationship that began on the wings of romance. Marriage followed quickly. In parallel with Sumon's escalating control, harassment and aggression, Rumana's response alternated between confusion and self-blame, disassociation and numbness. The pattern of behavior, and the narrative, is one common to most abusive relationships. However, questions beg to be asked. Human behaviour is complex. What triggered Sumon's coercive and controlling behaviour? Or his sense of a loss of control? Might there have been opportunity for intervention before it came to a case for the law, that could have led him to take accountability for and modify his behaviour? And, which could have led to positive change and healing past harms? What about resources for treating mental health, substance abuse and the effects of trauma?

I had almost completed this book when a student at the University of British Columbia and a friend of Rumana's returned from visiting Bangladesh and reported to her that cruel gossip was still circulating there. The friend's aunt had asked if she knew Rumana Monzur. Hardly did she reply yes when the aunt said, "What a shame, she is living her life and her husband is dead. All of Chittagong knows how she had an affair, how she pretended to be blind. How else could she have become a lawyer?" A belief that women are subordinate to men may have led some to conclude that Sumon had to have been a husband wronged. The divergence from fact speaks to inequality, exacerbated by economic disparities, of access to education and to knowledge.

The impetus for a book was Rumana's. In 2017, by then having taken up Canadian citizenship, Rumana was soon to begin a second career of law. She wanted her young daughter to know that her strength to overcome the trauma of the attack and learn to live in darkness came from the values of generations of her family, of living a life with meaning. She approached Jackie Kaiser, who is also my agent. My first conversation with Rumana was in her family's townhouse in a student housing complex at the University of British Columbia. She began to share the story of her marriage. I spoke of the act of writing, where narrow truths give way to wider ones. She insisted that I should have "creative independence." The shortened daylight of winter faded to darkness. Rather than ask if I might turn on a light, I continued our conversation. In those moments, I felt a keen bond of writer to subject.

I had hoped that the family who survived Sumon would agree to be interviewed. During my research trip to Dhaka, sadly, Sumon's father, Kabir, passed away. I elected to not make contact in consideration of a grieving family, who had lost a son and brother and, now, a husband and father. My subsequent entreaties to the Kabir family went unanswered. Finally, by grace of a lifelong friend of the Kabirs, I had a brief phone conversation with two of the family. It was apparent that Sumon's accusations of infidelity against Rumana remained front of mind and that emotions still ran high. The family said they would call back if there was to be a further conversation. They did not. When my book was soon forthcoming, an intermediary informed Sumon's mother on my behalf and let her know that I was available if she wished a word with me. Word came back that she wanted to speak with me at some point. At the time of this writing, this has not happened.

I offer some explanations of word choices in these pages. I refer to the war in 1971 as the War of Independence; it is also known as the Liberation War. Where I quote from press conferences and interviews by traditional and online media in Dhaka, I do so according to how English-language media in Bangladesh reported it in translation. By way of example, on Sumon's arrest, he spoke in Bangla to the assembled press. I report what he said in English translation. The reader may also find it helpful to have an explanation of the usage of proper names. Because surnames are more common than first names, parents may elect to use the father's first name as a surname for their children. Rumana's father did so for her. In keeping with how the two fathers were known, I refer to their respective families as the Monzurs and similarly, the Kabirs. I refer to the Kabir children not by their formal names, but by how they were known. The media and online posts in Dhaka used the formal name of Sumon—Hasan Syeed—or added Sumon to it—Hasan Syeed Sumon. As for place names, I use the names most common at the time, with the exception of the Bangladeshi capital. I refer to it throughout as Dhaka; in fact, it officially changed from its English spelling, Dacca, in 1982

acknowledgements

TO UNDERTAKE THE RESEARCH FOR THIS BOOK REQUIRED trust between Rumana Monzur and myself. It found root in mutual respect for each our own inquiries and deepened in the six-and-a-half years it took me to write *Out of Darkness*. I thank foremost Rumana and her parents. From my many interviews with them, my research rippled outward. In Dhaka, I relied on Rashed Maqsood and his wife, Samia Faisal, who were generous and obliging, and Faiham Sharif, whose lively mind and commentary entertained, to help me retrace Rumana's footsteps in her birth country, including on the fateful days in May and June of 2011. I thank Rumana's extended family, childhood friends and her former students and colleagues at Dhaka University, all of whom were open and forthcoming. I also benefitted from conversations with people in Dhaka engaged in human rights, law, journalism and governance. For inspiration and expertise, I owe particular thanks to Sara Hossain, Monzoor Hasan, Ifti Rashid, Heather Cruden, Elaine Nickerson, Alex Neve and Dr. Robert Boeglin. In Canada, Henry Yu, the principal of St. John's College at the University of British Columbia, provided vital information and, together with Alice Lam, extended every courtesy to me. Residents of the college from Rumana's time and her friends and others who were part of her life in Vancouver were important to my research. I also thank Farrukh Mohsen, who, in his abiding humanity, facilitated my efforts to reach out to the family of Rumana's former in-laws.

Two people for whom I have great affection helped make possible this book and helped coax forth a story: my agent, Jackie Kaiser, and my editor at Random House Canada, Craig Pyette. Jackie, always caring and attentive, brought Rumana and me together. Craig, with his trademark patience, again brought his instinct for the power of a story. I could not have undertaken the level of research I did were it not for a grant in 2017 from the Canada Council for the Arts and a sojourn that same year as the 2017-18 writer-in-residence at the University of Calgary. Thank you to Jacqueline Jenkins, the then-chair of the English Department, and the community in Calgary, including the inimitable Winnie Chow. Photos of Rumana in hospital in Dhaka are courtesy of Sk Enamul Haq/*The Daily Star*. Rumana at work as a lawyer is reprinted by permission of Aaron Vincent Elkaim/*The New York Times*/Redux. The remaining photos are courtesy of the extended Monzur family, Shehneela Tilat, Farruhk Mohsen, Faiham Sharif, Mahmudul Hoque Moni, Sarah Meli, Mohsen Seddigh, and Paul Joseph of UBC Media Relations.

I thank my family with all my heart. *Out of Darkness* may be several books on from my first, but no matter where my family live—as close as my husband, Roger, in the same home, or as far away as our grown children, Jade and Kai, in another city or country—they each live with my making of a book. Roger read the manuscript and made valuable polishing comments. For all the trials of writing, including the long hours into the night and draft after draft, the reward is the love of my children and their support for what I try to do. They are the ones who teach me about belief. I know Rumana would say the same.

© Monique de St Croix

DENISE CHONG is the author of prize-winning and bestselling books that portray the lives of ordinary people caught in the eye of history. Her previous books have been translated into many languages and include her family memoir, *The Concubine's Children*, which is being adapted for film; *The Girl in the Picture*, about the napalm girl of the Vietnam War; and *Egg on Mao*, a story of love and defiance in China of 1989. In 2013, she was appointed an Officer of the Order of Canada for "writing books that raise our social conscience." She lives in Ottawa.